Building
a Professional Culture
in Schools

Building
a Professional Culture
in Schools

edited by
ANN LIEBERMAN

TEACHERS COLLEGE PRESS

Teachers College, Columbia University
New York and London

Published by Teachers College Press, 1234 Amsterdam Avenue, New York, NY 10027

Library of Congress Cataloging-in-Publication Data

Building a professional culture in schools / edited by Ann Lieberman.
    p.   cm.—(Professional development and practice series ; 1)
   Contents: 1. Making the case for professionalism / Kathleen Devaney & Gary Sykes—2. School as a place to have a career / Milbrey Wallin McLaughlin & Sylvia Mei-ling Yee—3. Whose culture is it anyway? / Myrna Cooper—4. Policy and professionalism / Linda Darling-Hammond—5. Assessing the prospects for teacher leadership / Judith Warren Little—6. Restructuring secondary schools / Holly M. Houston—7. School, a community of leaders / Roland S. Barth—8. Teacher leadership / Ann Lieberman, Ellen R. Saxl & Matthew B. Miles—9. Unlikely beginnings / Lynne Miller—10. Leading cultural change / Phillip C. Schlechty.
   Bibliography: p.
   Includes index.
   ISBN 0-8077-2901-9.   ISBN 0-8077-2900-0 (pbk.)
   1. Teachers—United States. 2. Teaching—Vocational guidance—United States. 3. Professional socialization—United States. 4. Teacher participation in curriculum planning—United States. 5. Teacher participation in administration—United States. I. Lieberman, Ann. II. Series
   LB1775.B85 1988   88-2843
   371.1'002373—dc19   CIP

Manufactured in the United States of America

93 92 91 90 89 88   1 2 3 4 5 6

Contents

Introduction

ANN LIEBERMAN

This book represents the bold thinking of a group of people who are involved as organizers, conceptualizers, and researchers in a development critical to education in our time—the building of a professional culture in schools. Rather than suggesting more courses, more tests, or more monitoring of the curriculum, the second wave of reform, as some are calling it, suggests a comprehensive view of restructuring schools. Involved in that restructuring is the building of a new set of relationships between and among all members of the school community, including an enlargement of the leadership team in schools, new roles for teachers and administrators, changed organizational arrangements, and even a rethinking of the substance of what is to be taught. New policies, often contradictory in their pursuit of simple solutions to complex problems, proliferate. New roles for teachers are appearing, often without examination of the consequences—both intended and unintended—and without the support and learning needed for success in these new positions. Across the country new coalitions are being fashioned, new ways of organizing districts and schools are beginning to surface, and, in some cases, traditional structures are actually changing.

This book is written by educators who are participants in this restructuring process, this second wave of reform: activists, researchers, academics, and unionists. Although they come from different places and disciplines, they hold in common the idea that professionalizing teaching and building a more collaborative culture in schools can profoundly change the way both staff and students in schools grow and learn.

The book is divided into two major sections: "Developing the Case for a Professional Culture" and "Building Collaboration and Expanded Leadership Roles and Responsibilities." In the first part, the authors examine questions of policy, research, and practice, seeking to determine the conditions that need to be present to enable the school culture to be changed. In the second part, we move from analyzing the issues surrounding student learning that suggest the need for structural change, to describing the existing school environment and the impact on it of new leadership roles for teachers, to documenting and interpreting an attempt to make comprehensive change in the culture of a school district.

The book opens with a chapter by Kathleen Devaney and Gary Sykes that sets forth the complexity of the task of building a professional culture. Starting with the view that the changing needs of students require teachers who are themselves changing and growing, they suggest that both students and teachers would be better served as members of a more professional culture.

Milbrey Wallin McLaughlin and Sylvia Mei-ling Yee argue for a new conception of the teacher's career as they analyze data from an in-depth study of teachers in northern California. Their very original thesis shows the need for understanding the multi-faceted, individual nature of a teaching career as well as the nature of rewards and advancements that must surround this conception of the teacher's work.

Myrna Cooper, in her provocative chapter, encourages us to look at the culture of the school as it is experienced by the people who live it. It is her view that the values and customs of the people in the schools are central to any meaningful changes that may take place. If change is to be sustained it must have the teacher-student relationship at the core.

Linda Darling-Hammond's chapter analyzes the difficult issues involved in professionalizing the teaching force and increases our awareness of the competing constituencies who must be considered in building a professional culture. Her careful analysis focuses on the importance of policies as they respond to state, community, and parental interests.

And finally, Judith Warren Little makes a strong case for focusing the effort for reform on the professionalization of teaching. Her definition and discussion of teacher leadership revolves around the organization of teaching and learning in a school as the *collective* responsibility of teachers. Based on data from several research studies, she concludes that teacher leadership has the potential to change the power of the prevailing culture in schools and, perhaps in a larger way, the teaching occupation as a whole.

The second part of the book includes several examples from research and practice in places where new structures, roles, and coalitions are being built. It examines different aspects of the school culture as they are affected by interventions that begin at the state, district, or local level and describes new ways of organizing schools and new roles that transform existing relationships.

Holly M. Houston begins this section with a description of an attempt to restructure secondary schools. Her chapter describes three key elements in a changed structure: the organizational, relational, and psychological. She shows us how teachers define the nature of their work and discusses the elements of leadership, evaluation, and decentralized responsibility through a composite view of several schools involved in the Coalition of Essential Schools network.

Roland S. Barth brings a new vision of how a "community of leaders" can replace the existing staff divisions and patterns of work in a school. Such a vision, while not easy to enact, can become a reality if members of the school community—particularly the principal and teachers—reexamine their responsibilities and commitments.

Ann Lieberman, Ellen R. Saxl, and Matthew B. Miles provide an in-depth look at the work, skills, and organizational behavior of a group of teacher-leaders studied over several years. Seeing these leaders in their own context, one begins to understand the complexity of the school culture and the necessity for both organizational structures that are collaborative (teacher centers, groups, advisory committees) *and* leadership roles for teachers who lead these structures. The qualities of these teacher-leaders, their particular knowledge and skills, are documented here.

Schools are embedded in a larger structure—the district. What is the role of the district in helping to build a professional culture? What kinds of changes are necessary in the personnel, perspectives, organization, and work of the district office? Lynne Miller describes such changes in an actual case, documenting the details of how the district became a starting point for developing a professional culture.

Phillip C. Schlechty, using the Charlotte-Mecklenburg Teacher Career Development Program, provides the reader with a fascinating and penetrating analysis of the process of cultural change in a large urban district. The interaction of all the constituencies involved in the educational enterprise and the attempt to plan for and think about institutionalization of this new effort provide us with an opportunity to struggle with the complexities of the elements of a professional culture and the strategies and processes of change that must be understood if the change process is to succeed.

Harry Judge provides a thoughtful afterword as he reflects on this group of chapters as a foundation for the work of building a professional culture in schools. Such work and thought, he points out, are not only going on in the United States, but in many countries throughout the world.

The book closes with an annotated bibliography of a collection of articles, papers, and books, loosely organized around the theme of this book. Patricia A. Wasley provides us with a broad beginning set of readings to further inform our debate and discussion.

Building
a Professional Culture
in Schools

PART I

Developing the Case for a Professional Culture

1

Making the Case
for Professionalism

KATHLEEN DEVANEY
GARY SYKES

We will not get very far in building a professional culture in public schools if we do not first convincingly answer the question: "Why?" Why should teaching now, after all these generations, put on the vestments—some would say trappings—of professionalism? These come with a high price tag, for individual teachers and for society. What is to be gained—not just for teachers, but for kids?

The question is perhaps long settled in the minds of most of the readers of this book. "Of *course* we must have teachers who are thoroughly schooled and helpfully inducted, who are autonomous and responsible, who are valued and treated as professionals!" But this view is not self-evident to all who participate in or observe teachers' work. If entertained at all, it is not clearly and firmly settled in the minds of citizens, lawmakers, bureaucrats, school board members, district administrators, school principals, or even of all teachers.

Certainly all teachers would endorse professional-level salaries, benefits, and perquisites; but professional-level responsibility for decisions about the classroom's and the school's instructional program? for setting and maintaining standards of practice among fellow practitioners? for continuous updating and upgrading of knowledge and skill? It is no slander to say that many, many capable, long-experienced teachers, upon pondering such obligations in return for professional salary and status, might decline the offer—or would at least think twice before accepting.

Thus there are two reasons for stopping at the start to answer, "Why?" The first is that ours is a publicly funded and locally governed educational system. Professional status will be expensive and must be paid for by local and state taxpayers. They will agree to meet the higher costs of professionalism only if they are strongly convinced of its utter urgency and if they understand that the enterprise of building a professional culture in schools is complex—it will not be accomplished in a couple of years with marginally increased funding—and will not make teachers less accountable to the public.

The second reason is that developing a work culture that is professional must be done in partnership with the workers themselves—teachers. Professionalism is a form of liberty that is not simply conferred; it is earned. Teachers themselves must not only be enabled; they must be convinced that tasks in their work can be accomplished only under professional standards, norms, and conditions. Then teachers themselves must set about achieving these.

In the past five years or so of rising calls for professionalizing teaching, several arguments have been marshaled in its favor. The case most frequently made might be headlined: "Recruiting and Retaining the Best and the Brightest." You have read the story (maybe you have written it): "Rising numbers and changing demography of the student body of American public schools, coupled with the impending retirement of the present generation of teachers, will create a high demand for teachers. But the present low status and tarnished image of teaching, coupled with the greater accessibility and attractions of other professions for able college students, is cutting the supply of new teachers. The best and brightest among young women, and immigrants' and minorities' sons starting their climb out of the working class, are no longer restricted to teaching; they are wooed by banking, law, medicine, corporate management, engineering, and other occupations where the work is better paid, better regarded, and less onerous. If we are to avoid a serious shortage, or a debilitating drop in the intellectual caliber of teachers, we must upgrade the rewards and conditions of teaching so as to attract able people."

This is an argument we titled the "blight on the apple for teacher" a few years ago (Sykes & Devaney, 1985), concluding that the blight must be cured by professionalization. Not only higher entry salaries, but prospects for higher career-long earnings, enlarged responsibility, and greater variety of work are needed in order to attract and retain able people in teaching. Thus along with calls for professionalism come recommendations for a staged career, for a career ladder (or "lattice"—opportunities to leave the classroom for a time to take up other responsibilities and then to return to the classroom), for differentiated staffing. In sum, this rationale for professionalism holds that teaching will be more attractive if it offers plentiful opportunities to use experience-honed talents and knowledge in service to students and to fellow teachers outside the classroom, as well as the chance to earn more money without leaving teaching for administration or higher education.

DIFFERING CONCEPTIONS OF TEACHING WORK

In 1984, when we began preparing background materials for the members of the California Commission on the Teaching Profession,[1] we wanted to help them to see whole and to compare the various changes that recently have been proposed for teaching—changes re- lating to teachers' day-to-day work routines, roles, and relationships, as well as changes proposed for the whole career. We put together two quite different conceptions of the role of the teacher.[2] We addressed both conceptions to the same goals of schooling:

> The first goal is *quality*: education that is *humane* (for the student's continuing education towards fulfillment of talent and interest, ap- preciation and contribution to the common culture, and responsi- ble participation in government), and education that is *practical* (enabling the student to read, speak, and write clearly, to use these skills as well as mathematical processes and rational habits of mind to solve unexpected problems; and to work with other people— all with the end of rewarding participation in the sophisticated Amer- ican economy). Regardless of subject matter, and across all sub- jects, the criterion of quality now is deemed to be higher-order thinking ability: beyond basics, beyond memorization, beyond test- passing: toward comprehending, connecting, inquiring, inferring, creating, and problem solving.
>
> The second goal is *equity*. This has meant, practically speak- ing, desegregation, fiscal equity, native-language instruction for non- English speaking students, and heterogeneous classrooms (includ- ing children with special needs). Today there are new overtones to equity: a school district does not achieve it unless it keeps the mid- dle-class population in the public schools, and unless it prevents students from dropping out of school at age 15 or from simply "doing time" until they receive meaningless diplomas. (Sykes & Devaney, 1984)

Although both addressed these same goals, our two conceptions of teaching stemmed from fundamentally different assumptions about the nature of learning, and thus they evolved into different structures for organizing teaching work.

Our first conception of teaching emphasizes a repertoire of tech- niques increasingly derived from social science. Teaching work is characterized as rationally planned, programmatically organized, and carried out on the basis of standard operating procedures. Teachers must be more than automatons following routines or functionaries carrying out orders—they must learn to decide when and how to pro- vide knowledge and apply technique. The knowledge and technique, however, are largely standardized, and the essential encounter between teacher and student is often described as "delivery." Teaching is essentially conceived as skillful transmission of preorganized knowledge.

Within this conception, the school district (perhaps in partnership with the state) is the locus of curriculum and instructional policy. Teaching effectiveness depends on the wisdom of the social science knowledge base selected and applied by the superintendent and central-office deputies; on swiftness and clarity in the transmission of management orders to school sites; and on accurate, swift feedback on results in performance.

Within this conception, teaching must be closely managed work. A new staffing pattern might involve a two-tiered arrangement: a large mass of "short-termers"—young college graduates temporizing in teaching until they decide on their eventual careers, "loaners" from business and industry, and retirees, and a smaller cadre of master teachers who function as intermediaries between administration and rank-and-file.

Short-term teachers would receive brief training and modest salaries; in all likelihood they would either exit teaching after a few years or prepare to move up. Master teachers would supervise the short-termers, model good teaching, conduct staff development, and participate in schoolwide decision making. They would make handsome salaries and would stay in teaching over their careers.

A contrasting conception of teaching emphasizes the continual and changing interplay between thought and action, based on close observation and reflection about the encounter or "match" between students and subject matter. Teaching is characterized as developmental—teachers basing individual technique on their personal learning style (for the teaching act is viewed not only as didactic but as problem solving), on experimentation, and on personal assessment of experience.[4]

Prescriptions from science and policy serve as goals and guidance, and it is assumed that the teacher must master a body of theoretical knowledge as well as a range of techniques; but teaching involves a process calling for intuition, creativity, improvisation, and expressiveness, and it leaves room for departures from what is implied by rules and formulae. Teaching is more than skilled transmission; it is principled action.

Within this conception, the local school is the place where the most influential decisions are made about the educational program. Decisions must fit within state and district frameworks, but the main determinant of students' educational programs is the teacher's judgment as to how to motivate these particular students and enable them to learn. Supporting each teacher's judgment are facultywide decisions—facilitated by the principal—on matters of curriculum, instructional method, school climate, communication with and involvement of parents, selection and assignment of teachers, inservice education, and teacher evaluation.

A career structure consonant with this orientation might involve a variety of advanced positions with increasing scope for expertise and greater responsibility. All teachers, however, would enter the profession by means of an extended preparation program, including a closely supervised residency. Beyond entry-level teaching, advanced assignments available on either part- or full-time, short- or long-term bases might include curriculum development, residency supervision, instruction of preservice students, collaborative research, staff-development planning and instruction, etc. and so on.

Playing out these two conceptions for the work of teaching shows that both of them allow a place for professionalism. In the case of our first version, professionalism is for a small cadre of career teachers who work as trainers, "masters," and supervisors of a much larger cohort of "generic" teachers, who are essentially technicians rather than professionals and who individually will not be expected to persist in teaching much longer than five years or so. In contrast, our second version of teaching implies professionalism on the part of *all* teachers. They work with substantial autonomy in their classrooms as well as substantial collaboration throughout their schools. They plan to make teaching a career.

IS LEARNING CONSUMPTION OR PRODUCTION?

Since 1984, when we spun out that pair of contrasting alternatives, Phillip Schlechty (1987) has offered a trio of different constructs of teaching work. One conception that Schlechty observes guiding the preparation of teachers and the practice of teaching is dedicated *service*. A second conception is teaching as skillful *performance*. The third is that teaching is resourceful *leadership*. All of these allow for skillful, responsible practice to emerge, but Schlechty argues that the leadership conception should be the ideal we use to guide the teaching occupation now, because the concept of teacher as leader considers the students not as clients or audience but as intellectual workers themselves—and this is what our society needs.

However one derives these differing constructs of teaching—whether as visions to which people with different philosophies of learning aspire or as versions of the teacher role that realistically capture the variety within actual practice—the features on which the competing concepts consequentially differ have to do with the teacher's stance toward students and with the student's stance toward the task of learning. Is learning at root a passive or an active endeavor—consumption or production?

This is a philosophical question that is also intensely practical. It segues into other questions: Do we *need* a professional culture in schools (the question we started with)? Do we need *all* teachers to be professional or just *some* teachers? Can the public afford professionalism for teachers? What are the hallmarks of a professional culture?

All of these questions—starting out with the ones about the nature of learning and teaching—ought to be addressed by politicians, bureaucrats, and citizens; for in public education it is not the intelligentsia and professoriat of the occupation itself who make decisions about the most effective construct for learning and thus for teaching; rather it is governors, legislators, state schools chiefs and their staffs—and then local school boards, school superintendents, and their staffs. These policy makers are in turn influenced by organized teachers and by those citizens and voters who can be persuaded to express strong support for public education. Organized teachers' demands and citizens' support thus have to be voiced in terms far more sophisticated than those we have been accustomed to if teachers are to attempt to build a professional culture in the public schools.

It is true that the argument for teaching being "professionalized" in order to attract and retain intelligent people does not require a complicated line of reasoning. But from acceptance of that argument it does not necessarily follow that the *culture* of the schools should be professional. As we have stated, it is possible to create advanced positions, perquisites, and responsibilities for an elite cadre within teaching who prescribe the work and oversee the performance of ordinary teachers. The concept of a professional cadre has the advantage of simplicity, holding out to capable and ambitious recruits the possibility of considerably increased lifetime earnings in teaching as well as providing skillful supervisors for a workforce or ordinary intellectual caliber, minimal experience, and limited commitment.

This version of professionalism does not require all teachers to strive toward standards of excellence and collaborative relationships, nor all teachers' participation in making the instructional decisions for their own classrooms and for their schools. In fact, to develop such professional attitudes and activities among a workforce comprised mainly of technicians might be difficult, if not impossible. And why bother? Professionalism on the part of all teachers—a professional culture pervading a school— is not required if one conceives of learning as straightforward consumption and of teaching as reliable service and skillful performance.

Since this is the conception that most laypersons do hold of learning and teaching, it will take a very strong case to convince politicians and bureaucrats and taxpayers that schooling requires a professional *culture*—something more than professional trappings. The case must be made that schooling needs professionalism on the part of *all* teachers, not just on the part of an elite cadre; and, since professionalism for all teachers would be costly, that this professionalism is needed for the sake of students' learning, not just for the sake of attracting people into teaching.

THE CASE FOR ALL TEACHERS BEING PROFESSIONAL

This case exists. It is clear and potent. It derives from two sources: economists' and demographers' portrayal of a markedly different economy and society for which our public schools must prepare the young, and cognitive scientists' recent findings on how human intellectual ability develops.

First, the part of the argument derived from economics: the United States will not be able to compete with other high-technology economies unless the schools produce a literate, responsible, inventive workforce. Educators with liberal-to-leftist political leanings tend to deplore this argument as crass, saying that education should be valued for more than economic profit. Indeed it should. But here the predictions of demographers enter into the argument in a way that directs quality schooling not primarily toward profits but toward self-sufficiency for a new generation of workers. Among these workers will be the heirs of the greatest immigration wave (Muller & Espenshade, 1985) in our nation's history—mainly from the Third World—and the children of the new, threatening-to-be-permanent underclass in our own country—undereducated, unemployed and seemingly unemployable, single-parent families (Hodgkinson, in press; Levin, 1986).

With this changing population, the United States participates in an economy that is not just changing but has already changed. This economy is not national but worldwide, so that we as a nation no longer control our economic life. Among the permanent changes cited by Peter Drucker (1987) are that "the primary-products economy (for instance oil and agriculture) has come 'uncoupled' from the industrial economy," and that "in the industrial economy itself, production has come 'uncoupled' from employment" (pp. C1, C8).

The significance of these changes for American society and government, barely contemplated let alone understood, is not that the new economy demands a lot of "yuppie-techie" engineer and MBA material from our public schools but that this economy cannot employ large numbers of blue-collar workers. "In all developed countries, 'knowledge workers' have already become the center of gravity of the labor force," Drucker writes (1987, p. C1).

This in turn means that those current American students who can see no place for themselves in school very likely will find no place for themselves in the workforce either. The threat to our open, comfortable way of life and government from throngs of uneducated, unemployed, poor, minority, and immigrant youth is simple: As a businessman member of the California Commission on the Teaching Profession put it in 1985, "We'll lose our society."

From this argument about the new economy and demography and the new nature of jobs arises a great cliché of contemporary education parlance: "critical thinking" by students and "problem solving" in the curriculum. The rhetoric is already shopworn even though it has not yet been translated into action, because the action required does not fit Americans' simple conceptions of teaching and learning.

A large and varied body of research by investigators of human cognition underlies the thrust toward problem solving. These social scientists look at intelligence as the ways that people mentally represent and process information. This information-processing conception of intelligence offers many insights on how teachers should organize and conduct their work of instruction so as to get students to do their work of learning—that is, to think critically.

INSIGHTS FROM RECENT RESEARCH ON COGNITION

From this research on cognition we have extracted seven sets of findings that throw light on the questions of what the most prudent constructs are for learning and teaching in our society today and why we need a professional culture in our schools.

Complexity of schoolwork.   The first insight we gain from the cognitive research is that *schoolwork is much more complex* than educators have typically assumed. In such areas as mathematical understanding, the knowledge and skills necessary to understand literary works, the apprehension of scientific concepts, and the ability to write, we are just beginning to produce accounts of the cognitive operations necessary to competence, and the picture is one of hitherto unsuspected complexity. Here, for example is one account of the composing process:

> As a cognitive activity, writing involves the use of specific kinds of knowledge that a writer has and is able to discover in constructing meanings and expressing them in writing. Underlying and enabling this use of knowledge are a variety of cognitive processes, including: discovering or generating an intended propositional meaning; selecting aspects of an intended propositional meaning; selecting aspects of an intended meaning to be expressed; choosing language forms that encode this meaning explicitly and, simultaneously, guide the reader/writer through different levels of comprehension; reviewing what has been written, and often revising to change and improve meaning and its expression. (C. Frederickson & Dominic, 1981, p. 2)

Writing is, quite simply, among the most complex of human mental activities. An appreciation of the cognitive complexity of academic tasks should sober and temper any estimates of the effects of simple factors on achievement. These findings are consonant with the view that learning is a matter of the student's complex construction rather than of simple consumption. They strongly suggest that teaching must be more than delivery of knowledge.

Problem structure.   Second, the research on cognition tells us that there is a *distinction between well-structured and ill-structured problems*. The former are

> clearly presented with all the information needed and with an appropriate algorithm available that guarantees a correct answer, such as long division, areas of triangles, Ohm's law, and linear equations. But many of the problems we face in real life and all the important social, political, economic, and scientific problems in this world are ill-structured. Schools seldom require students to solve such fuzzy problems—problems that are not clearly stated, where the needed information is not all available, there is no algorithm, and there may not be a single answer that can be demonstrated to be correct. (N. Frederickson, 1984, p. 363)

In the past, teachers have mainly been expected to concentrate students' attention of *well*-structured problems, and students have gained little practice or experience in confronting the sorts of problems widely encountered in technical and professional work in our society. Schlechty's image of the schoolroom as a workplace and students as intellectual workers under the organization and leadership of professional teachers seems to fit here.

Learning strategies.   A third set of findings differentiates the components of human cognitive activity. For example, one scheme distinguishes "metacognition," "performance," and "knowledge acquisition" as separate components within problem solving. The investigators call attention to the *executive skills by which individuals frame and monitor their own thought processes* and activities. Efficient learners have mastered these and other metacognitive strategies and so are better able to direct their own learning. Some teachers have an intuitive feel for these matters and can help students with them, but for the most part instruction ignores these critical components of cognition. Instruction that construes learning only as knowledge acquisition and performance is thus inadequate to help students learn how to learn on their own (Bereiter & Scardamalia, 1987).

Domains of knowledge.   A fourth line of provocative and illuminating research compares expert with novice performance on such tasks as playing chess, writing compositions, solving geometry and physics problems, and so on. This and other research has revealed some important facts about the role of knowledge in problem solving.

Cognitive abilities are specific to particular domains of knowledge—they do not easily transfer. So, for example, the chess grandmaster will be inept at the Japanese game of *Go. Highly specific prior knowledge* is critical to problem solving; *naive knowledge*—common sense, intuitive notions that we all have—is quite persistent and often faulty. This is especially true in science, where most children and adults have misconceptions about such physical phenomena as light, gravity, space and so on.

The teacher's task, then, is not simply to pour information into the students' heads, but to overcome their flawed but powerful prior ideas with scientifically valid concepts. Students who do not possess the appropriate knowledge structures are likely to use memorizing strategies to accomplish tasks and so be unable to use what they can state about a field actually to solve problems.

Other research, especially in mathematics, has revealed that students also invent faulty procedures for solving problems, procedures that often go undetected by teachers and tests. This theme—the importance of prior knowledge—suggests, first, that good teachers must become adept at discovering what their students know as a basis for (re)educating them and, second, that we probably cannot teach general problem-solving skills and expect their useful application in various domains. Good problem solvers are deeply knowledgeable about their areas of expertise. These findings strongly point to professional need for depth of knowledge and ways of working for all teachers, not just for a top rung on the career ladder.

Social- and cognitive-skill requirements.   A fifth insight from the research on cognition is that in actual work and life, *solving problems requires a mix of social and cognitive skills*. Anthropologists have studied the display of intelligence in cross-cultural, cross-situational perspective (see Erickson, 1984). One of the principal themes in this work is radically transforming our perceptions of intelligence as essentially fixed. Rather, purpose and features of the situation serve as cues for intelligent behavior (see also Rogoff & Lave, 1984).

For example, a child can display arithmetic competence while dealing with change in a grocery store, and yet seem to lack that ability when doing similar arithmetic problems on a worksheet or at the chalkboard in a classroom. In many practical situations, individuals work together in framing and solving problems, so a person can compensate for cognitive weaknesses of certain kinds by relying on others who are strong in such skills, while themselves supplying what they are strongest in. This social feature of cognitive competence is also present in the tutoring situation, where the child has rights to ask for a range of kinds of help.

Conceiving of intelligence as a situationally specific, collective, and negotiated enterprise has significant implications for teaching. This view perhaps suggests that we must emphasize collaborative rather than individual learning in the classroom, structuring learning tasks cooperatively rather than competitively. This line of research also substantiates a view of the schoolroom as a buzzing, busy intellectual workplace, with the teacher not as the service giver or lecturer or performer, but as the organizer and instigator of students' collaborative work.

Task-focused instruction.   A sixth principle from the new research on human reasoning is that *the basic unit of education is the task*. This conception draws attention to (1) the products students are to formulate, (2) the operations that are to be used to generate the product, and (3) the "givens" or resources available to students while they are generating a product (Doyle, 1983). Herbert Simon (1980), Nobel laureate in economics and polymath scholar, comments:

> We can best think of most skills—both general skills and competence in specific subject matter—as being represented in productions rather than propositions. . . . We need to teach our students that this is the form that most professional knowledge takes, so that they do not mistake learning propositions for acquiring basic skills. I continue to encounter many students who . . . wonder why, after they have memorized some material with great thoroughness, they cannot pass examinations that require them to solve problems. (p. 93)

The implication of this focus on the task—on the work that students do in school—is twofold. First, tasks govern the selection of information and the choice of strategies for processing that information. The task constitutes the kind of event experienced by the learner. Second, students learn what tasks lead them to do. They will acquire the information and the skills necessary to accomplish the tasks they encounter in school.

Clearly, this emphasis on tasks suggests the classroom as workplace, students as intellectual workers, and teacher as organizer and leader of the work, rather than the classroom as assembly line delivering knowledge packets to consuming students.

Direct vs. indirect instruction.   Finally, a seventh set of investigations address the *question of whether cognitive skills can be taught directly* in school. Some psychologists believe this is possible, and there are programs in existence that attempt this. But if cognitive skills are specific to particular domains and rely heavily on knowledge, then the best approach is to teach critical thinking and problem solving within each discipline in the curriculum (but see Sternberg, 1987, for a discussion of this issue). However, there are as yet no clear guidelines on how to teach children reasoning within specific content areas, on when to introduce such reasoning into the curriculum, or on how to transfer such learning in one subject to nonrelated settings.

Furthermore, some research indicates that so-called indirect instruction, which provides students the opportunity to experiment, to invent, and to discover, works better with students of high ability. Low-ability students may be unable to profit from loosely structured learning situations because they lack "the general understandings and processes that enable them to formulate their own generalizations or procedures necessary to accomplish academic tasks under indirect conditions" (Doyle, 1983, p. 177).

Simply to provide opportunities to work on ill-structured problems, therefore, may stimulate some students but prove merely frustrating to others. Yet direct instruction in the component cognitive processes typically fails to produce lasting, transferable benefits. Cognitive science cannot at this time produce a technology for teaching higher-order skills. In the absence of a standard technology, we need the independent and collaborative judgments and actions of intelligent, experienced, and resourceful teachers—who are themselves confident problem solvers—to induce higher-order thinking in our children.

The evidence from cognitive science suggests an agenda for schools that will require difficult changes and high costs. Educators resist changes; politicians and citizens resist big pricetags. The instinct to preserve the familiar is a reflex: "Hey, now, it's not all bad! Our schools have served us well in the past. What we need is to recapture past standards of excellence and rigorous methods, taking some cognitive findings into account, sure, and reasonably increasing our commitment of funds so we can secure teaching talent, but not, for goodness' sake, tramping off in some radical direction."

We have a wealth of informed opinion dissenting from this position of shaping up the status quo. The dissent is grounded in differing conceptions of what students must learn and of how teachers must teach. Larry Cuban (1984), for example, writes,

> The contradictions between district and school organizational arrangements and current cognitive theories that stress thinking as an active, holistic, inquiring process demanding the student's total involvement is staggering. (p. 672)

Further,

> The bulk of instructional time finds students listening to teachers talk, working on tasks that require little application of concepts, imagination, or serious inquiry. Description after description documents a Sahara of instruction demanding little thought from students beyond information already learned. What emerges unblurred is what Theodore Sizer calls "a conspiracy of the least," a tacit agreement between teacher and student to do just enough to get by. (p. 661)

Walter Doyle (1983), whom we have already drawn on, concurs:

> The tasks that cognitive science indicates are likely to have long-term consequences, such as those involving higher level executive routines, are probably the most difficult to manage in classrooms. Tasks that leave room for student judgment are often hard to evaluate and have a greater probability of evoking attempts by students to circumvent task demands. (p. 188)

As such strong commentary indicates, a great weight of evidence demonstrates that the familiar delivery/consumption construct for teaching and learning affords little or no opportunity for critical thinking. Students decode rather than comprehend books; memorize and practice the rules of grammar rather than write and edit their own compositions; study science as low-order facts rather than as inquiry, and so on. The teacher relies on methods that draw the focus of the whole class to herself or himself and to the textbooks as the source of knowledge, via lecture and demonstration, simple factual questions, workbook exercises, and regurgitation of texts.

FEATURES OF SCHOOLING THAT OBSTRUCT CRITICAL THINKING

This pattern has been remarkably stable since the inception of the common school (Cuban, 1983). It rests on concepts of learning as consumption and teaching as delivery of packaged knowledge, which in turn have formed a set of sociological features of schools that are as pervasive as chalk dust. Like chalk dust, these familiar features of school organization will obscure the sketching of a new profile of professionalism for teaching. Six of these factors stand out in particular.

Numbers of students.   One teacher confronts 25 to 35 students. We have just reviewed how complex are cognitive skills and their development. Now consider how to intervene sensitively with more than 20 individuals simultaneously, when the processes you are trying to nurture are invisible. *This most common format for schooling—one teacher alone attempting to hold to pinpoint focus a group of students, many of whom see no point in being there—sets real limits on what can be accomplished.*

The imperative for order.   For teachers, the task of overriding importance is gaining and maintaining the cooperation of students in activities that fill the daily class time. Because teachers must do this not for individuals but for large groups of students, they quite naturally select activities that minimize distraction, noise, motion, and the need for teachers' concentration to be many places at once. Research (see Goodlad, 1984, Chapter 4) indicates that students spend 60 to 70 percent of class time listening to the teacher and doing seatwork in which they complete assignments, check homework, take tests, and so on. They spend another 20 percent of the time in transitions between activities, a figure that is fairly constant across high- and low-ability classes.

Teaching methods that encourage students to solve problems and think critically, to work together rather than alone, are in the beginning much more difficult to organize and manage. Such methods require social skills that many students do not possess; they depend on social norms that teachers and students alike are not used to, habits they have not developed. Those teaching methods that provide the greatest control are also, as an unrelieved diet, least conducive to the acquisition of higher-order skills, but they are familiar, comfortable, and in the past have served the demand for order. *This tension between the need for order and the call to pursue higher-order skills is endemic to school organization, a predictable, durable feature of classroom life.*

Dependence on textbooks.   A large amount of classroom time is structured around printed materials in which curriculum knowledge is packaged—often poorly or inappropriately for particular students. "Analyses focusing on discourse properties and cognitive demands," notes Doyle, "indicate that school texts are not clearly written and often unwittingly pose complex logical and inferential tasks for students" (1983, p. 181).

Studies of basal reading texts, for example, demonstrate that few provide enough direct instruction in comprehension processes, instead offering practice and assessment exercises (Durkin, 1981). Since they tell stories or present information that students find insipid or irrelevant, they constitute no incentive for students to learn to read.

In other subjects, schools' insistence on texts—manipulations of symbols—stands in contrast to the outside world's manner of teaching—reliance on tools and other extensions of human intelligence in the context of group work.[4] In today's competition for the attention and concentration of students who feel little internal or external compulsion toward academic success, the schools lose. *Texts and workbooks are the principal technology of instruction, and in many cases they ill serve to promote cognitive development.*

The accountability system.   Students quickly come to recognize that school involves only an exchange of performance for grades. Students are constantly evaluated formally and informally. This encourages them to avoid ambiguity—they seek precise answers and precise formulae for generating those answers. They are afraid to take risks. Teachers' stringent evaluative criteria result in even good students' concluding that they cannot afford to experiment or speculate, for then their grades may fall. In the negotiation of classroom life, students put pressure on teachers to reduce ambiguity and risk so that they can succeed at the game. *The accountability system exerts a powerful influence on teachers and students alike, pulling both away from the sorts of tasks that are complex and difficult to assess*—such as wrestling with ill-structured problems, conducting experiments, discovering solutions, and so on. Many visitors to classrooms have commented on the bargain or deal struck there: students behave themselves and offer at least minimal attention to teachers, who, in return, water down content, reduce assignments, and make minimal intellectual demands on them (see, for example, Powell, Farrar, & Cohen, 1985; McNeil, 1986; Sedlak et al., 1986).

Influence of tests.   Contributing to this last problem is the nature of the tests that are common in schools today. Standardized tests are now widely used to hold teachers and schools accountable—raising test scores is rapidly taking its place alongside maintaining order as an imperative in schools. *But the tests direct attention to low-level skills and facts, and so drive teachers and students alike to attend to what is tested.* Teaching to the test may not be a bad thing, but it all depends on the test. We now have a serious mismatch between the new agenda of higher-order skills and the accountability technology in place, which ignores such skills almost entirely (N. Frederickson, 1986). Furthermore, as Edward Deci and others have demonstrated in a variety of experiments (Deci & Ryan, 1985), external accountability systems tend to undercut the intrinsic motivation of teachers and students alike and thus to distort the learning process.

Press for basic skills.   Finally, there is even some evidence that the very system we have in place to teach basic skills efficiently in the early grades may work to hinder the acquisition of higher-order skills in the later grades. Tests and instructional methods in the elementary grades concentrate almost exclusively on applying rules in order to read, write, and do arithmetic. States and school districts test relentlessly for these things. *Students consequently become "ad-*

dicted" to the basics and develop little capacity or inclination later on to engage in tasks requiring real reasoning.

These common features of schooling derive from the humble beginnings of public education, when teachers were workers only slightly more qualified as scholars than the oldest of their grammar school students, and from the huge size and variety of the student population today, given America's commitment to educate all its people. But these features of schools also derive from the fundamental conception of learning as straightforward, simple acquisition of facts and skills and of teaching as straightforward, simple delivery, performance, and technical/humane service. This conception of learning and teaching is similar to a lot of our common-sense conceptions of science, pointed out by the cognitive researchers: it is naive, intuitive, based in the individual's own limited experience—and wrong.

THE CHALLENGE FOR THE FUTURE

These seemingly immutable features of schooling appear to be teamed against the seemingly unachievable new group of higher-order thinking skills that society is calling on schools to teach. In a way, it's "the old familiars":

Lone teacher, many students
Lecturing and seatwork
Prepackaged, mainly symbolic print materials
The teacher/student bargain: easy grades for good behavior
Testing that "dumbs down" instruction
Students' early addiction to simple skills

versus "the new problem solvers":

Helping students make complex constructions of knowledge
Requiring students to tackle *ill*-structured problems
Preparing students to organize and monitor their own learning
Stoking problem solving with highly specific prior knowledge
Emphasizing collaborative and situation-specific learning
Setting students to work on tasks that incorporate skills

Such a confrontation appears to spell certain defeat for the problem-solving agenda. It need not be so. The items on the "old familiars" team have taken their present form from old conceptions that learning is the acquisition of knowledge and teaching is the straight-forward delivery of knowledge. If we turn our heads around and use a conception of learning as production and teaching as leadership, these seemingly intractable traditional features of schooling might be modified so that the higher-order thinking agenda could be realistically pursued.

This is not to say the task is easy. It will take tough higher-order thinking and problem-solving work from the inside, not mandates from the outside, by knowledgeable, experienced, proficient, thoughtful, committed, and energetic workers—teachers. Such teachers are not likely to be enlisted as change agents from the outside in the huge numbers we need. It is more likely that they will be identified, recognized, and developed from within workplaces that require, nourish, and encourage teachers to invest their skill, thought, idealism, and cooperation. Simultaneously to stimulate and support such teachers is the reason that a culture of professionalism must be built in schools and school districts.

Attributes of this professional culture in a school need not be newly conceived or intuited. Characteristics of and conditions for professional work in schools have been observed and are described in the following chapters in this book. However, such schools are neither common nor widespread; and in any event, social cultures cannot be copied—they must grow themselves. Each school must build its own work culture, unique and appropriate to its own population of students and teachers and to its community's goals and resources. In the absence of models to copy, a professional culture must be purposefully built from firm premises about how particular students best learn and how teachers best teach vis-à-vis an appropriate, sophisticated learning agenda. To acknowledge, elaborate, and insist upon these principles as the prerequisites for teaching our youth to think, to work, and to govern themselves should be the first task in building a professional culture in a school.

NOTES

1. The California Commission on the Teaching Profession was a state-level commission in California charged with studying the condition of teaching and making recommendations for change. See the references for the commission's final report.

2. The literature on teaching is filled with distinctions similar to these. For a discussion that parallels ours, see the article in the references by Ke-

pler-Zumwalt. For an even broader treatment that considers teaching as work, craft, profession, and art, see the article by Mitchell and Kerchner.

3. An analysis of professional work that elaborates these ideas, stressing the need for practitioners to be reflective and systematically to draw on their own experiences, has recently been elaborated by Don Schon in a pair of books. See the references.

4. In her presidential address to the American Educational Research Association in Washington, DC, on April 22, 1987, Lauren Resnick stressed the importance of both tools and work in groups for the exercise of intelligence, citing a wide range of recent research in cognitive psychology that explores these themes.

REFERENCES

Bereiter, C., & Scardamalia, M. (1987). An attainable version of high literacy: Approaches to teaching higher-order skills in reading and writing. *Curriculum Inquiry, 17*(1), 9–30.

California Commission on the Teaching Profession. (1985). *Who will teach our children?* (Staff report). Sacramento: Author.

Cuban, L. (1983). *How teachers taught: Constancy and change in American classrooms, 1890–1980.* New York: Longman.

Cuban, L. (1984). Policy and research dilemmas in the teaching of reasoning: Unplanned designs. *Review of Educational Research, 54*(4), 655–681.

Deci, E. L., & Ryan, R. M. (1985). *Intrinsic motivation and self-determination in human behavior.* New York: Plenum Press.

Doyle, W. (1983). Academic work. *Review of Educational Research, 53*(2), 159–200.

Drucker, P. (1987, March 11). Behind the changed world economy. *San Francisco Chronicle*, pp. C1, C8.

Durkin, D. (1981). Reading comprehension instruction in five basal reader series. *Reading Research Quarterly, 16*, 515–544.

Erickson, F. (1984). School literacy, reasoning, and civility: An anthropologist's perspective. *Review of Educational Research, 54*(4), 525–546.

Frederickson, C. H., & Dominic, J. (1981). *Writing: The nature, development, and teaching of written communication* (Vol. 2). Hillsdale, NJ: Erlbaum.

Frederickson, N. (1984). Implications of cognitive theory for instruction in problem-solving. *Review of Educational Research, 54*(3), 363–408.

Frederickson, N. (1986). Toward a broader conception of human intelligence. *American Psychologist, 41*(4), 445–452.

Goodlad, J. (1984). *A place called school.* New York: McGraw-Hill.

Hirsh, E. D. (1987). *Cultural literacy.* Boston: Houghton-Mifflin.

Hodgkinson, H. (in press). The schools we need for the kids we've got. In N. Magum (Ed.), *The schools we've got, the schools we need.* Washington, DC: American Association of Colleges for Teacher Education.

Kepler-Zumwalt, K. (1982). Research on teaching: Policy implications for Teacher Education. In A. Lieberman, L. Fischer, & M. McLaughlin (Eds.), *Policy making in education* (Eighty-first Yearbook of the National Society for the Study of Education, Part I, pp. 215–248). Chicago: University of Chicago Press.

Levin, H. (1986). Educational reform for disadvantaged students: An emerging crisis. (Search Series.) Washington, DC: National Education Association.

McNeil, L. (1986). *Contradictions of control: School structure and school knowledge.* New York: Routledge & Kegan Paul.

Mitchell, D. E., & Kerchner, C. T. (1983). Labor relations and teacher policy. In L. Shulman & G. Sykes (Eds.), *Handbook of teaching and policy* (pp. 214–238). New York: Longman.

Muller, T., & Espenshade, T. J. (1985). *The fourth wave: California's newest immigrants.* Washington, DC: Urban Institute Press.

Powell, A. G., Farrar, E., & Cohen, D. K. (1985). *The shopping mall high school.* Boston: Houghton-Mifflin.

Rogoff, B., & Lave, J. (Eds.). (1984). *Everyday cognition: Its development in social context.* Cambridge, MA: Harvard University Press.

Schlechty, P. (1987, January 30). Speech presented to the Holmes Group, Washington, DC.

Schon, D. A. (1983). *The reflective practitioner: How professionals think in action.* New York: Basic Books.

Schon, D. A. (1987). *Educating the reflective practitioner.* San Francisco: Jossey-Bass.

Sedlak, M. W., Wheeler, C. W., Pullin, D., & Cusick, P. (1986). *Selling students short: Classroom bargains and academic reform in the American high school.* New York: Teachers College Press.

Simon, H. A. (1980). Problem-solving and education. In D. T. Tuma & R. Reif (Eds.), *Problem-solving and education: Issues in teaching and research.* Hillsdale, NJ: Erlbaum.

Sternberg, R. J. (1987). Teaching critical thinking: Eight easy ways to fail before you begin. *Phi Delta Kappan, 68*(6), 456–459.

Sykes, G., & Devaney, K. (1984). *The role of the teacher—Two versions.* Unpublished background paper prepared for the California Commission on the Teaching Profession.

Sykes, G., & Devaney, K. (1985). A blight on the apple for teacher. *Education and Urban Society, 17*(3), 243–249.

2

School as a Place to Have a Career

MILBREY WALLIN McLAUGHLIN
SYLVIA MEI-LING YEE

What is a teaching career? And what makes a satisfying one? These questions are at the heart of proposals to reform the teaching profession and attract talented teachers. The answers framed by policy makers reflect two substantively different conceptions of career.

CONCEPTIONS OF CAREERS

The first is an *institutional* view that sees career in terms of organizational structures and rewards. This notion of career defines "advancement" as progression through a series of hierarchical functions, "success" as attainment of a slot at the top of the system, and "reward" as differential monetary recognition. Career is conceived in largely external terms of vertical mobility. For example, consider this statement by an occupational sociologist:

> With reference to occupational careers in organizations, the theoretical model involves entry into a position that requires the performance of occupational duties at the lowest rung of the occupational ladder. This is followed by a sequence of promotions into high-level positions within an organization, leading eventually to the pinnacle, and finally to retirement . . . this generalized model calls for upward progression from the bottom to the top. (Slocum, 1966, p. 5)

This traditional conception of career motivates many education personnel policies and reform efforts. In the early 1980s state educational policy makers set out to reshape the flat opportunity structure of the teaching occupation by providing financial incentives and advancement opportunities to teachers. They embraced strategies such as career ladders and merit pay in the hope of enlisting the commitment of experienced teachers to remain in the profession. At the top of the ladder are jobs that are basically administrative and quasi-supervisory, promoting teachers out of the classroom.

A second, different conception of career is *individually based*, taking meaning from personal motivations and goals. In contrast to the first view, this subjective notion of career relies on an internally defined sense of advancement and satisfaction. It may or may not generate the vertical or hierarchical career path that is the centerpiece of the first view. The extent to which it does depends on an individual's goals and values (Schein, 1978). As a consequence, this notion of career is difficult to standardize and implement wholesale. Policies based on this conception of career stress multiple rewards and individual voice in identifying them, while moving the institutional or structural definition to the background.

Which of these different conceptions most nearly fits teachers' notions of a satisfying career? We explored this question in a study involving 85 teachers in five diverse northern California school districts.[1] Teachers, we found, base their notion of both career and professional satisfaction squarely within this second, subjective conception. Most of the teachers we interviewed, when asked what they hoped to be doing in the next five years, replied that they wanted to stay in the classroom and do what they enjoy most—teach. Most were interested neither in moving vertically into quasi-administrative or expanded teaching functions nor horizontally into administrative or central-office resource positions. Career, for the majority of these teachers, clearly was conceived in terms of classroom teaching and continued direct involvement with youngsters. As one teacher put it:

> I am stuck on teaching. I really don't want to do anything else.
> I enjoy being a teacher and never want to be an administrator.
> There is something wrong with the system when administrators
> see it as punishment to be sent back to be a classroom teacher
> and when people think that there is something wrong if you are
> still a teacher after so many years.

Only 6% of the teachers reported that it was likely they would apply for a principalship; several of these added, however, that they hoped for teacher-administrator positions that would allow them to continue some instructional contact with students. These people were committed to working with students but also desired some influence on the larger workings of the schools.

For some teachers, professional advancement meant new or expanded teaching roles. Specifically, nearly a third said they probably would apply for mentor-teacher positions, while a smaller proportion (8%) reported some likelihood of applying for resource-teacher positions. However, these teachers retained a strong commitment to classroom teaching. Several saw these expanded roles, by giving them a larger view of educational or organizational processes, as an enhancement of their classroom effectiveness. A portion of the teachers who aspired to expanded roles clearly wanted to continue in or return to the classroom. So even though some teachers wanted expanded or new roles, a vertical job structure did not fit their vision of career advancement.

This typically horizontal, internal view of a career outlined by teachers we interviewed tracks closely with research on teachers and other professionals. Research on reward structures in public schools, for example, suggests differences between motivational patterns of professional and production-oriented organizations (Spuck, 1974). Many people are drawn to the teaching profession by a strong service ethic or a strong client orientation and attribute greater importance to intrinsic motivation or reward (Lortie, 1975; Swanson-Owens, 1986). The strongest incentives for teachers derive their power from enabling teachers to reap psychic, intangible benefits from making a difference in the classroom (Lortie, 1975).

Similarly, research on female elementary school teachers demonstrates an internally defined notion of career success—personal satisfaction derived from becoming "great teachers" through achievements with students—that does not hinge on vertical mobility (Biklen, 1986). New recruits to teaching from more "prestigious" fields, such as law, accounting, and engineering, also explained their career shifts in terms of teaching's intrinsic rewards—making a difference in someone's life. A former accountant reflected: "I feel like I'm doing something worthwhile. . . . It's certainly not the money" ("Fresh old faces," 1987, p. 2a). A successful attorney turned history teacher echoed this sentiment: winning in court "was all about money. It didn't seem to me that sixty years from now I'd say, 'Hey, I won all these lawsuits and won a lot of money and that was worthwhile'" ("Fresh old faces," 1987, p. 2a). This former attorney is now engaged in what she thinks is important—leading students to think critically about social issues. A teacher returned to teaching after a stint in the business world echoes this sentiment:

> I left education and came back. I commuted to the city, wore silk blouses and enjoyed an increase in status. The real reason I

came back was that even though I had a very glamorous job in the outside world, I missed the human purpose of teaching.

Teachers, then, conceive of career and define career satisfaction largely in subjective terms—making a difference, sharing a discipline they love. Through these attitudes, teachers generate an *expertise-based, individually determined* notion of career; advancement is framed in terms of an ongoing process of professional growth, and success means effectiveness in the teaching role. The flat occupational structure that characterizes teaching has no necessarily positive or negative relationship to a career for most teachers. Instead, teachers focus attention on the individual meaning that professional roles and experiences have for them.[2] Their careers are individually constructed and experienced. In contrast to a hierarchical, institutionally structured notion of career, this conception depends on professional growth and efficacy.

How, then, from this perspective, does a teacher achieve a rewarding career? If "career" for teachers is not defined primarily as it is in many private sector activities—as upward movement—or as it is in many semiskilled occupations—more money—what are the attributes of a teaching position that promote this subjective, expertise-based conception?

FACTORS SHAPING A TEACHING CAREER

Two individually experienced, position-related factors emerge consistently from research on teaching and from organizational research as critical to an individual's effectiveness, satisfaction, and growth: *level of opportunity* and *level of capacity*.[3] These behavioral attributes of a position vary significantly across institutional settings and play a primary role in defining an individual's career as a teacher and the satisfaction derived from it.

Level of Opportunity

Level of opportunity means the chance to develop basic competence; the availability of stimulation, challenge, and feedback about performance; and the support for efforts to try new things and acquire new skills. Level of opportunity is central to an expertise-based notion of career because it determines the extent to which an individual can develop increasing degrees of professional competence and reach new levels of mastery. Level of opportunity means much more than the availability of weekend workshops or afterschool staff development sessions. Many factors—both informal and formal—comprise important opportunities. Our teachers mentioned a variety of sources of significant professional growth beyond the usual credential programs or school inservice activities: for example, attending conferences, participating in informal mentor relationships, sharing ideas with other teachers; observing other classes and being observed; changing subjects, schools, or grade levels. One teacher explained what helped her be her best with students:

> There are a lot of things that go together. It is hard to isolate a few things. I think it is important to be up to date through the professional development programs that are available. [It is also] the willingness of teachers to help each other. I think on this staff if you have a problem you can go to a teacher and ask for help and they will help you without making you feel dumb.

Opportunities to improve performance, particularly in the context of collegial interaction, are also valued rewards in themselves. Another teacher explained what she considered most rewarding in her work, in addition to "seeing student growth":

> [The most rewarding things for me are] being exposed to some of my colleagues that I have respect for and learn a lot from; [and] the problem solving regarding particular children that is done with my colleagues. We regularly get together before school and talk about children with special problems.

Opportunities and support for professional growth are particularly critical for beginning teachers. Teachers often referred to the stress of their first year on the job. The conditions under which some young teachers operated necessitated strategies for physical and emotional survival that precluded the kind of reflective growth good teaching requires. A high school teacher offers a positive example of professional development opportunities early in the career:

> I think the most important [learning] was the year I started to teach. This school district let me develop very slowly and positively. They surrounded me with very good teachers and started me on a limited schedule. Out of five periods, two periods were team teaching with almost all observation.

Teachers with rich opportunities to grow and learn are enthusiastic about their work and are motivated to find ways to do even better. But teachers with low levels of opportunity become burned out, just make it through the day, and trade on old skills and routines. They wind up feeling stuck in deadend jobs, going nowhere in terms of their career.

Level of Capacity

Capacity is the second aspect of a teaching position that shapes a teacher's sense of career and satisfaction. Also called "power" by some analysts, capacity comprises teachers' access to resources and the ability to mobilize them, the availability of the tools to do their job, and the capability to influence the goals and direction of their institution (Kanter, 1983; Stein & Kanter, 1980). A number of teachers pointed to the latter aspect of capacity as the most important change policy makers could promote to improve classroom teaching:

> Organizational direction [is critical]. If teachers are part of the decision-making process they are enthusiastic about bringing about [the changes necessary to improved practice].

Conversely, other respondents pointed to the frustration associated with a lack of capacity to shape their environment:

> Too many extraneous people are involved in making decisions [about curriculum]. They don't know the first thing about what they are talking about.

> [The least rewarding aspect of teaching is] attempting to deal with district administration and to some degree school site administration. It is tremendously frustrating. Teachers have very little input into decisions. . . . [For example,] there is a $5 million fund for building repair and there is no [teacher] input, no committee is being formed to discuss it.

Another important aspect of capacity is access to resources and the ability to mobilize them. Teachers who feel they lack adequate materials to do their job, who have little control over their institutional setting or resources, quickly become discouraged, bitter, and frustrated. A teacher from an urban school spoke about the devastating effect this had on her:

I think that schools could be a very progressive force—but not
with the [lack of] resources they currently have. I feel angry
and depressed and frustrated. It is a very difficult situation for
those teachers who care.

Another teacher in a school where books did not arrive until two
months after school started remarked: "At the time, I felt like I was
trying to give my best, and we didn't even have books. [As a result,]
a lot of teachers lost interest in teaching." Still another teacher spent
his first years with no textbooks for the students and teaching outside
his area of specialization. He remarked in retrospect:

You can only learn to be a teacher if you have a supportive nurturing environment. If you are a soldier in a war zone, you
don't plant a garden. If you do, the garden doesn't do very well.

As obvious as it seems, access to resources is often neglected in
discussion of motivation; yet it is as important as any reward for work
improvement (Staw, 1983). One teacher stated that it was "having the
tools of the trade—books, paper, and pencils" that helped her to do
the best job she could. Without these tools, teachers are set up for
failure and professional frustration.

Teachers with a sense of capacity tend to pursue effectiveness in
the classroom, express commitment to the organization and career, and
report a high level of professional satisfaction. Lacking a sense of
power, teachers who care often end up acting in ways that are educationally counterproductive by "coping"—lowering their aspirations, disengaging from the setting, and framing their goals only in
terms of getting through the day. Teaching thus is apt to become just
a job, not a career.

SCHOOL ENVIRONMENTS THAT SUPPORT A CAREER

What kinds of institutional settings are associated with these be-
havorial aspects of a satisfying teaching career? What kinds of schools
provide levels of opportunity and capacity to teachers adequate to
support professional growth and accomplishment?

Five interrelated qualities of the school environment emerge from
our research and related studies as central to enabling a sense of
professional progression and effectiveness and thus to creating a sat-

isfying teaching career. Schools where teachers can establish a sense
of career are typically:

Resource-adequate (as opposed to resource-deprived)
Integrated (as opposed to segmented)
Collegial (as opposed to isolated)
Problem-solving (as opposed to problem-hiding)
Investment-centered (as opposed to payoff-focused)[4]

Adequacy of Resources

A *resource-adequate* environment is one that provides the minimum tools and conditions necessary to teaching. Absence of the bare
minimum frustrated many of the teachers in our study, most especially teachers located in urban, inner-city schools. For example, a
high school teacher explained how an insufficient number of biology
textbooks meant she had to use two different editions for a class,
which meant having to identify two different sets of page numbers
and correlating problem sets. A colleague in another school also
pointed to the demoralizing impact of insufficient science materials:

> For me the least rewarding aspect of teaching is the fact that
> there is so little material to use in the area of science. Last
> week my class [with 31 students] was examining tissues and
> had only 12 microscopes, so more than half the students had to
> wait at least 20 minutes before their turn—this kills their enthu-
> siasm . . . and the lesson loses a lot. [When we do dissections] I
> pray all of my students won't come to class [since I have only 6
> dissection pans]. Those are the kinds of things you deal with.
> You know, those are the things that make you not want to come
> to work.

A history teacher who was not provided paper, pencils, or history texts
during his first year likened his experience to having land mines
placed in his path as a teacher. He concluded with anger and resent-
ment, "Don't criticize me for not being able to run with the ball."
Gross deficiencies such as described by these teachers impede
teachers' efforts to provide even an adequate level of instructional
activity for their students and leave them feeling effectively powerless.

However, our research also indicates that resources by themselves do not empower teachers or contribute to a higher level of professional satisfaction. We talked with teachers in schools that would be considered resource-slim who expressed excitement and enthusiasm about their jobs; we also met teachers in schools that were relatively resource-rich who expressed cynicism and frustration about their effectiveness and about teaching. We saw that given the bare essentials to get on with the job, other nonmaterial aspects of the institutional setting defined teachers' sense of their careers and level of satisfaction. For example, when asked about factors that made her as effective as possible, a high school teacher responded:

> working as a member of a group as opposed to working as an individual . . . sharing ideas and concerns with colleagues. Materials are important but not as important [as these factors].

Similarly, answers to a survey question about the importance of various considerations as supports for improved teaching revealed that only 20 percent of the teachers ranked "improved instructional resources" as first or second in importance. In contrast, 55 percent of the teachers placed "increased input into decisions that affect the school and classroom" as first or second in importance; 48 percent ranked "more time for reflection on teaching practices or planning with colleagues" at or near the top. And, in fact, these teacher preferences are reflected in the institutional features that follow.

Common Goals

An *integrated school environment,* the second element of a school setting supportive of a teaching career, is characterized by unity of purpose, clear organizational guidelines and goals, and a collective sense of responsibility. In their study of effective schools, Rutter et al. (1979, p. 192) emphasize this aspect of the school setting:

> The "atmosphere" of any particular school will be greatly influenced by the degree to which it functions as a coherent whole, with agreed ways of doing things which are consistent throughout the school and which have the general support of all staff.

These features set the stage for professional challenge, growth, and accomplishment, because they establish shared expectations and a sense of group purpose. Thus, teachers can gauge their performance not only against individual goals, but also against goals established for the school as a whole.

An integrated environment also provides a degree of comfort and certainty to teachers as they strive to acquire new skills and strategies. It does so because the institutional "rules of the game" are clear, thereby directing and bounding teachers' efforts. On this point, one teacher recalled how she was nearly driven from the profession when she was assigned to work in a segmented environment where the teachers were divided and where bad feelings, due to misunderstandings, inconsistencies, and blocked communication, were pervasive. Demoralized by this environment, she felt thwarted in her efforts to improve and to do her best.

Another teacher underscored the importance of institutional agreement: "The number one way to help teachers to be effective is to make sure there is a consistent, schoolwide set of rules that are followed." A colleague added:

> Teachers need to know what the policy is and to be assured that it will be enforced so they know how to handle a number of issues that arise in the classroom.

An integrated environment supports opportunity for professional challenge and growth in other ways. An integrated environment frames performance and accomplishment as a group (not just as an individual) responsibility: the group's purpose drives individual actions. Thus collective rather than individual accounting for school outcomes characterizes an integrated environment; problems with a teacher's performance are regarded as the responsibility of the group rather than failure on the part of the individual teacher. In segmented schools, teachers see their role confined by the four walls of their classrooms; in an integrated institutional setting, teachers see themselves as a part of a cohesive effort.

The principal plays a key role in creating a collective sense among the faculty. Too often teachers feel a "them—us" relationship with the administration. One teacher spoke about how her principal succeeded in creating a sense of group purpose in the school:

> The current principal works so hard and is so visible that teachers are motivated to work harder, too. Also, she talks to teachers as equals, not down to them. She says things like "what are *we* going to do," "*we* have a problem," "this is what *we* need to do, I can't do it myself," "this is something *we* have to live with."

Ironically, in segmented environments, the "system" often is trusted more than the individual teacher and functions such as teacher evaluation are designed to protect the system from the individual (McLaughlin & Pfeifer, 1988). The institutional focus turns to catching and routing out "incompetents" instead of nurturing the growth of a competent collective of teachers.

In contrast, where the group's purpose is framed in terms of improving the quality of education in the school, innovation, challenge, and experimentation with new ideas become the norm rather than the province of an isolated individual. Having common goals and objectives so that all the faculty is headed in the same direction not only creates a sense of solidarity around a shared purpose, it is also a source of motivation and reward in itself (Mitchell et al., 1983). Consequently, motivation is fostered in an integrated environment because individual growth is considered integral to institutional achievement.[5] An elementary teacher highlighted these aspects of an integrated school environment:

> [Discussion of instructional matters with other teachers] is a structured part of the school. We have a principal's meeting and on alternative weeks, cluster meetings by grade levels. We meet to discuss children, their progress, anything we want to discuss. These meetings run from 3:30–5:00 once a week. Sometimes we meet [as a whole faculty] to address issues we all want to hear about—like human relations, critical-thinking skills, math and language-arts successes. One thing we did was a peer observation triad. We would go and observe and take copious notes about their teaching and their interactions with the kids and then meet and discuss it. We are the only ones [in the district] who have done it. It grew out of our own loneliness [in the classroom]. [As a result] there are a lot of rich opportunities for learning in this school and that's a part of the job satisfaction.

In such an atmosphere, the general level of opportunity for an individual teacher—in terms of stimulation and challenge—is high. And individual power or capacity is enhanced by the collective, cohesive nature of the school's purpose—as is collegiality, a third institutional element fundamental to a satisfying career as a teacher.

Collegiality

A *collegial* environment provides multiple opportunities for in-teraction and creates expectations of colleagues as regular sources of feedback, ideas, and support. A collegial environment enhances both level of opportunity and level of capacity for teachers, because it serves as a critical, essential source of stimulation and motivation. Dedication to high standards of performance is more easily promoted through shared professional norms than by bureaucratic sanctions and controls (Van Maanen & Barley, 1984).

Developmental relationships, such as between a mentor teacher and protégé(e), can be a powerful stimulus for change and learning. These relationships, however, do not have to be formally assigned ones, as in mentor programs. In fact, voluntary or naturally occurring collegial relationships may be more effective than organizationally imposed ones (Kram, 1985).

A high school teacher described a confluence of collegial activi-ties, both voluntary and arranged, that made her early years exciting and exceptionally productive. She made an important transformation in her teaching strategy from a "strictly academic" teaching style to a "more caring, holistic, individual approach," which enabled her to reach students better. She made this significant change when she was taken under the wing of a veteran teacher, who was also undergoing an evolution of teaching styles and who volunteered copies of her materials. In addition, she had the opportunity to observe other dy-namic teachers and to meet every two weeks with other members of the English department to share ideas and to develop curriculum jointly.

This teacher exemplifies the views teachers expressed in our survey. We asked about the importance of informal conversations with colleagues as compared to more formal sources of professional de-velopment. With possible responses of "very helpful," "somewhat helpful," and "not very helpful," 45% of the teachers said that infor-mal conversations with colleagues were "very helpful"; an addi-tional 33% rated this form of collegial interaction as a "somewhat helpful" source of professional stimulation. In contrast, courses at nearby universities or colleges were marked "very helpful" by only 22% of the respondents; district-sponsored activities were ranked "very helpful" by 8%.

In schools with low levels of collegial exchange, it is difficult to create shared norms or to build a sense of common purpose for in-structional improvement. A high school math teacher complained:

I'm confined too much to a class with not enough time to interact with colleagues. We are like separate ships. We need to talk
about kids and instruction and be in the same boat together.

In more isolated environments, teachers do not often get beyond
complaining about difficult kids. In contrast, in schools with high
levels of collegial interaction, discussion among teachers centers more
around instructional planning and improvement of practice (Rosenholtz, 1986). For example, one teacher pointed to her school's high
level of collegial interaction as an important ingredient in instructional success: "We have learned to use each other as resources. There
is a commitment here of teachers to work on doing better."

Other research shows how more successful schools are differentiated from less successful ones by the norms of interaction and continuous improvement (Little, 1982). Contrary to conventional wisdom,
which holds that teachers resist collegial comment and involvement,
many of the teachers we interviewed wanted more feedback from
colleagues because they recognized the limitations inherent to working alone within a classroom. For example, a typical teacher commented:

I'd like more people to come and visit my classroom—to look,
visit, comment. Not to visit with an evaluative purpose, but
with the purpose of commenting on what's going on in the
classroom. I'd really like feedback from my peers.

A suburban teacher spoke in similar terms about her need and criteria for a mechanism for reflection:

I want nonthreatening feedback from someone who has the
time to really take a hard look. It would have to be someone
whom I respected and looked up to, and they would have to
value the same things I do in teaching. I need a comfort zone, a
framework around me within which I have the freedom to be
myself—to use my own judgment and get trust and respect.

Colleagues, in short, provide both the stimulation central to opportunity and the feedback and comment that enhance individual capacity or power. One teacher put it this way:

Coming to this school [with its high level of collegial interac-
tion] had a tremendous impact on my attitude as a teacher. I

found the staff as a whole more happy, more excited about
teaching, more creative. In turn I became more excited and innovative about my own teaching . . . and less drained at the
end of the day.

Isolated teachers, in contrast, lose out on a very special source of
growth and motivation—their colleagues—and are left effectively to
their own devices to create satisfaction or to forge a teaching career.

Problem-Solving Orientation

Careers and professional satisfaction are also enhanced by environments that are *problem-solving* rather than problem-hiding, a
fourth institutional feature associated with a rewarding teaching career. A problem-solving environment is characterized by a strong
sense of group purpose (present in integrated and collegial environments) that encourages teachers to reflect on their practice and explore ways to improve it on an ongoing, rather than episodic, basis. It
is an environment in which it is safe to be candid and to take the risks
inherent in trying out new ideas or unfamiliar practices. A problem-
solving environment assumes constant change and revision—or
professional growth—as the norm and thus establishes conditions
central to a high level of opportunity for individual teachers. For example, many teachers in a school characterized by problem-solving
norms pointed to problem-solving activities among the faculty as the
most rewarding aspect of teaching.

Conversely, in problem-hiding environments, teachers hide their
problems and then hide the fact that they are hiding problems.
"Everything's fine" becomes the standard response to administrative
or collegial inquiry about classroom activities, and the classroom door
closes out candid review or comment, thus surrounding and isolating
practice. An elementary school teacher described just such a setting:

Most teachers [in our school] don't know what other teachers
do. One learns to keep one's mouth shut about what your kids
are doing. It's a problem of ego. Teachers resent [your com-
ments] unless you are really good friends.

Problem-hiding environments typically are segmented settings in
which each individual worries about him- or herself, with no assumed need to worry about others or the performance of the organization as a whole. And because success is seen exclusively in
individual, rather than in institutional, terms, incentives direct indi-

viduals to portray success and bury disappointments or less-success-
ful activities.

In a problem-solving environment, teachers do just the opposite.[6] Individual problems are often aggregated to the institutional
level to be examined as a problem for the organization as a whole—
inadequate staff development, inappropriate backup materials, problematic pupil placements, for example. Individual problems also typically are treated as a group responsibility—the group's self-interest
requires that problems be recognized and addressed. Rosenholtz
(1986) describes a similar phenomenon in what she calls a "learning-
enriched" environment. In such settings, she found no teachers willing to define ineffective practice as an individual's problem or to point
out a "bad" teacher. Rather, disappointing classroom activities were
approached as fixable and within the purview of the group.

Reward Structure

Finally, an environment that promotes individual opportunity and
capacity is *investment-centered* rather than payoff-centered. Teachers are rewarded for growth, risk taking, and change rather than only
for successful past practice. A payoff-centered environment, where
strategies such as merit pay, summative evaluation, or bonuses reward successful practice, ironically encourages precisely what these
policies hope to discourage—a backward-looking point of view, hiding of mistakes or disappointments, "show-and-tell" on evaluation
day.

Payoff-centered reward systems make it impossible to produce
integrated, collegial, and problem-solving schools. Merit pay encourages competitive instead of collaborative relationships among the
faculty (Bacharach et al., 1984; Porwoll, 1979; Lawler, 1981). Moreover, merit pay and bonus plans operate as disincentives for teachers
to be open about problems or to approach others for help (Bacharach
et al., 1984). Many career-ladder schemes are basically merit pay in
disguise. While possibly an incentive for the portion of the teaching
staff who make it to the top, ladder schemes discourage those who do
not (Freiberg, 1985; Kanter, 1977). Ironically, career ladders deny careers to a substantial proportion of teachers, given the inherent quo-
tas on the top rungs of the advancement system (Johnson, 1986;
Bacharach et al., 1986). One respondent commented on the logic of
"paying off" good teachers with promotion out of teaching:

Unfortunately, many people think of growth as an opportunity
to leave the classroom. This way of thinking is what's destroy-

ing the public schools. The notion of getting good teachers into administration is a very negative notion; teachers should be encouraged and given the opportunity to remain in the classroom.

Rewards such as extra pay can actually depress a teacher's involvement, because the provision of monetary rewards removes the spirit of volunteerism and the sense of self-efficacy that are important intrinsic motivators (Berman & McLaughlin, 1978; Deci, 1976; Pfeffer, 1981). Investment in teachers is investment in the future. It implies a long-range view of nurturing the development of teachers and their interest in continuous improvement. And it rewards teachers by making possible what matters most to them—personal satisfaction from a job well done, from making a real difference in student learning.

An investment-centered approach also encourages teachers to stretch themselves beyond what they know and to seek what one of our teachers called ongoing "professional refreshment." An outstanding high school teacher with 16 years of experience related how opportunity for development and the capacity to do her job are critical to her sense of growth and career:

> I still love teaching. I like working with young people and watching people learn. [After my first six years of teaching] I got burned out, and thought about leaving. I had reached my stagnation point. I got tired of doing the same old thing, not growing professionally. I took a sabbatical and [when I returned] became involved in a new way of teaching with other teachers [cooperative learning]. That gave me a fresh start again. Now I see professional growth meaning revitalization, learning new things, new approaches, meeting with colleagues, being part of decisionmaking which affects my classroom—decisions about policy, curriculum—and not just accepting dictates. (Yee, 1987)

Teachers who say they love their work typically spoke of the need for challenge and periodic change to avoid boredom, getting "in a rut," or becoming "robotic." They often mentioned assignment changes or temporary assignments as a stimulus to learn new things and renew their commitment to teaching. A veteran teacher described the effect of her change from teaching first grade:

> The principal gave me a change which I needed. It was like starting teaching all over. I was bursting with enthusiasm, which I needed. It was fun to get new material. We all need

change once in a while. Coming to a new school was also a good change. I think I would like to work for the district some time and try my hand at curriculum development, because that would help my teaching, too. It would help me to look at my work from another point of view and give me its freshness.

Investment in teachers—attention to their long-range growth needs—prevents burnout and reduced involvement by providing jobs with a high level of opportunity and power. It also means creating a work environment that is resource-adequate, integrated, collegial, and problem-solving—in other words, an environment in which a teacher can have a rewarding career.

CONCLUSION: TOWARD CAREERS, NOT JOBS

Career satisfaction for teachers hinges on the ability to pursue the personal values and beliefs that led them into teaching—to be of service and to make valued contributions to young students. The notion of career, as formulated by a majority of teachers, is subjective and individual. By itself, an organizational view of career that centers on status, money, and hierarchical advancement is too restrictive to motivate most teachers, who see their careers in terms of developing new levels of classroom-based expertise. Career, for teachers, is a constructed reality, a consequence of the interplay between individual goals and the school setting, not an institutional given or a rung on a career ladder. Rather than a positional view of career, with a long-term series of jobs, this subjective view of career implies a dynamic, developmental process that is constructed from features of the work environment—level of opportunity and level of capacity. And career development for teachers is an ongoing process, not an episodic event—an aspect seldom considered seriously by policies to promote teachers' professional growth and satisfaction (Bacharach et al., 1986).

The subjective nature of career underscores the need for policy to address the diverse nature of career orientations and individually valued rewards (Derr, 1986). Wholesale solutions, particularly those that place primary emphasis on traditional promotion systems, misspecify the incentives that motivate teachers and the nature of a satisfying career. A view of career that is individually defined and based in evolving levels of expertise highlights the need for a professional development strategy that is based on a system of multiple rewards and development resources, one that includes in its offerings opportunities for lateral and temporary moves as well as for continuous stimulation and development (Schein, 1986). School environments that are investment-centered, problem-solving, integrated, resource-adequate, and collegial offer the variegated, individualized kinds of incentives called for. These kinds of schools enable a teaching career.

Unfortunately, most teachers work in schools where these features are uneven or absent. Most schools, independent of financial resources, are segmented, egg-crate institutions in which teachers are isolated; objectives are framed in individual, not institutional, terms; problems are hidden rather than examined; and rewards are associated with past performance, not future challenge. As a result, we conclude that most teachers have jobs not careers.

Should this really matter in the scheme of things? Are we talking about anything much more than teachers' "happiness quotients"—a desirable end to be sure, but hardly a compelling issue for policy? We believe it should matter, because whether teachers have jobs or have careers has important consequences for the institution of education and for society's objectives as well as for the individual.

Individual teachers who experience teaching as a job, rather than as a career, generally feel bitter, frustrated, and unhappy in the classroom. They feel they are "stuck" not "moving."[7] In a people-dependent enterprise such as education, such perceptions have direct impact upon the organization's mission and goals. Stuck employees tend to lower their aspirations, become apathetic, and settle for "just getting through the day." The energy, enthusiasm, and persistence characteristic of effective teachers is difficult to mobilize and sustain for individuals who perceive themselves and their professional activity as stagnant or thwarted. The classroom consequences for students are obvious. As John Dewey warned in 1916, if teaching is not stimulating to teachers, then we can hardly expect them to make learning very interesting to students.

In contrast to teachers who feel stuck in their jobs, individuals who feel they are moving, who feel a sense of continuing challenge and growth, generally aim for more, try harder, and express a high level of commitment to their organization. For these reasons, teachers who feel a sense of professional movement—who have a sense of a viable career—are more likely to be effective in motivating students and reaching youngsters with diverse needs. Whether teachers have jobs or careers, whether they feel they are stuck or moving—these affect the fundamental purposes of education, because these feelings affect the energy, interest, and commitment brought to the classroom.

Other important implications flow from the extent to which teachers experience a career based in growing expertise and individual competence. The degree to which schools can respond effectively to changing conditions and pressures on the system depends ultimately on the response of individuals in the classroom. Teachers teaching in classrooms is what education is all about. The ability of the institution to change and to adapt turns on the ability and willingness of teachers to change and adapt. Individual competence and motivation are thus among the most important assets of a school. The vitality of today's schools as well as tomorrow's hinges to a significant degree on the extent to which teachers have a rewarding career. In education, where teachers comprise the technology, the link between individual responses to challenge and change and organizational effectiveness is direct and irreducible.

Further, the demands of policy makers and the public for "greater accountability" are met most effectively when teachers are engaged in a satisfying career. Both quality and control in the school organization are enhanced when motivation and standards are internalized, because the most powerful accountability mechanisms come from professional norms and standards. Career, in the individual, subjective, expertise-based sense elaborated here, functions as an unobtrusive, collective form of organizational control.[8] Accountability rooted in the professional orientation of teachers provides a form of control much more secure when classroom doors are closed than that vested in formal roles, sanctions, or authority.

In multiple ways, it matters then, whether or not school is a place to have a career. It matters to the satisfaction and vitality of the individual. It matters to the enthusiasm, aspiration, and commitment evident in the classroom. It matters to the ability of the educational institution to adapt and respond effectively to changed circumstances and environmental pressures. And it matters to institutional accountability—to the fit between organizational concerns for quality and individual activities.

The task before policy makers and practitioners, then, is to develop strategies and policies that acknowledge the multifaceted, individual nature of a teaching career and that organize rewards and advancement around the challenge of the work itself. Moving to an expertise-based, subjective view of career requires thinking broadly about the multiple sources of motivation and support for professional development that operate in the school and about the design of school settings that nurture individual opportunity and capacity, and so foster a rewarding teaching career. Institutional or structural solutions have a role to play, but are marginal only to career satisfaction for most teachers.

NOTES

1. This two-year study, which involved intensive interviews with teachers at all grade levels in school districts of different socioeconomic status and size, explored sources of teachers' satisfaction and effectiveness. It was sponsored by the Walter S. Johnson Foundation and carried out by Milbrey McLaughlin, Annette Lareau, R. Scott Pfeifer, Deborah Swanson-Owens, and Sylvia Yee of Stanford University's School of Education.

2. A number of analysts explore this notion of an internally defined career and career satisfaction. See, for example, Van Maanen and Barley (1984), Schein (1978), and Stebbins (1970).

3. The discussion that follows was stimulated by Rosabeth Moss Kanter's analysis of innovation and entrepreneurship in American corporations, *The Change Masters*. Kanter identifies opportunities for development and power as positional attributes associated with individual-level satisfaction, innovativeness, and high levels of contribution to the organization. This framework is elaborated in Stein & Kanter (1980). These themes appear in other frameworks and under other labels in analyses of teacher incentives and satisfaction (for example, Johnson, 1986) and of effective staff-development programs (for example, Lieberman & Miller, 1979).

4. These distinctions combine and elaborate analyses developed by Susan Rosenholtz (1986), Rosabeth Moss Kanter (1983), and Milbrey Wallin McLaughlin and R. Scott Pfeifer (1988).

5. Susan Rosenholtz (1986) elaborates this notion in a setting that she calls a "learning enriched environment."

6. This analysis draws on Kanter (1983).

7. Kanter (1983) uses these terms to describe different levels of employee motivation and commitment.

8. John Van Maanen (1977) elaborates this notion of control and the power of aligning individual incentives with institutional objectives.

REFERENCES

Bacharach, S. B., Conley, S., & Shedd, J. (1986). Beyond career ladders: Structuring teacher career development systems. *Teachers College Record*, 87(4), 563–574.

Bacharach, S. B., Lipsky, D. B., & Shedd, J. B. (1984). *Paying for better teaching: Merit pay and its alternatives*. Ithaca, NY: Organizational Analysis and Practice.

Berman, P., & McLaughlin, M. W. (1978). *Federal programs supporting educational change: Vol. 4. The findings in review*. Santa Monica: The Rand Corp.

Biklen, S. K. (1986). I have always worked: Elementary schoolteaching as a career. *Phi Delta Kappan*, 67(7), 504–512.

Deci, E. L. (1976). The hidden costs of rewards. *Organizational dynamics*, 4(3), 61–72.

Derr, C. D. (1986). *Managing the new careerists: The diverse career success orientations of today's workers*. San Francisco: Jossey-Bass.

Freiberg, H. J. (1985, December). Master teacher programs: Lessons from the past. *Educational Leadership*, pp. 16–21.

"Fresh old faces turn to teaching." (1987, April 13). *San Jose Mercury News*, pp. 1a–2a.

Johnson, S. M. (1986). Incentives for teachers: What motivates, what matters. *Educational Administration Quarterly*, 1986, 22(3), 54–79.

Kanter, R. M. (1977). *Men and women of the corporation*. New York: Basic Books.

Kanter, R. M. (1983). *The change masters: Innovations for productivity in the American corporation*. New York: Simon and Shuster.

Kram, K. (1985). *Mentoring at work*. Glenview, IL: Scott, Foresman.

Lawler, E. E. (1981). *Pay and organizational development*. Reading, MA: Addison-Wesley.

Lieberman, A., & Miller, L. (Eds.) (1979). *Staff development: New demands, new realities, new perspectives*. New York: Teachers College Press.

Little, J. W. (1982). Norms of collegiality and experimentation: Workplace conditions of school success. *American Educational Research Journal*. 19(3), 325–340.

Lortie, D. C. (1975). *Schoolteacher: A sociological study*. Chicago: University of Chicago Press.

McLaughlin, M. W., & Pfeifer, R. S. (1988). *Teacher evaluation: Improvement, accountability, and effective learning*. New York: Teachers College Press.

Mitchell, D. E., Ortiz, F. I., & Mitchell, T. K. (1983). *Work orientation and job performance: The cultural basis of teaching rewards*. Riverside, CA: University of California Press.

Pfeffer, J. (1981). *Power and organizations*. Boston: Pitman.

Porwoll, P. J. (1979). *Merit pay for teachers*. Arlington, VA: Educational Research Service.

Rosenholtz, S. J. (1986). *The organizational context of teaching*. Interim report to NIE, Grant #NIE-G-83-0041.

Rutter, M., Maugham, B., Mortimer, P., Ouston, J., & Smith, A. (1979). *Fifteen thousand hours: Secondary schools and their effects on children*. Cambridge, MA: Harvard University Press.

Schein, E. (1978). *Career dynamics: Matching individual and organizational needs*. Reading, MA: Addison-Wesley.

Schein, E. (1986). Increasing organization effectiveness through better human resource planning and development. In A. Leibowitz, C. Farren, &

B. Kaye (Eds.), *Designing career development systems*. San Francisco: Jossey-Bass.

Slocum, W. L. (1966). *Occupational careers: A sociological perspective*. Chicago: Aldine.

Spuck, D. W. (1974). Reward structures in the public high school. *Educational Administration Quarterly, 10*, 18–34.

Staw, B. (1983). Motivation research versus the art of faculty management. *Review of Higher Education, 6*(Summer), 301–321.

Stebbins, R. A. (1970). Career: The subjective approach. *Sociological Quarterly, 11*, 32–49.

Stein, B. A., & Kanter, R. M. (1980). Building the parallel organization: Creating mechanisms for permanent quality of work life. *The Journal of Applied Behavioral Science, 16*(3), 371–387.

Swanson-Owens, D. (1986, April). *Teachers' perspectives on teaching: Enduring and emerging themes*. Paper presentation at the annual meeting of the American Educational Research Association, San Francisco.

Van Maanen, J. (1977). Summary: Towards a theory of the career. In J. Van Maanen, *Organizational careers: Some new perspectives* (pp. 161–180). New York: Wiley.

Van Maanen, J., & Barley, S. R. (1984). Occupational communities: Culture and control in organizations. In B. M. Staw (Ed.), *Research in organizational behavior* (Vol. 6, pp. 287–365). Greenwich, CT: JAI Press.

Yee, S. (1987). Teacher turnover: Career commitment and professional involvement. Draft of doctoral dissertation, Stanford University, Stanford, CA.

3

Whose Culture Is It, Anyway?

MYRNA COOPER

It is common to focus the discussion of professional culture in schools on authority and decision making (hegemony, differentiated roles and responsibilities), control of access (entry, testing, certification, professional boards), models of professionalism and collegiality (medicine, higher education), and quality issues (building a knowledge base, increasing effectiveness).

The discussion is generally initiated outside the schools and away from teachers. It is naive to suggest—as has been done by organizational leaders, political representatives, and technical experts in research or organizational development—that the occasional presence of one teacher on a blue-ribbon panel alters this. Each of these representatives may have an agenda and priorities whose paths to professionalism reflect their settings and interests. For example, legislators professionalize by imposing rules and standards; interest group leaders, by strengthening participation and influence and by increasing rewards and incentives; and technicians (researchers, etc.), by manipulating formats, arrangements, and structures. While each of these approaches—rules, authority, structures—makes a contribution to the whole, none of them *is* the whole, and all are essentially external to how schools and their inhabitants really behave. If we are to get a fuller sense of how best to support professional growth in schools, we must examine the themes and vocabulary of school culture with less prejudice about schools and more openness to how things really happen in schools. This is a mild way of suggesting that we not impose solutions and that we recognize that outside-looking-in is different from inside-looking-around.

School people have surely not prospered, or even benefited, from "received" culture and imposed wisdom. Yet school inhabitants have lived as though they were unsophisticated natives ministered to by well-meaning missionaries who exude paternalism. Practitioners have had their shortcomings and inadequacies catalogued and classified and, sadly, have come to accept the blueprint of their deficiencies as though they had drawn it themselves. They have become passive and dependent in pursuit of their own voices.

At the same time, they have been "done to" so often that they are beyond illusion. Faced now with a new language of change, they are rather reserved in their embrace. Secretly they are skeptical, wondering at this sudden interest in their professionalism and their culture, when for years their behavior has been standardized and prescribed. As a breed naturally suspicious of cant and accustomed to being run over by hurtling bandwagons, they rummage in the new greenmarket of change for something practical to help them work.

Reflection on the effects of reforms in the schools, on appropriate professional models, and on the meaning of professionalism is not limited to external agents. By assimilating perspectives closer to the field of inquiry and by questioning some of the mainstream assumptions about schools and school cultures from that perspective, we can add vitality to this undertaking. Such observations may bring a *divergent* wisdom to the dialogue. Here are some such divergences.

Divergence #1.   Cultures are not made; they are born and grow. A professional culture, any culture, is not built the way a house is built, essentially by the overlay of construction artifacts on a passive, cleared plot, as if there were no culture inherent in the institution in the first place (i.e., no glimmer of professionalism) and no necessary interaction with that culture. A culture exists in history.

Divergence #2.   One cannot define a professional culture without positing a belief system or ideology. Most discourses on schools and professionalism confound by this stark omission, for there are no "systems" that are not belief systems. What, then, does this culture *in vacuo* really portend? Clearly, it means to say that the change intended is no change in the content or convictions of the system. For, absent a set of beliefs, we are left with what we had before, i.e., we retain the mainstream canons of the environment of the school(s).

Divergence #3.   Most current reforms of schools miss the mark. They aim at eliminating differences, not altering similarities. Yet one is led to believe that respect for creativity and diversity are aspects of professional culture. In such an environment, one would seek to discourage lock-step curricula, relationships, examinations, and so on. A role in making decisions about problems for which prescribed solutions exist is meaningless.

Divergence #4.   Whose culture is it, anyway? If teachers are told what to be professional about, how, when, where, and with whom to collaborate, and what blueprint for professional conduct to follow, then the culture that evolves will be foreign to the setting. They will once again have "received" a culture.

Divergence #5.   Status (reward) and control are not the characteristics of professionalism; they are the byproducts. To focus teachers on the trappings without the substance is to leave everyone unprepared for the inevitable political embarrassment.

Divergence #6.   Professional cultures in schools are viewed monolithically. For example, the cultures of elementary and secondary schools differ substantially. If we viewed schools as *living* organisms rather than ground for overlays, we could begin to think of these differences as opportunities to enter into the life of schools. In fact, are we not simply viewing schools as political rather than anthropological subdivisions? Respecting individuality is as important with respect to schools as it is with respect to children.

Divergence #7.   Much is said about the norms of collegiality, concerning which we are asked to examine the college-of-education model. This is probably because college faculty have, by and large, an important voice in delimiting curriculum and dispensing tenure. But collegiality is more than political advantage. It is not clear that the higher-education model is an apt one. Competition, the absence of sharing, and a general scrambling for recognition and advantage are hallmarks of all too many education faculties. Moreover, education faculties often underemphasize instruction and resist demonstration, observation, and evaluation; they rarely engage in training of faculty. What is even more lamentable, education and other faculties tend not to be student- or client-centered. The emphasis, then, is not on norms of collegial practice, but rather on norms of institutional protocol.

Divergence #8.   Neither are norms of collegiality cross-cultural. Higher-education missionaries to the lower schools sustain relationships with the natives only so long as the grant lasts. Once the money disappears, so do they. The broader opportunity of interinstitutional and multilevel collegiality is rarely addressed and almost never essayed.

Divergence #9.   Most professional culture building proceeds on the assumption that schools are similar venues, responsive to causal processes on a single plane. As a result, goal-setting models of the old positivistic school dominate teacher-empowerment activities. But these models presuppose that similarities in schools are what is critical. Two problems arise. First, schools are alike only in gross characteristics, differing in ethos, population, staff, character, climate, structure, circumstance, and history. Differences can be critical. Second, it is well known that teachers do not begin the instructional process with rational goal setting but with needs and activities; they rely heavily on intuition. Idiosyncrasy makes their culture distinctive.

Divergence #10.   The milieu of schools is written in the lives of children as well as professionals. Yet the lore on school professional culture ignores the client. The notion of service, the personal nature of the relationship to youngsters and families, the caring and bonding context of the event are embarrassingly absent. Have we extracted the least admired characteristics of the professional models, characteristics that divert teachers from their core tasks with children?

Divergence #11.   In the right pursuit of control over their professional destiny, teachers and other school personnel try to imitate the professions that are respected in our society. They observe that these professions offer status, independence, rewards, and power. However, to conclude that these are the criteria for a profession would be mistaken. It would confuse cause with effect. As we will see, the medical model *can* rightly instruct us.

Divergence #12.   We have, perforce, placed a higher assessed value on what is more costly to obtain. Now it is time to value the medical model of a professional culture for reasons more profound than that of status or control. These have to do with the quality and depth of practice and the values of the professional.
  The reputation that has provided status and reward for physicians and that has enabled them to control access to the profession, as well as the curriculum of access, stems from the following:

1. Concern for performance and reliable means to measure performance
2. The independent exercise of choice in determining treatment and an array of acceptable options from which to choose
3. Standards of practice (and see 8, below)

4. Respect for the common tongues within the profession, for the shared knowledge base, for the multiple languages of method and analysis as well as the multiple ways of thinking about subjects
5. An authentic collegiality, based on the foregoing, the norms of which are determined not by the needs of the professional but by the needs of the client
6. A focus, therefore, on the clientele
7. Acceptance of the public nature of the practice: maintenance and sharing of case records and histories, observed surgery, clinical conferencing
8. A code of conduct (an oath), a set of precepts to secure objectivity, and a clarity about primary purposes (i.e., to preserve life) that do not alter when legislatures or hospital administrators change
9. An exclusive attention to client need independent of local priorities, external mandates, and other extraneous considerations

By contrast, we have regarded Soviet medical and scientific practice as being unethical and unprofessional (e.g., Soviet psychiatry, the biologist Lysenko) because we detect political or ideological motivation and bias in the practices and findings.

The medical concern for detached performance is made clear in the systematic process of developing a treatment plan. Diagnosis commences with a thorough history. Where necessary, prior treatment agents are consulted. Assessment instruments are standard and examination protocols, universal. While intuition is respected (as a special talent), it is always based on a full menu of information. Methods of diagnosis, treatment plans, and instruments (tools, medicines) are sufficiently diverse and variable so as to make the practitioner's decision critical.

Moreover, the client within the medical field expects certain things of the practitioner:

1. An array of strategies: tailored to the patient
2. Thorough assessment: decisions based on evidence
3. Reliability: stability of procedure and prescription
4. Consistency: maintenance of a level or standard
5. Regularity: evenhandedness of treatment
6. Availability: accessibility of practitioner or a nominee, and/or alternatives for meeting needs

7. Trustworthiness: fidelity of action and confidentiality, non-
    judgmentally respectful of intimate relation
8. Responsibility: implicit recognition that patient welfare is an
    absolute criterion

The question is not whether every practitioner meets this medi-
cal-professional ideal. The question is whether the patient's expectation can be regarded as realistic and whether its existence is a
natural outgrowth of past practice. In fact, medical practitioners *have*
established a level of expectation within their discipline because they
have, *as a rule* (not without exception), exhibited the listed characteristics. Rewards have flowed from the characteristic practices, not
vice-versa.

It takes no highly developed power of inference to get the message from the foregoing. The reader is invited to apply these standards, expectations, and characteristics to the culture of education to
see how long a road is yet to be traveled to perfect a professional culture.

Divergence #13.   In our haste to embrace such attractive catch-
words as *empowerment* and *leadership*, we have perhaps overlooked
the real essence of hegemony. Empowerment is less than power. To
be a colleague, a helper, a "developer" does not a leader mean. So
long as teachers are political subjects and philosophical objects, their
strivings for an independence of culture and action will be frustrated.

Teacher "power" in the present wave of reform is essentially derived power—it is empowerment, the licensing by others (authoriza-
tion) to act somewhat free of direction in specified areas of
performance (something like a medical *student*, or at best, a clinical
intern). Moreover, to have authority *delegated* is not the same as to
have authority. It is very clear that that which is given may be with-
drawn.

At the same time, delegated authority has other limitations as
well. It generally lacks scope and scale. For example, the delegated
authority to select a social studies textbook for a grade has very little
to do with curricular control as long as textbook production is the
province of for-profit publishers whose products are amalgams of political, social, and religious ephemera. Certainly a teacher may choose
or reject the better-written text or the one that is less rich in activities, but none of this has any bearing on the meanings, values, or belief systems which have been predigested by the book-production

process. In fact, it is very possible that a book which deviates from the mainstream point of view may not even be on the list of approved books that the teacher is examining.

Essentially, the current empowerment of teachers in such areas as curriculum, school improvement, and professional development is *received* power, limited by others' decisions and subject to cancellation if extended beyond defined boundaries. Similarly, it is a misnomer to describe as leadership roles for teachers such tasks as staff developer, mentor, coach; that is to mislead by misnaming, for the essence of these roles is collegiality and collaboration in an evaluation-free context. Such roles provide supportive, authoritative assistance, but not direction or determination. They are essentially egalitarian. Semantics aside, were these teachers to be perceived as centers of power (which is the way leaders are perceived), then, very likely, from their colleagues' point of view, they would be less trusted and less credible; from the administrators' point of view, they would be a threat. In fact, particularly entrepreneurial staff-development workers frequently encounter resistance when they seek to extend the boundaries of their authority in either direction.

Divergence #14. The key relationship in schools is that between child and teacher, and that relationship is more comparable to a family than to an institutional model. Relationships internal to schools are based on human service; the corporate model is as alien as the factory model has been acknowledged to be. It is possible that the emphasis on the culture of professionalism has actually overshadowed the real nature of school culture, the ground of which is family ecologies rather than professional ideologies.

Perhaps what is needed after all is not a professional culture in schools but a school culture that has been freed of organizational and mechanical overlay. Teachers' satisfaction, as researchers observe, is not solely a product of professionalization, but of the fulfillment derived from positive relationships with children and the sense of efficacy drawn from helping children grow and succeed.

In professional settings, when teachers are moved to share, it is usually because they are *proud of something they have done with children*. No amount of posturing about new roles and responsibilities can even begin to approach that powerful motivation to be professional. By the same token, the greatest fear and frustration teachers have is not the denial of professional opportunity (though this is of value), but the concern engendered when they feel powerless to resist the actions of other authorities who do not exist in relationship to children and whose decisions teachers may view as potentially damaging to children. In this case, teachers often, regardless of professional sophistication, perform a protective role not unlike that of parents who, irrespective of parental skill, sense the need to shelter their young. When teachers are trapped between what their judgment tells them should be done and what is actually done, and when they see no recourse, they become alienated and disaffected. It is that feeling which some wrongly call lack of commitment and others, burnout.

Divergence #15.   What made other professions distinctive was soundness of practice. It follows, then, that the proper focus for teachers should be the extension of power over the content and practice of teaching. Indeed, one might well urge those who pursue this power to beware, for should they succeed then they would be subject to the same snares as more established professions. The vulnerability to malpractice proceedings that is so present in medicine says something instructive about medical practice. It says that there are established and defined norms, procedures, and practices that no *competent* member of the profession would fail to apply. Malpractice implies the presence of a standard of practice against which to measure professional judgments. We will know that teaching is a profession when a malpractice suit becomes plausible.

Divergence #16.   The ancillae to a professional culture for teachers are the activities in which teachers engage that are not concerned with direct teaching. Such functions as membership on school task forces, problem-solving committees, school-improvement panels, and site-management collaboratives, as well as participation in curricular and programmatic development, are associated with professionalization. In this regard, the model is once again the higher-education faculty in which extraclass activities frequently absorb more of the faculty's energies than does teaching.

There are ironies in this seemingly worthy aspiration. For one thing, as we have noted, the higher-education model is hardly the model for instructional commitment or excellence because college faculties trail well behind elementary and secondary faculties in recognizing the importance of commitment to teaching and of teaching as a strategic practice requiring methodological decisions. Nor is it actually clear that a college instructor's main business is to instruct. Apocrypha aside, college faculty activity is most intensely involved with research, writing, committees, and other aspects of "professional life." Faculty exposure to students is often less frequent than faculty interaction with peers or with no one. One might suggest that such faculty maintain office hours not to convey accessibility and presence but to overcome inaccessibility and estrangement. It is worthy of mention that, with some notable exceptions, many reputable (and some disreputable) institutions of higher education use junior faculty primarily for direct instruction (often in large student groupings) and reserve senior faculty for more intimate instructional work with a graduate student elite.

Without attempting to evaluate the reason for these longstanding practices, one can at minimum conclude that if that be a professional culture, then teachers might wisely seek their culture elsewhere.

One need not reject completely the value of broadened professional activity. Teachers often enjoy and feel good about participation in schoolwide developmental work and clearly, as the most likely advocates for children, have something important to contribute. But the culture of schools may not be able to accommodate too generous a dislocation of teacher energy. On the one hand, too fertile a contribution may create a culture shock when empowerment encroaches on power. On the other hand, people have only so much energy to expend. What is given to school improvement may be taken away from bonding and caring.

The definition of a right role for teachers in this context is less than clear. If systems are serious about harnessing teacher wisdom and sensitivity for decisionlike events, then how is it that no developmental effort is devoted to providing teachers with the skills that accompany this kind of leadership? If they are to share in the experience of leadership, will they be provided with the background that informs the experience? Lacking the skills and supports, teachers will inevitably encounter the same kinds of frustration and powerlessness that teachers not supported in the classroom feel. In a way, they are being set up to fail by those who have a stake in not sharing power.

Similarly, if such participation is a right role (still an open question), then why is it customarily treated as an afterthought or addendum to *regular* teachers' work after school, for a week in late August, one day every other month, and so on? Much invention is devoted to making sure that participation in decision making is *not* a natural part of a teacher's life. In a sense, such an ambiguous approach really assures that teachers will have the worst of both worlds—distracted from the teaching mission while inadequately assimilated into the leadership role.

Divergence #17.   A professional culture is not built solely out of an environment and tasks. It is also a product of the background of the individuals in the setting, and that background draws much from the communal experiences of the profession. For doctors, lawyers, and other professionals, the culture that emerges rests on the rigor both of their training and of their rites of passage into the community. These experiences forge a bond within that fraternity that links its members in subsequent practice. Each culture embodies criteria of membership that are achieved only when the process of assimilation into the culture has been sufficiently thorough and comprehensive and serves to distinguish those within from those outside. That may come to be the last piece of the puzzle of a professional culture in schools.

*   *   *

Seventeen provocations ago, this chapter undertook to challenge glibness in talking about school culture and the inhabitants of schools. It is hoped that the reader, having examined the divergences, will recognize that the question of building a professional culture is methodologically complex, politically sensitive, and intellectually intricate. This chapter has attempted to take the question out of the vacuum of form and place it in the vortex of substance, to create a recognition of the social context of schooling and the centrality of children to schools. In the process, we have seen that many models for school culture are less helpful than we would have wished, while others may have been admired for the wrong reasons. We have gently questioned assumptions about the structures and relationships within schools relative to such matters as power and purpose.

We have concluded that neither changed roles for teachers nor (superficially) changed structures in schools can of themselves change anything *that matters*. Change, to mean anything, must itself have meaning, and the meaning we have located falls on a line between the rigor of professional practice and the familial bonding nature of teacher–student interaction. We are of one mind with Nietzsche, who said, "Whoever is a teacher through and through takes all things seriously in relation to his students—even himself" (*Beyond Good and Evil*, Part four, 63). In the final analysis, there is no professional culture for teachers save what is conferred through their students. If participation in the profession, in decision making, in the rites of power and control helps children, then a professional culture will have meaning. That being the benchmark, the effort will not be self-serving.

4

Policy and Professionalism

LINDA DARLING-HAMMOND

Why should we seek to create a professional culture within schools? This question is the first order of business for those who would reform education through a new construction of teaching. The answer, though not mysterious, is not altogether straightforward. Establishing a professional culture within schools may produce teaching that is more knowledgeable and responsive to student needs; it will also disturb the delicate balance between state, community, and parental interests as they are currently configured and deployed in defining schooling. Disturbance produces opportunity for sabotage as well as for progress; it also creates resistance. Hence the arguments for professionalization must be clear, convincing, and responsive to these other interests. The methods must be systemic and thorough as well as persuasive. Otherwise, efforts to reshape the norms, incentives, and roles that comprise a school's culture will be short-lived.

Building a professional culture within schools also requires building a professional structure for the occupation of teaching both inside and outside the schoolhouse walls. As we have seen during a number of other reform movements over the past century, some small number of schools can effect major transformations in their character and effectiveness. But absent alterations in the school environment, few can sustain these changes; and rarely do they permeate the system as a whole.

The form and culture of schooling are shaped by many forces outside the school building itself. Community values and major societal trends are among these forces; policies defining who will teach and how they will do so are factors that increasingly predict the possibilities for and constraints on improving schooling. This chapter examines the policies that currently shape what goes on in schools and discusses the kinds of changes in the policy framework surrounding schools that would be needed to support and sustain a professional culture centered on student learning.

THE CURRENT POLICY CONTEXT

Over the last two decades, state and federal regulation of schools has burgeoned. Following the federal initiatives on behalf of under-served students during the 1960s, state policy makers began to extend their educational lawmaking activities first to equity issues (desegration, school-finance reform, and education of the handicapped) and then to productivity issues. With increased federal and state funding of local schools came pressures for accountability. As a consequence, the 1970s saw a proliferation of laws and regulations seeking to prescribe not only school inputs, but school procedures and even student outcomes as well.

State Regulation of Schooling

Between 1969 and 1974, state legislatures enacted at least 66 laws encouraging school accountability through management and budgeting reforms, planning and evaluation procedures, and statewide assessment of student performance (Darling-Hammond & Wise, 1981). By 1979, all 50 states had undertaken some legislative or state board initiative to set standards for schools or students, usually in the form of minimum competency testing. By 1983, most states had put in place mandates prescribing school curricula, planning activities, evaluation procedures, and student promotion or graduation requirements (ECS, 1983).

The buzzwords of the 1970s were *back to the basics* and *accountability*, reflecting the policy makers' view that schools had accommodated too many frills and would, left unchecked, shirk their basic mission. To assert control over the schooling enterprise, lawmakers sought to promote uniformity and efficiency in education by outlining in greater and greater detail what schools should do and how they should do it (Wise, 1979). By implication, they removed from professional educators authority and responsibility for determining how to conduct their work. As Porter and colleagues (1979) put it: "The accountability movements of the 1970s view teachers not as autonomous decisionmakers but as agents of public school policymakers, agents subject to hierarchical controls" (p. 4).

By the early 1980s, a growing sense of malaise about the health of the educational system had produced a new cycle of reform reports and legislative initiatives. *A Nation at Risk*, a 1983 report of the National Commission on Excellence in Education, pointed to declines in student scores on tests of academic ability and higher-order thinking skills in its call for higher standards to turn back "a rising tide of mediocrity" threatening to engulf American schools. Since dubbed the "first wave" of educational reform in this decade, the Excellence Commission and its progeny focused on the need for more governmental regulation to improve schools—primarily through more courses and tests for students and greater standardization of school curricula.

In response to *A Nation at Risk* and the subsequent batch of "excellence" reports, states intensified their efforts to reform the schools. The Education Commission of the States (1983, pp. vi–vii) categorized these activities as follows:

1. New state-developed curricula or curriculum guides, often coupled with "coordinated instructional delivery systems"
2. New requirements for local district and school planning, and expanded state review of local instructional programs
3. Comprehensive school improvement programs, usually requiring a process of local needs assessment, program redesign, monitoring of student performance, and changes based on evaluation data
4. State dissemination and adoption assistance programs
5. Student testing programs and new requirements for the uses of student test data for decisions pertaining to both students and programs
6. New certification and training requirements for teachers
7. Initiatives aimed specifically at improving mathematics, science, and technology instruction in schools

As these enactments demonstrate,

> Increasingly, criteria for and decisions about curriculum, instruction, certification, funding, and evaluation are being made at the state or federal, not the local level. Decision makers are more likely to base their decisions on a cross-unit rather than a within-unit perspective. Such actions have reduced discretion at the local school district level. One consequence has been a clash between the values advanced to justify increased state control, namely, equality, accountability, and efficiency, and the values of freedom of choice and differentiated treatment, which are embodied in justifications for local school control. Another consequence has been that state governments are becoming more involved in the details of teaching, testing, and the curriculum than they ever have before. (Airasian, 1987, pp. 400–401)

These state initiatives, by and large, reflect a theory that greater specification of school inputs, processes, and outcomes will improve school effectiveness. While school effectiveness may or may not improve, there are other effects of these actions. As Wise (1979) notes:

> The more educational policies are promulgated by higher levels of government, the more bureaucratic will become the *conception* of the school. Education is seen as serving narrowly utilitarian ends employing rationalistic means. . . . To the extent that educators accept the bureaucratic conception of the school, the more bureaucratic will schools become *in fact*. Quasi-judicial procedures, rigid rules, pseudoscientific processes, and measurable outcomes *can* be implemented. . . . To the extent that the public or its representatives insist upon *measuring* the effects of educational policies, the goals of education will be narrowed to that which can be measured. (pp. 201–202)

The problem with the policy makers' search for a better "system" for schooling is that, while policies must be standardized and uniform in their application, students are not standardized in their needs and abilities. The further this model of educational reform is pushed, the less well served many students will be. The limits of "legislated learning" have been noted by subsequent reformers, who have begun to reformulate the educational "problem" in ways that suggest different policy strategies.

The "New View" of School Reform

A "second wave" of American educational reform was heralded in 1986 by reports from the Carnegie Forum on Education and the Economy, the National Governors' Association, the Education Commission of the States, and the Holmes Group of education deans, among others. Though differing in some specifics, the group of new reformers is united in its insistence on the need to improve education by improving the status and power of teachers and by "professionalizing" the occupation of teaching.

Couching their arguments largely in economic terms, the reformers propose that America's future economic welfare depends on educating most students, rather than only a few, for verbal and technical proficiency and for creative work; this requires teachers who themselves possess these capacities and who can inspire critical inquiry among students, rather than merely marching them through texts and drills. Furthermore, it requires teachers who can understand the minds of a wide range of students and thus be able to forge those connections that make knowledge the possession of the learner, not just the teacher. Such well-trained teachers can be recruited in suf ficient numbers only if the teaching occupation offers adequate compensation and a professional work structure within which they can accomplish these challenging goals.

Furthermore, in a marked departure from other recent reform movements, the new reformers argue that decisions about education must be decentralized and professionalized. That is, they must reflect teachers' and principals' best professional judgments on behalf of students rather than adhering blindly to rules and procedures that emanate from higher bureaucratic offices and government agencies. These regulations, it is believed, stifle educational innovation and negate local educational leadership, creating a situation in which "everyone has the brakes but no one has the motors" to make schools run well (Carnegie Forum, 1986).

In policy terms, the second-wave reformers suggest greater regulation of teachers—ensuring their competence through more rigorous preparation, certification, and selection—in exchange for the deregulation of teaching—fewer rules prescribing what is to be taught, when, and how. This is, in essence, the bargain that all professions make with society: for occupations that require discretion and judgment in meeting the unique needs of clients, the profession guarantees the competence of members in exchange for the privilege of professional control over work structure and standards of practice.

The theory behind this equation is that professional control improves both the quality of individual services and the level of knowledge in the profession as a whole. This occurs because decision making by well-trained professionals allows individual clients' needs to be met more precisely; and by making "effectiveness" rather than "compliance" the standard for judging competence, it promotes continual refinement and improvement in overall practice.

It is this theory that guides current efforts to restructure schools so that they may support professional judgments that serve students well. To buttress confidence in professional decision making, structural reforms—such as the creation of a National Standards Board for Teaching and the revision of teacher preparation programs—have been proposed. Until the public trusts teachers to make appropriate decisions, deregulation of teaching is unlikely to occur. However, so long as compliance with teaching prescriptions guides school practice, more effective means for structuring teaching and schooling will be difficult to create and sustain.

THE REFORM DILEMMA

Herein lies the dilemma for educational reform. We have developed a system of schooling that relies on externally developed policies and mandates to assure public accountability. We give voice to democratic control over education through legislation defining what is to occur in schools, administered by bureaucratic agents who prescribe regimens and reporting systems. Within current governance and administrative structures, teachers are accountable for implementing curriculum and testing policies, assignment and promotion rules, and myriad other educational prescriptions, whether or not these treatments are appropriate in particular instances for particular students. As a consequence, teachers cannot be held professionally accountable—that is, responsible for meeting the needs of their students; they can only be held accountable for following standard operating procedures.

This situation not only constrains teacher decision making, it also works against the interests of students and the knowledge base of the profession. As Sykes (1983) notes:

> Administratively mandated systems of instruction not only hinder teachers' responsiveness to students, but over time discourage teachers from learning to be responsive, from developing sensitivity to individual differences, and from broadening their repertoire of approaches. Ultimately such systems become self-fulfilling prophecies: routinized instruction, and the attendant loss of autonomy, makes teaching unpalatable for bright, independent-minded college graduates and fails to stimulate the pursuit of excellence among those who do enter. Over the long run, then, the routinization of instruction tends to deprofessionalize teaching and to further discourage capable people from entering the field. (p. 120)

While the new reformers recognize that public education has become overregulated and that the teaching occupation has become unattractive to many talented college students, their reform proposals at the same time urge greater involvement of policy makers in shaping schools and greater involvement of teachers in shaping teaching. Consequently, we see states passing laws that pay lip service to teacher professionalism while, with the other hand, they enact greater restraints on curricula, textbooks, tests, and teaching methods.

Teachers who feel the tug of professional accountability describe in graphic terms the ethical struggles they experience when asked to conform to policies and procedures that they know may be educationally counterproductive, and at times even damaging to their students (Darling-Hammond & Wise, 1985; Darling-Hammond, 1985). Those who know the most about good teaching and who care most deeply about their students are apt to subvert policies when they need to and to say they will leave teaching if teaching content and methods are further regulated.

This frustrating state of affairs occurs when states or local school boards adopt inappropriate or poorly constructed textbooks and mandate their use, when standardized curricula are required for students who are not standardized in their needs and stages of cognitive development, when tests that deemphasize the development of higher-order skills and performance abilities are used to gauge progress and support decisions about students and teachers, and when scheduling and assignment practices reduce teachers' opportunities to create viable conditions for student learning. Those who resist these practices are often deemed troublemakers, although their challenges to standard operating procedures are precisely what meaningful educational reform and the advancement of professional practice require.

Indeed, the very definition of "professionalism" in teaching has been turned on its head in public schools. Rather than connoting a high level of training and knowledge applied to practice that must, above all else, serve the needs of clients in intellectually honest ways, many policy makers and administrators use the term to mean unquestioning compliance with agency directives. Evaluation criteria stress good soldiership and conformity with district policies over knowledgeable advocacy and use of appropriate teaching practices. The "professional" teacher in common parlance is one who *does things right* rather than one who *does the right things*.

The problem with instructional policies is not that they are not well-intentioned and sometimes even well-informed; it is that policies by their nature must be uniform, operational through a bureaucratic chain of command, and implemented in a standardized fashion to produce easily measurable results. Effective teaching, on the other hand, requires flexibility, a wide repertoire of strategies, and use of judgment in complex, nonroutine situation where multiple goals are being pursued.

Furthermore, policies that define practice are necessarily backward-looking: they must rely on the technologies and knowledge available at any point in time. Slavish adherence to their requirements prevents growth of knowledge and improvement of practice. When policies are created by nonprofessionals unaware of the contingencies that influence appropriate decision making or the possibilities for improvement in effective practice, these effects are only exacerbated. If medical practice, for example, were regulated by nonprofessionals through policy mandate, we might still be treating fevers by applying leeches.

Ironically, increasingly prescriptive policies created through the political process in the name of public input and accountability have begun to reduce schools' responsiveness to the needs of students and the desires of parents. In the cause of uniform treatment and in the absence of choice among schooling alternatives, large numbers of students "fall through the cracks" when rules, routines, and standardized treatment prevent schools from meeting their individual needs. Those who can afford to do so leave for private schools. Those who cannot are frequently alienated and ill-served.

Michael Lipsky (1980) explains that this dilemma operates in all "street-level bureaucracies," where workers must make decisions responsive to the individual needs of clients while also required to follow highly prescriptive agency procedures that are general and uniform. The result is a dual accountability paradox:

> Street-level bureaucrats have responsibility for making unique and fully appropriate responses to individual clients and their situations. . . . These considerations cannot be sensibly translated into authoritative agency guidelines, although it is on behalf of their agencies that street-level bureaucrats are accountable to clients. It is a contradiction in terms to say that the worker should be accountable to each client in the fashion appropriate to the presenting case. For no accountability can exist if the agency does not know what response it prefers, and it cannot assert a preferred response if each worker should be open to the possibility that unique and fresh responses are appropriate. (Lipsky, 1980, pp. 161–162)

He describes how efforts to exert management controls can ultimately subvert the quality of services by reducing workers' accountability to clients and to professional standards of conduct. This occurs when goal clarification reduces the scope and mission of public services by deemphasizing areas that are not the focus of performance measures, and when procedural constraints result in inappropriate treatment of clients.

It would not do, however, to point to the limits of bureaucratic controls without acknowledging their reason for being. The tensions between bureaucratic controls and the demands of professional work are difficult and sometimes counterproductive, but given the current structure of the teaching occupation, they are inevitable. We must understand why such forms of control exist if we are to think productively about how they might be changed.

RATIONALES FOR BUREAUCRATIC CONTROL OF TEACHING

The rationales for bureaucratic decision making are at least threefold. Legislative control over public education policy making is a means for ensuring that education serves the public welfare. State legislative and local school board policies give citizens a voice—through their elected (or, sometimes, appointed) representatives—in deciding what type of education is needed to prepare at least minimally educated citizens and to provide educational services more or less equitably. As we have noted, although public controls have long existed, broad policies guiding resource allocations and general programs have increasingly been augmented by policies that dictate the substance of teaching practice as well as the organizational features of schools.

Furthermore, because public education is equally available to all without charge, schools and teachers are not acquired through a fee-for-service market that would provide a sort of accountability through choice—for those who could afford it. Bureaucratic structures for administering schools are meant to foster uniformity and efficiency in the provision of educational services. To create uniformity, teachers are bureaucratically accountable for doing certain specific things in standardized ways. Thus equal treatment is at least prescribed, if not always ensured.

Efficiency is desired both to safeguard taxpayers' pocketbooks and, as the term is used in some state constitutions, to ensure that educational programs achieve their desired effects. Some recent school finance rulings have interpreted the state's responsibility for equal provision of "thorough and efficient" education to include mandates encompassing precisely what education is to be offered and how it is to be offered efficiently. This often leaves little room for other goals, programs, or teaching strategies that might be more effective in some circumstances and for some purposes, but risk being "wasteful" in making a beeline toward that state's objectives.

The rationales for legislative and management controls—public voice, uniformity, and efficiency—ultimately lessen the involvement of teachers in a broad spectrum of important teaching decisions. The basic reason, though, for these top-down and increasingly prescriptive approaches is that policy makers do not trust teachers to make responsible, educationally appropriate judgments. They do not view teachers as uniformly capable, and they are suspicious about the adequacy of teacher preparation and supervision. These doubts are a measure of the weakness of the professional structure in education and its ability to offer alternative means for guaranteeing quality.

Yet policy makers experience their own dilemma when they seek to achieve school improvement at a great distance from the targets of their efforts. Tom Green describes the delicate balance between policies that seek to accomplish that which is consonant with their intrinsic limits and those that seek to do too much:

> Public policy is a crude instrument for securing social ideals. We would not use a drop-forge to quarter a pound of butter or an axe to perform heart surgery. Public policy is the drop-forge or the axe of social change. It is not the knife or scalpel. That is to say, public policy deals with gross values. It deals with the common good, not with my good in particular or my neighbor's or the good of us both together. Policy deals always with what is good in general, on the whole, and for the most part. . . . It is true that government can't do everything we desire, and therefore, it is equally true that public policy is not the fit instrument to secure all our desires. For example, even if we knew what is needed to make every school excellent and every teacher a paradigm of wisdom in the care of children, it would remain doubtful that we could express this knowledge in public policy and thus secure the good we seek. . . . Minimizing evil is a proper aim of public policy. Maximizing good is probably not. The latter assumes that we may shape the axe into a scalpel. (Green, 1983, pp. 322–323).

Despite the limits of bureaucratic controls for enforcing educational quality, they cannot be abandoned if there are no other accountability mechanisms to take their place. State policy makers cannot spurn their constitutional obligation to provide an adequate public school system available to all on equal terms; nor can we turn back the clock to those times when the meaning of an adequate education was much leaner than it is today. Arguably, the only way out of the teacher's dual accountability dilemma and the policy maker's frustration with inadequate tools for reform, is to ensure competence in the teaching force, thereby reducing the need for bureaucratic controls designed to prevent incompetence.

PROFESSIONALIZING POLICIES

Many proponents of professionalization view increased teacher authority and autonomy as the major goals of this course of action. The idea is that giving teachers more "freedom" will empower them to do what is best for students. This simple construction, however, is dangerous and one-sided. It does not adequately answer the obvious question, "What if more authoritative and autonomous teachers do not do what is best for students?" Having weakened other alternative sources of authority, how will we ensure that students' needs are given voice and their interests are served?

Indeed, in other public service occupations, autonomy is the problem that professionalism is meant to address. It is precisely *because* practitioners operate autonomously that safeguards to protect the public interest are necessary. In occupations that have become professionalized, these safeguards have taken the form of rigorous training and selection, screens to membership in the profession, and ongoing peer review of practice. Collective autonomy from external regulation is achieved by the assumption of collective responsibility through self-governance (Darling-Hammond, 1986b).

There are at least three elements that are prerequisites to professional claims for self-governance:

1. Knowledge of those principles, theories, and factors that undergird appropriate decisions about what procedures should be employed—and knowledge of the procedures themselves
2. The ability to apply this knowledge in nonroutine circumstances, taking relevant considerations into account
3. A commitment to do what is best for the client, not what is easiest or most expedient

Members of the public will not—and should not—trust an occupation to govern itself unless they can be assured that all practitioners will possess the requisite knowledge, ability, and commitment to do what is best for clients. This last requirement is the most important. As Sykes (1984) notes:

> What marks a professional's relation to the client is a high degree of trust. We consult physicians, lawyers, and the clergy on matters of the utmost importance and trust their judgment. In turn, the professional is not out to please clients but to do what is best for them. Quacks and charlatans pander to the populace, professionals do not. Their authority rests not only on their proven effectiveness but on a willingness to insist on what they judge is best. This extends to the occupation itself: professionals must be willing to evaluate other members of the profession to point out ignorance and expose malpractice. To resist quacks and to transmit professional knowledge and service ideals requires a supporting organization

which helps instill these ideals. Professionals then form a community within the community, one of whose functions is to enforce high
expectations. (p. 3)

The development of that supporting organization, the "community within a community" of which Sykes speaks, is the first task of
reformers who would professionalize teaching. Though necessary and
important, it is not sufficient that such communities be formed only
within individual schools—for without a superstructure that enforces
and transmits professional standards of practice throughout the occupation as a whole, efforts within schools will eventually be under-
mined by changes in personnel and by the press of regulations that
work against these efforts. How, then, should we proceed to develop
that supporting organization? What policies are required to support a
professional community?

Policy Goals

The goals of professionalizing policies are to protect the public
by ensuring that (1) all individuals permitted to practice in certain
capacities are adequately prepared to do so responsibly; (2) where
certainty about practice does not exist, practitioners will, individually and collectively, continually seek to discover the most responsible course of action; and (3) as the first two points suggest,
practitioners will pledge their first and primary responsibility to the
welfare of the client.

The first of these goals—that *all* individuals permitted to practice are adequately prepared—is absolutely crucial to attaining the
conditions for and benefits of professionalism. So long as anyone who
is not fully prepared is admitted to an occupation where autonomous
practice can jeopardize the safety of clients, the public's trust is vio-
lated. So long as no floor is enforced on the level of knowledge
needed to teach, a professional culture in schools cannot be long
maintained, for some practitioners will be granted control and autonomy who are not prepared to exercise it responsibly.

This is a key issue in teaching, where 46 states maintain emer-
gency licensure procedures and 23 have recently sanctioned a dou-
ble standard for entry by adopting alternative certification provisions
(Darling-Hammond & Berry, in press). These allowances are deemed
necessary to ensure an adequate supply of teachers, but by failing to
distinguish the roles and responsibilities special entrants are qualified to assume, they fundamentally undermine the presumption that

all professionals holding the same office will share common knowledge and commitments. They permit autonomous practice by those who have not satisfied the prerequisites for public trust.

This is a situation in which the alternatives available within the current structure of teaching seem constrained to distasteful trade-offs. If one admits untrained teachers to full membership in the occupation, the risk of uninformed practice—and student mistreatment— is high. If one does not, and a shortage of teachers results, the alternatives are also suboptimal: enlarged class sizes, constricted program offerings, misassignment of current teachers. This bind occurs because current school and teaching structures do not yet envision diversity of service-delivery structures and roles and do not permit of professional supervision.

In other professions, differentiated roles and responsibilities have gradually emerged as a means for balancing the requirements of supply and qualifications. Those not fully certified or less extensively trained are limited to performing tasks for which they have been prepared, and they practice under supervision. Complex decisions are reserved to those certified to make such judgments. The Holmes Group's suggestion that untrained college graduates be hired only as instructors who practice under the supervision of certified teachers is a step toward protecting the public interest (Holmes Group, 1986).

The second and third goals—that professionals will continually seek to discover what is the most responsible course of action and that their first obligation will be to the client's welfare—suggest that norms of inquiry and ethical conduct are extremely important. But because knowledge is constantly expanding, problems of practice are complex, and ethical dilemmas result from conflict between legitimate goals, these requirements cannot be satisfied by codifications of knowledge, prescriptions for practice, or unchanging rules of conduct. Instead, the transmission and enforcement of these norms must be accomplished by socialization to a professional standard that incorporates continual learning, reflection, and concern with the multiple effects of one's actions on others as fundamental aspects of the professional role.

Professions seek to accomplish these goals by creating structures and processes by which standards of professional practice and norms of professional conduct are defined, transmitted, and enforced. Professional bodies, such as professional standards boards and accrediting agencies, are the primary vehicles for articulating and enforcing standards. Training and socialization processes, such as preparation programs, supervised internships, and continuing education requirements, are the primary vehicles for transmitting standards. Norms of responsibility for the welfare of clients are buttressed by peer control over preparation and entry and by peer review of practice. These require a certain convergence of knowledge, view, and purpose among those who set and enforce standards, those who train practitioners, and those who practice.

This is a tricky business, because—though perhaps not immediately apparent—the propositions advanced above suggest that, on the one hand, appropriate practice cannot be reduced to rules and lodged in concrete; on the other hand, there must be means for reaching a common definition of inappropriate practice and for encouraging the pursuit of what is right, even where that is not a routine judgment. While standardized practice is not adequate, we cannot accept the notion that *any* practice is appropriate. What is sought can be achieved neither through more precise legislation of practice nor by total discretion for teachers. Instead, we are seeking to vest in members of the profession a common set of understandings about what is known *and* a common commitment to test and move beyond that knowledge for the good of individual students and the collective advancement of the profession. Both common and uncommon practice must be guided by considerations of what is known and what serves the welfare of students.

Shared knowledge and shared commitment to extend that knowledge depend in large part on shared membership in a group that articulates and supports their pursuit. The structure of the profession is critical here, for it defines the group's boundaries and its reach. Teaching has suffered from the lack of such a professional structure—a community within the community—by the balkanization of the occupation and by its failure to seek resolution of competing claims for accountability and autonomy from within and without.

There is no single institution for teaching—no analogue to a bar association, medical board, or architectural registration board—that can lay claim to representing or enforcing the common claims of members of the profession to knowledge and standards of conduct. Teachers' unions represent the employment interests of those individuals called teachers, who arrive at this title by various routes; administrators' unions do likewise for those teachers who have been "promoted" by school boards. Other professional associations for teachers require no prerequisites for membership. State licensing bodies represent the lay public as its views are given voice through legislatures and state boards of education. Teacher educators need not even meet the lay public's standards for licensure.

Most organizing rubrics for group membership are based on employment status—acquired through variable means—or on self-selection by claims to interest in the education enterprise. Because no common structure or standard exists for defining entry into the *profession* (and such standards as do exist do not govern rights to practice), occupational status becomes the primary determinant of organization. Furthermore, the associations that represent the interests of those people employed as school teachers, principals, supervisors, superintendents, and teacher educators do not consider themselves as representatives of a common profession with common understandings and purposes; much of the time they view themselves as engaging in competing claims to authority by virtue of role rather than expertise.

This situation undermines the development of shared knowledge and the norms of inquiry and ethical conduct that must undergird a profession. Too often, judgments about appropriate conduct are subject to unguided individual proclivities, and claims to authority are subject to occupational status rather than expertise or responsibility for client welfare. This deprives the public of a powerful means of accountability, and it deprives the profession of an identity and a voice. The resolution of this dilemma depends on both the substance and the governance of policies defining who will teach and how.

Policy Content

It is easy to talk of raising standards for teacher preparation and entry. It is even relatively easy, as we have seen, to pass laws requiring more selectivity in entry and more specific coursework for teacher education. However, once the trappings of rigor have been adopted, the basis for confidence in a profession is that these standards can in fact be shown to enhance the knowledge and ability of those admitted to practice.

In the last few years, virtually all states have changed their requirements for teacher certification. Twenty-seven states now regulate admission to teacher education; most have made changes in course requirements for certification; standards for state approval of teacher education programs have also become more highly specified. Forty-one states have imposed tests for initial teacher licensure, and three have imposed tests for continuing licensure. Twenty-five states have created programs for the supervision of beginning teachers, in most cases tied to the acquisition of a continuing teaching license (Darling-Hammond & Berry, in press).

These changes indicate real efforts to regulate entry into the occupation of teaching, one of the important prerequisites for establishing a profession. However, the changes have come largely from legislatures and state agencies, and they do not reflect a consensual view either within the profession or across states of what a prospective teacher ought to know and be able to do. Most of the tests are basic-skills examinations; existing tests of general or professional knowledge tap very little of what might be called a knowledge base for teaching.

Currently available instruments for evaluating prospective teachers' readiness to practice do not allow for demonstrations of teacher knowledge, judgment, or skill in the kinds of complex situations that characterize real teaching. Where performance assessments have been required, they have tended to adopt behavioral indicators that presume little need for teacher reflection, flexibility, or judgment (Darling-Hammond, 1986a; Shulman, 1987; MacMillan & Pendlebury, 1985). Indeed, by positing unidimensional responses to simplistic questions or evaluation criteria, these measures may discourage the use and acquisition of that kind of knowledge which surpasses and should underlie technique—that which would predispose candidates to a reflective and client-dependent conception of teaching.

These first-generation "standards" have quite often been adopted with more speed than deliberation and, by and large, without meaningful involvement on the part of educators. They have served political purposes well—imposing screens to justify greater investment in teacher salaries—but have not yet sought to serve professional purposes. Most of the discourse about these measures has focused on pass rates and cutoff scores, rather than on content.

There are two functions of professional requirements. One is to sort and screen candidates. Many believe that an increase in standards has occurred when greater screening takes place. This conjures up a vertical image: standards go up or down; there are cutoff scores or course counts that may be raised or lowered to allow more or fewer people to pass. This function serves a symbolic purpose, providing selectivity for entry, irrespective of the substance of the measure. As long as a cutoff level is applied, some individuals will pass and others will not. The level of the standard can be changed simply by changing the rates of passage.

The second major function of professional requirements—and the most important one for creating professional standards—is defining the knowledge base for defensible practice. Preparation requirements and examinations are a major means by which a profession makes an explicit statement about what is worth knowing and how it should be known and demonstrated. This statement exerts a powerful influence on training and practice independent of cutoff scores or pass rates.

When candidates prepare to take the bar examination, for example, they know they will have to study constitutional law, torts, contracts, tax law, criminal law, and so on. Regardless of the pass rate for that exam in a given year, candidates know that they will have to demonstrate their knowledge of these topics in particular ways. They will not only need to be able to identify facts about legal rules and cases, they will also have to apply this knowledge in essays responding to case scenarios. The examination provides an explicit standard of knowledge that influences legal training and practice in important ways, regardless of the vertical standards used to determine who will be licensed.

Professional tests are designed and controlled by the members of a profession. Teacher tests currently are not. They are purchased by state departments of education from test developers who respond to different imperatives. By and large, the tools that have thus been developed give little support to the notion that a knowledge base for teaching—grounded in an appreciation of how children learn and how content is transformed into understanding--exists or needs encouragement. They serve poorly, if at all, the function of informing preparation and practice.

This situation perpetuates an already acute problem: the public does not trust the standards it has set for teachers. Although states have long regulated the content of teacher preparation and the requirements for licensure, there is so little public confidence in these standards that many believe better teachers might be had by eliminating or skirting these requirements altogether. Alternative certification and other loopholes are the result of this lack of trust. The curious outcome is that tests which avoid pedagogical problems are seen as a substitute for pedagogical preparation. When the secret gets out, public confidence will only plummet further.

More important, so long as standards for entry into teaching do not provide reasonable assurance that teachers can make complicated educational decisions, they will not be entrusted to do so. So long as their supervisors are not held to a similarly rigorous standard, their decisions on behalf of teachers will fail to take account of important teaching considerations. In the final analysis, it is those decisions made outside of schools that may prevent the exercise of professional knowledge and commitment within classrooms. As Dreeben (1987) aptly notes:

> Teaching entails the utilization of educational resources that both
> enable instruction to occur and constrain it. Otherwise excellent
> teaching can be hamstrung by poorly conceived textbooks fash-
> ioned by publishers, ill-advised book acquisition policies by school
> systems, inadequate allocations of time to curricular areas, destruc-
> tive scheduling, inappropriate assignment of students to classes and
> tracks, and the like. . . . No amount of renaming the categories of
> teachers or stiffening entrance examinations to the occupation is
> going to provide remedies for problems in how school systems al-
> locate and use the resources for mounting instructional programs.
> (p. 363)

Influencing the means by which these decisions are made is the
point of the current school reform movement. Legitimizing the involvement of teachers in the making of educational decisions is the
point of professionalization. The key issue is who will regulate what
aspects of the educational system. A fundamental part of the answer
is who the public will deem is best qualified to make these decisions. The *quid pro quo* for shared decision making is meaningful
standard setting within the profession.

Until the content of standards becomes the subject of debate and
transformation by members of the profession, standards will serve
only short-term political goals. In the long term, professional standards must demonstrate to educators and the public that they in fact
produce improvements in the quality of education. This will necessitate greater attention in the coming years to matters of policy substance in addition to form. It is at this juncture that the involvement
of the profession is critical, for state policy can constrain but not construct the conditions under which knowledge about teaching is produced, transmitted, and employed on behalf of those students who are
its ultimate beneficiaries.

Policy Governance

The discussion above constitutes an argument for professional
control over professional standards. The argument further supports
claims that establishing a professional culture in schools would provide a stronger and more effective means for accountability than
would seeking more detailed prescriptions for practice. But such a
culture cannot be sustained without both meaningful standards for
entry to teaching and conditions of work that support the use of
professional knowledge. The latter cannot be achieved without deregulation of teaching and the creation of alternative guides to practice.

The lessons offered by other professons suggest that:

- Rigorous training and selection, along with continuing education, are prerequisites for professional control over technical decision making.
- Professional control over technical decision making cannot be sustained without the articulation, transmittal, and enforcement of standards of practice.
- Standards of practice and professional accountability cannot be sustained without ongoing peer review of practice and substantial peer control over both the "production process" and the membership of the profession.

In circular fashion, these lessons reinforce the view that teachers' efforts to restructure schools must be accompanied by equally strenuous efforts to restructure the profession itself. And a critical element of such restructuring is not only the assumption of professional control but the assumption of responsibility, as well, for the conduct of oneself and one's colleagues. For this to occur, many of the policies currently controlled by political bodies must come to be shared with teachers. This is not a simple undertaking.

Occupations that have become professions have substituted professional accountability systems for bureaucratic accountability systems. The bargain entails rigorous, professionally determined standards for education, internship, and licensure to guarantee that all members of the profession are competent to exercise good judgment, in exchange for professional control—monitored through peer review of practice—over the structure and content of the work. Members of the profession are held to professional standards of practice but not to uniform treatment of all clients. Indeed the latter, because it would be inappropriate to clients' needs, would constitute unprofessional practice. Democratic oversight occurs through public representation on such bodies as licensing boards and hospital boards, where public input into professional standard-setting processes occurs; technical decisions are delegated to the members of the profession itself.

There is ample evidence that these mechanisms have improved the general standard of practice in other occupations that have become professions, by strenghtening the knowledge base, enhancing the competence of individual practitioners, and creating norms for ethical practice. However, this has sometimes occurred at the expense of widespread access to services, resulting in higher costs and unequal distributions of practitioners as a function of limits on entry. Furthermore, third-party review mechanisms, with increased public oversight, have been introduced in a number of professions (medicine and accounting, for example) when peer-review structures seem to have failed to prevent malpractice, inappropriate treatment, or excessive costs.

There are a number of reasons why the particular modes of professionalization adopted by other occupations such as medicine, law, accounting, and architecture are not fully adaptable to or desirable for public school teaching. First, public education is not only a publicly funded service (also true of an increasing share of medical services and some legal services); it is a right and an obligation made available to and *required of* its clientele. Because education is a right, it must be made available to all on equal terms. Because it is an obligation—an activity which is compulsory for children for most of their youthful years—the state must guarantee certain safeguards to ensure that no harm is done.

In addition, the state makes education compulsory in order to serve its own needs for an educated citizenry: socialization to a common culture, literacy as a basis for democratic participation, and training to serve economic ends. There are limits to the degree of control that the state is likely to delegate to any other source of authority, professional or otherwise. Other sources of authority include parental authority to decide what education best meets the needs of children (and serves the tastes of the parents) and community authority to decide what education best meets the local community's view of what education is desirable. These are not only balanced against the views of professional educators, but are also circumscribed by state regulation.

Indeed, as education has become more fundamental to the welfare of both individual citizens and the state, the relative authority of parents and local communities has been lessened along with the authority of professional educators. Thus, we see increased attention to proposals for choice in public schooling alongside proposals for increased professionalization. Both in a sense are arguments for more leeway in addressing the individual needs of students. Often, choice and professionalization are advanced together (see, e.g., Carnegie Forum, 1986) in the belief that greater diversity in schooling cannot be allowed or sustained unless students and parents can choose the form of schooling that is appropriate for them. Without some element of either choice or bureaucratic control in the system, images of heightened professionalism provoke fears that a professional cult will ignore the views of parents and the local community.

The legitimate demands of federal and state governments, local communities, parents, and professionals to determine the form of education that is most suitable, most fair, and most effective for a wide range of goals cannot be ignored. These forces pulling on public schools must be satisfied in any systemic answers to the reform dilemma. If one accepts the argument that a strengthened professional structure will improve the quality of education received by students, the task then becomes the creation of a policy setting in which such a structure can be supported without undermining other social goals.

That public control and professional control over education may be at odds is rarely acknowledged in current debates about school reform. Yet failure to resolve the tension between the two will torpedo the reform agenda in the 1980s, just as it did in the early years of this century, when Horace Mann, John Dewey, and others argued for virtually identical proposals. As historian Lawrence Cremin (1965) notes, this tension

> has been at the heart of the popular education system from the very beginning. On the one hand, there is the prerogative of the public to set policy, determine direction, and fix support: we speak of public *control*, not merely public sponsorship or public influence. On the other hand, there is the prerogative of the teaching profession to govern its own work, set standards, and determine the nature of teaching practice: the teacher is committed to teaching truth as he sees it and to following truth wherever it leads. (pp. 90–91)

Cremin argues that a democratic society should support schools that must then be left free to criticize the society that supports them. This is probably not possible. But we can do better than we have in the past to make more compatible the visions of reformers and the needs of various publics for school accountability.

First, we can create teaching standards boards—as six states have and as the Carnegie Task Force is seeking to accomplish at the national level—to give voice to professional standards and give form to professional responsibility. Second, we can reduce the inefficient and counterproductive balkanization of the occupation by holding all members to a common standard and allocating responsibility according to expertise rather than role. This can be achieved by enforcing cross-cutting professional certification standards for teachers, principals, and teacher educators that will both produce shared understandings and legitimize the notion of peer review throughout the profession. Finally, we can envision shared governance approaches—such as those evident in a few states and local districts—

that provide effective voice for parents and the public by establishing parity in decision making rather than allocating power.

To secure meaningful and lasting educational change in this country, we must be prepared to create new and ultimately more productive forms of governance and accountability for public schools that will allow teachers to practice professionally in the interests of students while preserving our democratic traditions. This can only be accomplished by pursuing jointly the separate prerogatives of policy makers and teachers and by enlisting public support and oversight of rigorous, professionally defined standards of practice.

REFERENCES

Airasian, P. (1987, May). State mandated testing and educational reform: Context and consequence. *American Journal of Education*, pp. 393–412.

Carnegie Forum on Education and the Economy. (1986). *A nation prepared: Teachers for the 21st century*. New York: Author.

Cremin, L. A. (1965). *The genius of American education*. New York: Vintage Books.

Darling-Hammond, L. (1985). Valuing teachers: The making of a profession. *Teachers College Record*, 87(2), 205–218.

Darling-Hammond, L. (1986a). Teaching knowledge: How do we test it? *American Educator*, 10(3), 18–21, 46.

Darling-Hammond, L. (1986b). A proposal for evaluation in the teaching profession. *Elementary School Journal*, 86(4), 1–21.

Darling-Hammond, L., & Berry, B. (in press). *The evolution of teacher policy*. Santa Monica, CA: The Rand Corporation.

Darling-Hammond, L., & Wise, A. E. (1981). *A conceptual framework for examining teachers' views of teaching and educational policies*. Santa Monica, CA: The Rand Corporation.

Darling-Hammond, L., & Wise, A. E. (1985). Beyond standardization: State standards and school improvement. *The Elementary School Journal*, 85(3), 315–336.

Dreeben, R. (1987). Comments on *Tomorrow's Teachers*. *Teachers College Record*, 88(3), 359–365.

Education Commission of the States (ECS). (1983). *A survey of state school improvement efforts*. Denver, CO: Author.

Green, T. (1983). Excellence, Equity, and Equality. In L. S. Shulman & G. Sykes (Eds.), *Handbook of teaching and policy* (pp. 318–341). New York: Longman.

Holmes Group, The. (1986). *Tomorrow's teachers*. East Lansing, MI: Author.

Lipsky, M. (1980). *Street-level bureaucracy*. New York: Sage.

MacMillan, J. B., & Pendlebury, S. (1985). The Florida performance measurement system: A consideration. *Teachers College Record*, 87, 69–78.

National Commission on Excellence in Education. (1983). *A nation at risk: The imperative for educational reform*. Washington, D.C.: U.S. Government Printing Office.

Porter, A. C., Schwille, J. R., Floden, R. E., Freeman, D. J., Knappen, L. B., Kuhs, T. M., & Schmidt, W. H. (1979). *Teacher autonomy and the control of content taught*. East Lansing, MI: Institute for Research on Teaching.

Shulman, L. (1987). Knowledge and teaching: Foundations of the new reform. *Harvard Educational Review, 57*(1), 1–22.

Sykes, G. (1983). Public policy and the problem of teacher quality. In L.S. Shulman & G. Sykes (Eds.), *Handbook of teaching and policy* (pp. 97–125). New York: Longman.

Sykes, G. (1984). *The conference*. Mimeographed. Stanford, CA: Stanford University.

Wise, A. E. (1979). *Legislated learning*. Berkeley: University of California Press.

5

Assessing the Prospects for Teacher Leadership

JUDITH WARREN LITTLE

This chapter begins with a simple proposition: it is increasingly implausible that we could improve the performance of schools, attract and retain talented teachers, or make sensible demands upon administrators without promoting leadership in teaching by teachers.

TEACHER LEADERSHIP AND THE PROFESSIONALIZATION OF TEACHING

Debate over the prospects for teacher leadership threads its way through larger discussions of the professionalization of teaching (see, e.g., Soltis, 1987). Three sets of professionalization problems form the context for questions of teacher leadership (see Figure 5.1). They are:

Conditions of membership in the occupation
The structure of the teaching career
Conditions of productivity in schools

Membership in the Occupation

Teachers have been invited—or pressed—to take a larger role in regulating membership in the teaching occupation. Teachers are increasingly involved in planning and conducting preservice teacher education. In some states, teachers now participate (or soon will) on assessment teams that make decisions governing teacher licensure.

This chapter is based on research conducted at the Center for Action Research, Boulder, Colorado, under Contract NIE-G-82-0020, and at the Far West Laboratory for Educational Research and Development under Contract 400-83-003, both with the National Institute of Education, U.S. Department of Education. The views expressed herein are not necessarily the views of that agency.

Figure 5.1.   Targets of Change in the Professionalization of Teaching Arenas for Teacher Leadership

Conditions of Membership in the Occupation
- Recruitment
- Preservice admission and exit standards
- Licensure/certification
- Testing and assessment tied to a knowledge base in teaching
- Teacher evaluation

Structure of the Teaching Career
- Structure of opportunity for advancement/promotion
- Structure of opportunity for expanded responsibility or job enlargement
- Access to meaningful (professional) reference groups in and out of school

Conditions of Productivity in Schools
- Structure of leadership and decision making that includes well-qualified teachers
- Administrators' roles in the support of teachers and teaching
- Collective responsibility for student achievement
- Reward structure that promotes teacher-to-teacher collaboration and accountability

---

Teachers and administrators in some districts have reached agreements governing teachers' participation in teacher evaluation. All of these changes are in accord with the recent proposition that, "it is only by regulating [those who become] *teachers* that we will be able to deregulate *teaching*" (Darling-Hammond, 1987, 356; emphasis in original).[1]

Restructuring the Teaching Career

Efforts to diminish the "careerlessness" of teaching (Sykes, 1983) have spawned a wide array of career-ladder plans and special roles or assignments for experienced teachers. Such plans typically present options for teacher leadership as possible steps in an individual career. Over time, according to most plans, some teachers will advance to senior positions on the basis of their demonstrated knowledge, skill, energy, and commitment. Their new positions will be recognized by distinctive titles, access to discretionary resources, and expanded responsibility and authority. The number of such positions will be limited, and teachers will necessarily compete for them.

The development of career-ladder and other incentive plans has been prompted by fears that attractive (and accessible) career options will lure both prospective and practicing teachers away from teaching and by hopes that the promise of career advancement will slow the attrition.

Career ladders and other competition-based incentive systems for teachers were announced with considerable fanfare following the flurry of reform reports in 1983,[2] but they have subsequently drawn criticism. It is probably a myth, Susan Rosenholtz (1985b) argues, that "competition between teachers for career advancement and higher pay is a sound way to improve the quality of their teaching" (p. 351) or that "career ladders and incentive pay will attract more academically talented people into the teaching profession" (p. 353). Further, critics have questioned the incentive value of plans that provide attractive options for only a small proportion of the teaching force, and then often after long tenure in the classroom.

Certainly it is hard to detect a groundswell of support from teachers for most of the career-ladder proposals; policy makers, educational reformers, and researchers have been the most vocal advocates.

The element of competition contained in career-ladder plans may be only one of several reasons for their lukewarm reception from teachers. The "promotion and advancement" vision of career reflected in such plans does not necessarily match teachers' conceptions of career. Studies of art and science teachers in British secondary schools conclude that professional identity and career satisfaction derive in part from meaningful contact with professional reference groups outside the school, for example, working scientists or artists or university-based educators (Bennet, 1985). American teachers interviewed by Stanford researchers appear to be less interested in hierarchically arrayed positions than in a richer pool of professional opportunities for all classroom teachers (Yee, 1986).

Conditions of Productivity in Schools

A third set of problems (and recommendations) centers on the professional environment of the school, or workplace conditions. Among the recommendations are ones calling for richer teacher–student ratios and greater amounts of planning and preparation time; these are conditions that would permit teachers time for critical reflection and closer collaboration. Other recommendations call for differentiated staffing or for school-level "lead-teacher" roles.

The idea behind such proposals is that promoting leadership by teachers in the context of the school will satisfy two needs: it will present attractive opportunities and rewards for teachers, and it will direct greater institutional attention to the quality of teaching.

Such recommendations treat leadership less as a matter of individual career trajectories than as a matter of rigorous professional relations among teachers. Teachers are expected to exert the kind of influence on one another that would enhance success and satisfaction with students. In that respect, workplace reform proposals challenge longstanding patterns of teacher isolation and individual autonomy. They fly in the face of most cultural, institutional, and occupational precedents (Feiman-Nemser & Floden, 1986).

Some recommendations, particularly those centered on differentiated staffing and the development of lead-teacher positions, have drawn the same criticisms as career ladders, and for some of the same reasons. On the whole, however, the workplace reform recommendations, like the career-ladder proposals, have been deemed by many states and localities to be important enough to deserve a serious trial (Darling-Hammond, 1987; Carnegie Forum, 1986).

PROFESSIONALIZING TEACHING BY PROFESSIONALIZING THE WORKPLACE

This chapter emphasizes the third of the three potential arenas for reform activity: conditions of productivity in schools. It is in this arena that the public interest in teacher leadership is most pressing. There are three main arguments underlying "school workplace" reforms.

First, experiments in teacher leadership will prove to be marginal and ephemeral if they are not demonstrably (and soon) linked to benefits close to the classroom. Teachers themselves test reform proposals by trying to anticipate the effect they might have in their own work. Other observers, including school board members and state legislators, will reasonably ask: What are the promised gains for students, their parents, and their communities when teachers assume greater leadership in the day-to-day life of schools?

Second, the work of schoolteaching is characteristically "professional" work; it is complex and subtle, requiring informed judgment by well-prepared practitioners in circumstances that are often ambiguous or difficult. Current arrangements often retard rather than advance teachers' professional capacities for sound judgment when they restrict opportunities for joint study and problem solving and when complex issues are tackled primarily through the exercise of bureaucratic rule making. The proposed alternative arrangements are held out with the promise that they will produce more successful solutions to problems of student learning and student socialization, at the same time that they build teachers' commitments to teaching.

Finally, we know something about the professionalization of organizations (Benveniste, 1987). These are reforms that are actionable. Despite some increase in real costs, they are reforms that will require clear vision, persistence, and good will far more than money.

In sum, the professionalization of the larger occupation rests in important ways on our ability to professionalize the organizations in which teachers work. Questions of theory, research, policy, and practice coincide in an examination of the prospects for professionalizing the daily work—and workplace—of teaching.

Even the most conservative of the workplace reform proposals requires that teachers, individually and collectively, act differently toward their work and one another. In some fashion or other, each proposal calls for teachers to take the lead in advancing the understanding and practice of teaching.

What are the prospects that such proposals, with their element of leadership by teachers, could be tested on a large enough scale in American schools to guide districts and states in their policy and program choices, or to guide professional associations in building their agendas?

The rest of this chapter assesses the prospects from one standpoint: the likelihood that teachers will accept one another's initiative on matters of curriculum and instruction and do so in ways that demonstrably affect their own classroom choices.

I have relied primarily on teachers' own perceptions of and participation in school leadership, collected as part of four separate studies.[3] The major source is a two-year study of instructional leadership in eight secondary schools. The study included leadership attitudes and practices by both administrators and teachers. The second is a study of "teacher advisors" who were charged with promoting and assisting teacher development in nineteen school districts. The third study examined the introduction of school-level instructional leadership teams in a single district. And the last is a two-year study of the California Mentor Teacher Program.

This collection of studies, and others' work on related topics, reveal some of the conditions required to promote and sustain rigorous professional relations among teachers that yield benefits for students.

WORK WORTH LEADING: TARGETS OF TEACHER LEADERSHIP

Leadership is an empty term when there is nothing to lead, nowhere to go, and no one who follows. Do teachers have reason to lead the work of teaching, and thus have reason to lead one another? Advocates of teacher leadership, it appears, have largely underestimated the magnitude of the change their proposals represent.

Are Schools Organized to Influence Teaching?

When we promote leadership by *teachers*, we may assume that such an arrangement is an alternative to present conditions—that principals, for example, may have to relinquish some of their own influence as instructional leaders in order to make room for teachers. There is some doubt, however, whether teaching is now led at all, in any meaningful sense, in more than a few exceptional schools.

History would lead us to be skeptical about schools' influence on teaching (Cuban, 1985). This is not to say schools are not organized. Schools have been increasingly well organized for several purposes that are dear to the public interest. Most are organized to provide a humane, safe, orderly environment for students to learn. More and more schools are organized to teach basic academic and social skills. Finally, most schools are organized to maintain good relations with parents and the local public.

Schools are organized, then, for many important functions. Influencing teaching—the long-term directions as well as the daily classroom decisions that affect students—is not typically one of them (Bird & Little, 1986; Feiman-Nemser & Floden, 1986). Teachers are far less likely to defer to another teacher's view of curriculum or instruction than to rely upon habit and personal preference. There is rarely anything in the immediate professional environment that overcomes the effect of other influences on teachers' decisions. Such influences range from the teacher's own experience as a student (Lortie's "apprenticeship of observation"), to students' attempts to "bargain" the curriculum, to teachers' interpretations of parental interests, to personal predilections regarding curriculum content, instructional method, or the social organization of students for learning.

Schools that are organized to influence teaching are relatively rare. There are few precedents in the occupation or in the organization of schools that would encourage teachers to take initiative with regard to the classroom choices made by their colleagues. The ar-

rangements that would underscore teachers' mutual interdependence, such as shared instructional assignments, are few. Traditional
authority relations in schools and districts, as well as conventional
teacher evaluation procedures, communicate a view of teaching as an
individual enterprise. Finally, few of these rare institutions appear
able to sustain their productive work norms and structures when the
building principal or key teaching staff depart.

Teachers Who Lead

Recall that the task here is to consider how teacher leadership
might be promoted in ways that improve productivity conditions in
schools. The target of teacher leadership is the stuff of teaching and
learning: teachers' choices about curriculum, instruction, how students are helped to learn, and how their progress is judged and rewarded.

Teachers who lead leave their mark on teaching. By their presence and their performance, they change how other teachers think
about, plan for, and conduct their work with students.

Teachers invited to lead may well fail to do so. Examples abound.
Leadership programs turn out to be mini grant competitions in which
successful competitors pursue topics and problems of individual interest and "lead" the same way they teach: alone. Or a position described as "mentor," bearing all the powerful imagery and promise
of that term, is steadily diminished in the eyes of teachers as its holder
is seen to do little more than ordinary curriculum writing ("extra work
for extra pay"). Or a teacher asked to assist first-year teachers worries
so much about being "threatening" that he or she turns out to be use-
less instead.

Teachers placed in positions that bear the titles and resources of
leadership display a caution toward their colleagues that is both
poignant and eminently sensible. The relation with other teachers that
is implied by terms like *mentor, advisor,* or *specialist* has little place
in the ordinary workings of most schools. Even the simple etiquette
of teacher leadership is unclear.

Teachers face a task of considerable magnitude in giving meaning to leadership within their own ranks. Imagine two teachers, one
of whom has been accorded a title of "master teacher." Having seen
each other teach rarely or not at all, the two teachers must worry about
what they will discover about one another. The leader must worry
about whether he or she has anything to offer that is not already fully
at the command of the person presumably to be led. Having seldom

or never talked about teaching in any depth, the two must now quickly learn to communicate in ways that match their complex and subtle sense of teaching; anything less will not satisfy them, because it will fail even to incorporate the accomplishments each has managed alone and because it will not take their work further than either one could carry it alone.

Teachers contemplating a rigorous mutual examination of their teaching may well have good reason to believe it will be difficult, even troublesome, and little reason to believe that the yield could be worth the trouble.

In a paper titled "The Lead Teacher: Ways to Begin," Kathleen Devaney (1987) describes six arenas in which teachers might reasonably demonstrate leadership at the school level. While some have more well-established precedents than others, each of the six has been described in prior studies of school organization. This is a plausible inventory of possibilities. It offers a balance between leadership that advances a school *program* by making it more suitable or rigorous, and leadership that moves *people* by strengthening their knowledge, skills, and commitment. In Devaney's view:

1. *Lead teachers continue to teach and to improve their own teaching.* They gain their legitimacy by remaining credibly in touch with life in the classroom. They work consistently to apply best practice, and they engage in planned experimentation, often as members or leaders of small groups of colleagues. The California Mentor Teacher Program requires that mentors continue to teach at least a 60 percent load. Programs that release teachers full time to work in a "mentoring" or "advising" capacity (see Kent, 1985) promote demonstration lessons and other classroom consultation as one means of establishing the mentor's legitimacy in the eyes of teachers.
2. *Lead teachers organize and lead well-informed peer reviews of school practice.* In practice, such activity has been most fruitful where it develops quickly from review to revision. In one school, teachers described two-year "innovation cycles." The cycle began when a group of five or six teachers decided that some aspect of student progress deserved their collective attention and set out to "get smarter" about the problem and the prospects for solving it. The cycle typically led to clearer formulation of the problem, potential avenues of improvement, skill training where appropriate, and selective classroom experimentation. Experiments that "worked" were marketed to others on the faculty. At the second-

ary level, we have observed reviews and improvement activities profitably organized by department as reviews of subject-area teaching. (For a discussion of the master teacher as curriculum leader, see Klein, 1985.)

3. *Lead teachers participate productively in school-level decision making.* They work with administrators and teachers to arrive at decisions that are well targeted, well informed, and well accepted. Shared decision making has taken a range of forms, from formally organized and specially scheduled goal-setting sessions to a once-a-week staff meeting that engaged principal and grade-level team leaders in the routine decision making that kept an entire school roughly headed in the same direction.

4. *Lead teachers organize and lead inservice education* that is meaningfully related to the student population and the school program. A faculty effectively organized for its own learning, it appears, can make reasonable use of external staff development options that would otherwise have weak effect (e.g., the one-time workshop).

5. *Lead teachers advise and assist individual teachers* through methods that have come to be called mentoring, coaching, or consultation. The literature on coaching has been growing steadily following Joyce and Showers' (1981) review of staff development practices, culminating in their prediction that classroom impacts would remain small unless skill training were accompanied by the kind of classroom assistance and consultation that would enable teachers to establish the "fit" between new ideas and established habits (see also Showers, 1983; Goodwin & Lieberman, 1984). On the whole, the logic underlying mentoring or coaching has been readily accepted (especially when applied to support for beginning teachers), but teachers have remained ill prepared and ill supported to assume mentoring responsibilities (Bird & Little, 1986).

6. *Lead teachers participate in the performance evaluation of teachers* by providing appropriate appraisal and feedback. Peer evaluation is promoted as one hallmark of a professionalized occupation, in which standards of performance are monitored by the members of the profession in exchange for substantial guarantees of (collective) autonomy. Evaluation of teaching and teachers is the most problematic of the proposed domains for teacher leadership, though not unknown in our own studies, in studies of effective teacher evaluation (Wise et al., 1984), or in current statewide reform initiatives (Connecticut State Department of Education, 1984).

TEACHERS' ACCEPTANCE AND SUPPORT OF LEADERSHIP BY COLLEAGUES

Much has been made of teachers' probable (and sometimes demonstrated) opposition to any large-scale change in the occupation or the organization of schools that would introduce status differences among teachers based on demonstrated knowledge and skill. And recently, administrators have made the news with their own opposition to leadership schemes that they believe will usurp site administrators' authority to conduct personnel and program evaluation.

In the past, studies of teacher leadership experiments at the school or district level have produced mixed results and limited practical guidance. One study of organized teacher teams in open-space schools documented teachers' ambivalence about team leaders assigned by building principals (Arikado, 1976), while other studies have attributed the vigor of a school program to the work of teacher-led teams in which the leaders were also designated by the principal (Lipsitz, 1983). There are more skeptics than enthusiasts represented in the literature, but it would be too strong an indictment to say it has been tried and did not work. There have been few serious trials.

This section examines the support for teacher leadership in the day-to-day social organization of schools. One can gauge the prospects for teacher leadership on a school-by-school basis in light of teachers' responses to two possibilities.

First, the prospects for leadership can be judged in part by whether teachers have developed, or are prepared to develop, a close working knowledge of one another's teaching, based on observation and in-depth discussion. To assess the prospects for leadership in a school, then, one might ask: Is the very act of teaching public enough (or might it become so) to support vigorous leadership that affects classroom practices?

Classroom observation among teachers serves as a bellwether practice: of all the possible interactions among teachers, it is perhaps the clearest signal that the traditional norm of privacy may have been displaced. A school's culture is conducive to leadership by teachers when teachers are in one another's classrooms for purposes of seeing, learning from, commenting on, and planning for one another's work with students.

Second, the prospects for teacher leadership can be judged by teachers' acceptance of initiative by specially designated leaders in their midst. Here, we examine the possibility that teachers who are recognized as leaders by some special title ("master teachers," "mentors," "teacher advisors") would, by word and deed, attempt to influence improvements in curriculum and instruction and thus influence the day-to-day classroom work of other teachers. A school's culture is conducive to leadership by teachers when such initiative is acceptable. To assess the prospects for leadership in a school, then, one might ask: What latitude will teachers accord a colleague who is clearly recognized as a "master teacher"?

Teachers' attitudes toward classroom observation, and their attitudes toward leadership initiative by specially selected teacher leaders, are not the only grounds on which one might assess prospects for leadership, but they are crucial ones. Teachers' acceptance of and participation in regular classroom observation reveals their fundamental orientation toward teaching as a private or public activity. Teachers' acceptance of initiative regarding curriculum and instruction reveals their orientation to the very idea of leadership, that is to the rights and obligations that teachers inherit by virtue of membership in the profession.

Making Teaching Public

Teaching has long been described as a private activity, both in planning and execution. Veteran teachers report having worked 30 years with no other adult in the classroom except on incidental business. Yet schools that are discovered to be vital, adaptable institutions have been consistently found to support vigorous professional exchanges among teachers. Teachers in these schools talk in depth about teaching and about students' progress, plan for teaching together, observe one another's work in classrooms, and learn from one another. They eschew oversimplified war stories that defy analysis, concentrating instead on straightforward assessments that reveal the true complexities of a situation and yield new options (see Rosenholtz & Kyle, 1984).

While classroom observation is clearly not the only route to a more public, collective version of teaching, we anticipate that the rate and rigor with which teachers watch and discuss one another's classroom work with students are important indicators of teachers' acceptance of teacher leadership.

The significance of leadership close to the classroom.   We consider the classroom observation data to be significant in principle for three reasons. First, structured classroom observations have been promoted as one of the most prominent and potentially powerful vehicles for instructional leadership. Second, classroom observation directly and literally tackles the main consequences of the closed classroom door. The closed door isolates students and fragments their learning; the closed door offers teachers only a truncated, impoverished understanding of one another's abilities and activities. Third, teachers argue that leaders must demonstrate that they have something to offer that is worth following—and that the demonstration will not be persuasive unless it is credible in the classroom. Teachers who aspire to lead must be able to display their own mastery of classroom challenges. They must be able to grasp and describe other teachers' intentions and accomplishments. And they must be willing and able to recognize and act on opportunities to improve their own and others' work with students. In the end, teachers are unlikely to accept leadership at too great a distance from the classroom.

Do good colleagues stop at the classroom door?   An exploratory study of interactions among teachers tells of Jim and Bill, whose close personal and professional relationship almost dissolved after Jim's first foray into Bill's classroom (Zahorik, 1987, p. 391). The study concludes that collegiality may stop at the classroom door. Others, too, have observed that what passes for collegiality may not add up to much (Hargreaves, 1984; Little, 1987; Rosenholtz & Kyle, 1984) and that access to classrooms is problematic (Little, 1985).

Across the country, schools are experimenting with peer observation, peer coaching, and other programs designed to get teachers into one another's classrooms. For teachers in many schools , the idea of classroom visitation has strong appeal. For an even larger number, I suspect, the idea is met with skepticism, indifference, or outright opposition. One might ask what prior experience those teachers have encountered that would lead them to respond in any other way.

In eight secondary schools, we examined teachers' assessment of the observation practices they typically encountered in their schools, and we asked teachers to indicate their relative approval or disapproval of specific classroom observation practices by department heads and by peers. Nearly 500 teachers in eight middle and high schools recorded their preferences and their actual experiences with regard to nine aspects of observation, including frequency and duration, methods of observation, arrangements for feedback or consultation, the nature of follow-up, approaches to praise and criticism, and the qualifications of the observer.[4]

The picture that emerges from the findings belies the stereotype of the closed classroom door. The door opens, it appears, to colleagues and other observers who will neither waste the teacher's time nor insult the teacher's intelligence. The door remains open when full professional reciprocity is established—when observers work as hard to understand and describe classroom events as teachers are working to plan and conduct them.

The precedent set by administrators.   When teachers consider observation by other teachers or by department heads, they look first to the precedent set by those who have observed them before. In most instances, the precedent has been set by administrators. For good or ill, the perspectives and practices of administrators carry substantial weight in teachers' estimates of the potential usefulness of observation by colleagues.

Among the eight schools in the instructional leadership study, the greatest support for observation of teachers by teachers came in two junior high schools in which administrators had worked hard to establish a record of thoughtful, thorough, well-informed classroom observation over a period of years. In contrast, teachers in the three urban high schools were generally unimpressed by any form of administrator observation they had had and were correspondingly unenthusiastic about observation by chairs or teachers.

Observers, whether administrators or teachers, have more latitude than they usually exploit. For almost every aspect of classroom observation, from how often it occurs to the nature of its link to formal evaluation, teachers approve a more rigorous scrutiny of classroom teaching than they typically encounter. In six of the eight schools surveyed, the greatest latitude is accorded to administrators; in two large suburban schools, department heads bear substantial responsibility for instructional leadership and supervision, and teachers reserved their highest expectations and most generous observation options for them. This pattern suggests that the greatest approval attaches to the role with formal and legitimate authority for observation; the preference for administrator over teacher as observer may well be an artifact of prevailing authority relations in schools, subject to systematic experimentation.

Does Classroom Observation Change Classroom Teaching?

Teachers find that spending productive time in others' classrooms is a labor-intensive business, one that is rarely accommodated well by the school's master schedule. Does spending time in others' classrooms yield enough benefits to compete well with other demands on teachers' time? How powerful is an observer's commentary as an influence on a teacher's planning and performance? Consider the following item as one measure of the relative salience of commentary on teaching: "In my school, teachers ignore feedback on their teaching."

In three urban high schools with no strong tradition of close involvement in classrooms (or, put another way, a longstanding tradition of independent/isolated work in classrooms), teachers and administrators are uncertain whether teachers take feedback seriously but are inclined to believe they do not. (In at least one of the urban high schools, administrators and department chairs are fairly certain that teachers *do* ignore feedback.) Observation is a ritual event, conducted only by administrators and associated almost exclusively with the triennial teacher evaluation.

Casual or infrequent classroom visitation, it appears, offers weak support for teacher leadership. (Indeed, there is some evidence that classroom observation of this sort may serve as a disincentive for teacher leadership, since it convinces teachers that they have little to gain from the occasions when teachers or administrators enter their classroom or presume to talk to them about their work with students.)

A strong contrast is provided by three small city schools, where secondary administrators (as part of an informal study group) have worked to make teaching "public" through frequent observation and discussion. Teachers in these schools firmly deny that teachers ignore feedback on teaching. The survey findings for these schools are consistent with case-study observation, and have led us to draw the following conclusion:

> In one of five [case-study] schools, classroom observation is so frequent, so intellectually lively and intense, so thoroughly integrated into the daily work, and so associated with accomplishments for all who participate, that it is difficult to see how the practices could fail to improve teaching. In still another school, the observation practices approach this standard. In three of the five schools, however, the observation of classroom life is so cursory, so infrequent, so shapeless and tentative that if it were found to affect instruction favorably we would be hard-pressed to construct a plausible explanation. (Little & Bird, 1986, p. 122)

Teachers who are newly selected in potential leadership roles—mentors, teacher advisors, resource teachers, and others—understand that the test of their worth will be in the classroom. But these emerging leadership roles have been ambiguous, particularly with regard to the expectations for entering other teachers' classrooms or becoming involved in any way with another teacher's work. (Mentors in California have been described as enacting a play for which there is no script.) Some districts have a long history of special-assignment positions that serve as an admirable precedent for the new generation of leadership roles. Some districts have developed the position of grade-level chair or department head as a good role model for successful leadership on curriculum, instruction, and classroom organization; more often, they do not. Individuals have been left to carve out identities and build support from teachers or administrators on a case-by-case basis.

In the absence of some commonly understood, affirmative ground for working with other teachers on matters affecting the classroom, most new leaders are hesitant to move toward another teacher's classroom unless invited, or to offer more than the most modest invitation to other teachers to observe them in their own classrooms. Teachers, meanwhile, refrain from making any request of the leader until they are certain of how it will be received and how it will be interpreted by others. In the absence of traditions for mutual work in classrooms, what transpires might be coined the "teachers' lounge waltz."

Teachers have more latitude than they have acted on to enter one another's classrooms. In any of the eight schools surveyed, teachers could enter one another's classrooms by satisfying stringent but quite practical conditions. These conditions establish professional reciprocity between observer and observed. For example, teachers who were observed wanted to be able to comment on the quality of the observation, in the same manner and spirit in which the observers would comment upon the teaching they witnessed.

Returning to the tale of "Jim" and "Bill" in Zahorik's recent study, I am led to underscore the importance of the ground rules and other preparations that make it acceptable to watch others at work. One might have concluded that collegiality need not have stopped at the classroom door, but that Jim and Bill's relationship—alleged to be a sturdy one—was barely sturdy enough to survive a clumsy first attempt at moving the action into the classroom.

In some schools, the entrance to the classroom is well trafficked. In one junior high school, for example, teachers reported that their high expectations for observation were in fact being met by colleagues who observe them. Teachers tended to observe one another in the course of work they were doing jointly to refine the curriculum—an endeavor that had already paid off handsomely in the form of increased test scores, improved daily classroom performance, and a virtual elimination of discipline problems. When participating in structured observations for one another (a kind of professional service), teachers took for granted that they would provide a written record of what transpired; they would take the time to engage in a properly thorough and deferential discussion afterward, concentrating on the response elicited from students. In order to see a set of related lessons unfold, they would devote at least 20 minutes to the observation and would try to observe for two or more days in a row. Further, teachers in this school have been known to observe and critique one another not only in classrooms, but also in conducting inservice workshops.

Teachers in all the surveyed schools shared high but reachable expectations when their colleagues observe. Teachers expect that:

- Observers will describe what they've seen and invite the teacher's commentary.
- Observers who find something to admire or praise will say so directly.
- Observers who have suggestions to make will help teachers to act on them by providing demonstrations or by joint planning.
- Teachers who observe will request feedback on their *observation* practices (reciprocity).

In follow-up videotape study of observation in action, we detected some of the moment-by-moment interactions among teachers that enabled leadership "close to the classroom" to emerge. This study of ten teacher advisors at work with teachers showed (1) how explicit ground rules built tolerance and trust and (2) how payoff escalated as teachers became "skillful pairs" with a common language and organized set of routines for describing, analyzing, and planning for teaching.

Taken alone, classroom observation (even at its most frequent and intense) is not an adequate avenue by which to expand a school's influence on teaching. Its most fruitful ground is the entire pattern of shared responsibility among teachers and the pattern of shared professional tasks, which give larger purpose to time spent in classrooms. Teachers' support for arrangements that bring them sensibly into contact with others, under conditions that they can reasonably accept, has been demonstrated in the data. Most responded that they "definitely would" agree to work with one or more colleagues under these conditions: "You and another member of your faculty have been asked to share your ideas and methods for teaching, to assemble the best methods that the two of you can come up with, and to use those methods and techniques well in your work. You will have some choice about the person with whom you are to work."

Acts of Leadership: Initiative by "Master Teachers"

A long-standing element of the culture of teaching is the maxim: "you don't interfere with another teacher's teaching." Teachers may offer their assistance to others under special circumstances and with special care. To a new teacher, it is widely acceptable to say, "Ask me if you need anything," but less so to say, "It's important to the school and to you that you get off to a good start here. I propose that we work together pretty closely for the first semester." In few schools would one teacher say to others, as a matter of course, "I've been studying some ways to help our kids with their writing, and I want to propose that we try some of them this year." In fewer still, "I've noticed that you've really been struggling with that class. Let me help." In the culture that prevails, "don't interfere" and "ask if you need help" bound teachers' initiative toward one another. Teacher autonomy, in this view, is interpreted as freedom from scrutiny and the right of each individual teacher to make independent judgments about classroom practice.

Missing from this scenario is an affirmative construction of professional obligations that is other than intrusive ("interference") or loosely invitational ("ask if you want"). The prospects for school-based teacher leadership rest on displacing the privacy norm with another that might be expressed this way: "It's part of your job to en-sure that all the teaching here is good teaching." Teacher autonomy, in this view, is interpreted as the right of the teaching *profession* to construct and uphold standards of good teaching (Sykes, 1983) and the obligation of individual teachers to examine closely their own and others' professional judgments. In schools, teachers would in fact ex-pect to be their brothers' keepers.

To examine the possibilities for a norm favoring closer mutual examination of teaching by teachers, this chapter stresses the central problem of *initiative* by teachers on matters of curriculum and in-struction. Initiative among teachers is construed here not as a prob-lem of individuals' character, energy, and knowledge (though certainly they matter), but as an institutional problem of teachers' ob-ligations, rights, opportunities, and rewards. Data from the two-year study of instructional leadership in secondary schools provide our first systematic test of teachers' acceptance of initiative by colleagues.

Teachers were confronted with the following statement, and then asked to judge a set of options for action: "In every school there are teachers who are known to be highly informed, creative, and skillful. These 'master teachers' routinely produce unusually good results. How should they and how do they interact with other teachers?"

Of the nine options that teachers were presented, the two most conservative options required almost no initiative on the part of the master teacher. They required at most that teachers recognize that some teachers in their midst might deserve the reputation of master teacher and that the master teacher "respond when asked by another teacher for suggestions, but otherwise not offer advice." Somewhat more initiative is envisioned by the options that place the master teacher at work with beginning teachers and then with experienced teachers, both at the behest of the principal. The most assertive options call for the master teacher to circulate materials, organize and lead inservices, and offer help independently to a teacher having difficulty.

Teachers in six schools ($N = 282$) recorded their relative approval or disapproval of each of the specific options and indicated the extent to which they encountered such behavior in their own school.[5]

A pattern of hesitant approval.   Teachers in five of the six schools did not flinch from the prospect that masterful teaching would be publicly recognized or that an acknowledged master teacher would be assertive in dealings with others. All but one of the nine options generated mean ratings from the group at large that were well into the "approval" range ($+1$ to $+3$). Nonetheless, the findings are best summed up as a pattern of hesitant approval. Teachers did not vigorously or uniformly embrace any of the options (none of the overall means exceeds 2.0, and the range of individual responses is considerable).

Judging by the three schools that offer both case-study and survey data, teachers' responses to others' leadership may correspond closely to their day-by-day experience as colleagues. The most confident endorsements of teacher-to-teacher initiative came from teachers in a junior high school that boasted a seven-year history of vigorous collaborative work among teachers. Elsewhere in the survey findings, teachers in this school were distinguished with regard to other professional practices: more than teachers in other schools, teachers here reported (1) two teachers getting together for a few minutes each day to share teaching plans for the day, (2) teachers negotiating ground rules to guide their work together, (3) teachers commenting on each other's course materials and tests, (4) exchanges of advice among experienced teachers, and (5) teachers praising one another's work. The most skeptical response came from an urban high school in which a variety of work conditions induced more competition than cooperation and in which teachers were formally observed only every three years.

Overall, teachers more readily gave their approval to those options that acknowledged a master teacher's skills and talents but did not anticipate truly assertive behavior toward other teachers. Offering help when asked, therefore, received uniformly high teacher approvals, while offering help without being asked drew the same level of approval from teachers in only two of the six schools.

Support for beginning teachers is one arena in which teachers have found status differences based on knowledge and skill to be defensible and leadership roles therefore sensible; these data are consistent with other case-study findings that support mentoring relationships directed at induction-year assistance. Thus teachers at five of the six schools registered solid support for the master teacher who helps a new teacher get off to a good start, while only two schools granted that same level of support for work to improve the performance of an experienced teacher.

As predicted, the school with the greatest shared responsibility for students, curriculum, and instruction (as determined by case-study findings) also showed the greatest involvement in leadership by teachers. In that school, teachers accept the principal's action in asking skilled teachers to present faculty inservice and said it happens often. Teachers give their approval to peers who circulate professional articles they have found useful. Teachers approve when some of their number are invited to provide inservice at other schools and believe that it happens reasonably often.

Yet even at this school, some doubt or hesitation remains about the possibility of the principal's asking a master teacher to meet regularly with an experienced colleague to help improve the other teacher's work; it almost never happens. The master teacher who offers help without being asked receives less approbation than the teacher who waits to be invited. And the master teacher who distributes copies of his or her own successful lesson plans may be looked at askance, although other professional materials a teacher has found useful or informative are welcomed.

Building on precedent: the department head.   When principals were recently encouraged to find ways of sharing their leadership with teachers (Acheson & Smith, 1986), one prominent suggestion was to capitalize on school-level positions that—at least in name, if not always in practice—already present opportunities for teacher leadership. Department heads, resource teachers, project directors, and grade-level chairs are among the examples of positions that may permit special recognition of talent and experience and that may have the requisite discretionary resources attached to them.

All six of the six secondary schools surveyed in the instructional leadership study gave some role to formal department heads, but only the two large suburban high schools emphasized the role of the department head as a leader in curriculum development and instructional supervision. In these two schools, department heads stood out as a distinctive reference group, more ready than teachers to approve of high initiative but still less cautious than the administrators. (In other schools, department heads' responses were virtually indistinguishable from those of other teachers.)

Asked about the possibility of giving assistance to an experienced teacher, department heads were more closely aligned with administrators than with teachers; judging by the responses, chairs were likely to overestimate the support they would receive from teachers for agreeing to work with a teacher in difficulty.

In questions targeted precisely to the department head's role, teachers were asked to review six options for behavior. Like the options regarding new leadership roles for classroom teachers, these reflect varying degrees of initiative. The most conservative (or lowest initiative) option called for the department head to act as a buffer, dealing with administration so that teachers can get on with teaching. Department heads were also depicted as encouraging participation in conferences or workshops, suggesting specific improvements to individual teachers, organizing teachers in small groups to study new options for teaching, arranging for a district supervisor to work with a department member, and using a department meeting to deliver a workshop.

The most aggressive profile of the department head came from one of the two suburban schools with a long history of using department heads to carry the weight of instructional leadership. Even in that school, however, support fell off when the chair was depicted as moving from one-on-one consultation to the leadership of the group as a whole. The lowest level of support for the department head came from the high school where that position rotates among teachers and is regarded as a "paperwork position."

When the options required group leadership (as in assembling a study group or conducting a workshop), schools with a strong recent history of teacher-to-teacher collaboration (but no particular emphasis on the department head position) stood out in their level of support; it appears that the collaborative history had established an environment in which the head's position could be invested with greater responsibility and latitude than it had enjoyed to date.

ASSESSING THE PROSPECTS FOR TEACHER LEADERSHIP

Teacher leadership has become a hot topic. Grand schemes, with equally grand titles, promise a new enticement for talented teachers and a new resource for the improvement of schools. In writing this chapter, however, I have had in mind a less grand scheme. I paint a picture of ordinary life in schools. And in doing so, I am led to draw four conclusions about the prospects for teacher leadership.

"High Gain, High Strain"

The *gain* in teacher leadership derives from teachers' classroom orientation, from their wealth of practical knowledge, and from their sheer numbers. The *strain* in teacher leadership derives from the inherited traditions of an egalitarian profession, from the persistent belief that teaching is just a matter of style and from the pervasive privacy and isolation of teaching. To talk in terms of teacher leadership is to introduce status differences based on knowledge, skill, and initiative in a profession that has made no provision for them.

The sources of strain often outweigh the felt gains, leading newly designated leaders to downplay their special status and the expertise that it signals.

The strains are compounded when teacher-leaders are recruited straight out of the classroom and attempt to earn their title after the fact with little preparation and support.

The strains are compounded when the principal is cut out of the action. Principals are pressed to be instructional leaders—and now are asked to move over and make room for teachers. When teacher leadership reaches the bargaining table, negotiators often require that the organizational "territory" occupied by teacher-leaders look so different from that occupied by administrators as to make any sensible discussion (or cooperation) between the two suspect. The more useful perspective is the well-led school.

Finally, the strains are compounded when the pace of implementation is fast—a year or less where legislative money is at stake.

To gain endorsements for a program, well-intended school professionals reach agreements that move a program forward but defeat the
interests of schools and students. (One example is the provision for
confidentiality regarding any dealings between a first-year teacher and
his or her mentor.)

Through the Eyes of the Principal

When confronted directly about the prospects of expanded
teacher leadership in their schools, what do administrators say?

Sweeping proposals for changes in teachers' titles, responsibilities, compensation, and relationships to principals have, predictably,
generated worried speculation in administrators and school board
members. Most commonly, administrators protest that a school's
standing in its community will be jeopardized by the public impres-
sion that no one is properly "in charge" and that the best teachers are
no longer available to teach children. Teachers' potential encroach-
ments on traditional domains of principals' authority, especially
teacher evaluation, have even led to legal opposition. Studies of larger
leadership initiatives, such as the California Mentor Teacher Program, detect considerable ambiguity in the teachers' new role and
uncertainty among teachers and principals about their proper relation to one another (Bird, 1985).

But sweeping proposals produce equally sweeping responses.
Case-study observations and closely situated survey measures have
permitted us to "get down to cases" with regard to administrators'
support of or opposition to specific teacher leadership possibilities.

Principals in case-study schools conceived and implemented a
range of faculty configurations that offered teachers both the reason
and the opportunity (including time) to lead. The configurations were
varied, including teacher-led interdisciplinary teams or subject-area
study groups, schoolwide instructional support teams, and intensified use of department heads. Asked in interviews and through survey measures about specific practices by which teachers, or principals
and teachers acting in concert, might take initiative to improve the
quality of teaching, principals responded in distinctly favorable terms.
These principals, like the principals of other team-based schools
(Johnson, 1976), were inclined to say that their influence over classroom teaching had been enhanced, not diminished, by involving
teachers in decision making on matters of curriculum and instruction.

Principals and assistant principals in six secondary schools were confronted with the same small set of "teacher-initiative" survey items that were presented to teachers in their school. The items explored faculty and administration approval for advice giving by recognized leaders and for assistance to both beginning and experienced teachers. They presented options that included leadership in curriculum and lesson development as well as formal inservice training.

In their responses to the selected teacher leadership options, administrators were more sanguine than teachers, displaying more support for teacher initiative than teachers themselves displayed and believing that such acts of potential leadership occurred with more regularity than teachers themselves reported.

It is probable that administrators' support for teacher initiative is overestimated by these findings. The consistently high approval rates among the administrators on survey measures (despite considerable variations in observed practice) suggest that we have not yet constructed a set of measures that will tap the threshold of administrator's tolerance for teacher initiative. There are no scenarios among these items, for example, that directly require administrators' support for peer evaluation by teachers. In addition, these measures capitalize on a long history of school-level autonomy that may be steadily eroded by initiatives that centralize curriculum policy, leaving neither principals nor teachers much of significance to lead.

The Public Interest in Teacher Leadership

Teacher leadership will be supported when teachers and school boards believe that it deserves local tax dollars: that public interest, professional interest, and personal interest all are served by singling out leaders from the ranks of teachers. The prospects for teacher leadership remain dim if no one can distinguish the gains made for students when teachers in large numbers devote their collective attention to curriculum and instruction. Each of the schools we have studied works with a staffing formula that makes the intelligent development of teacher leadership an exercise in creative organization (and occasionally creative insubordination). Underlying the staffing formula is a public conception (legitimized in board policy) of teachers and teaching that is satisfied almost exclusively by time spent in classrooms with children.

The most volatile issue in formal teacher leadership initiatives has been teacher selection. Witness the elaborate arrangements for the selection of mentor teachers in California and the careful provisions made for selection and promotion in the first stages of the Charlotte-

Mecklenburg career-ladder plan. The selection of leaders has been cast both as a technical problem (what are the acceptable criteria for performance?) and as a political problem (who will teachers accept as leaders, if anyone?), and substantial space has been devoted to describing its solutions (Schlechty, 1984).

One might see the selection problem, however, as an artifact of isolated work in schools, a problem that only arises when teachers have no sensible grounds on which to grant or deny someone the right to lead them. Thus classroom teachers who are recruited or selected into positions with titles that signal leadership (mentor) display a wondrous ability to diminish their new status and to downplay the leadership opportunities and obligations that (inescapably) accompany the title (Bird, 1985). To the extent that the selection problem remains at the forefront of discussions of teacher leadership, and elaborate selection strategies remain the heart of implementation plans, we can expect that the prospect of teacher leadership will decline.

What will defeat teacher leadership? Past efforts have had a "checkered history" (Griffin, 1985, p. 2), and current initiatives proceed by fits and starts (Bird, 1985). School-level arrangements that have fostered leadership by teachers, with apparent benefit to students, have proved fragile and unstable (Little, 1987; Cohen, 1981). The professional teacher responsibilities and relationships anticipated by the Carnegie Forum and by many state initiatives (including California's Mentor Teacher Program) are a sufficient departure from current practice to produce a backlash (Bird, 1985).

Among the conditions that will advance or erode the prospects for teacher leadership, these five are prominent:

1. *The work that leaders do:* Prospects will be diminished by describing as "leadership" tasks that are trivial and inconsequential, that are only peripheral to the important problems and tasks that schools and districts face, or that do not match in their own complexity the intellectual and social demands of teaching and learning. Prospects will be advanced by work that is widely and properly held to be important and difficult.
2. *The symbolic role that leaders assume:* Prospects will be rapidly lessened if teacher leaders serve as "hit men," engaged in activities designated to fix, punish, or remove the incompetent or intransigent. Prospects will be strengthened by roles that invest leaders with dignity and by activities that show them to be exemplars of rigorous, rewarding professional relationships.

3. *Agreements for getting started:* Teacher leadership will be jeopardized by well-intended but restrictive agreements (compromises) concerned largely with protecting the separate interests of teachers and administrators. A more sturdy platform will be provided by public, and concrete, demonstrations of shared interests and by specific ground rules for doing business together in the leadership of schools. For example, the relationship among principals, first-year teachers, and mentors can be thwarted by blind adherence to a confidentiality rule, but made effective by a careful consideration of each person's obligations to both of the others.

4. *Incentives and rewards:* Prospects for teacher leadership must be judged in large part by the incentives for teachers to favor collaborative work over independent work and to lend their support to teachers who take the lead on some shared task or problem. There are substantial disincentives in the present organization of work in most schools. Among the most powerful examples is Cusick's (1983) description of the disincentives to cooperation created by the proliferation of electives in the high school curriculum. Faculties that are relatively cohesive or polarized over appropriate ends and means for student learning are likely to provide quite different environments for teacher leadership, but those relationships have gone largely unexplored (see Metz, 1978).

5. *Local policy support:* Prospects for teacher leadership will be directly affected by district policies and practices, particularly those governing the principalship: the recruitment, selection, placement, and evaluation of building principals, and the provisions, if any, for transitions in leadership. In prior studies, effective but atypical faculty configurations have been quickly unraveled when the building principal departs (Cohen, 1981; Little, 1987) unless districts place special emphasis on preserving teacher leadership and evaluate principals accordingly (Little & Long, 1985).

Organized Preparation and Support

In effect, districts and schools face a two-part challenge. Policy and program support can be organized to meet both. One challenge is to introduce capable people to a new role. Leading a group, a school, or an occupation is not the same as teaching a class well. Training programs for new teacher leaders ensure that leaders have something to offer by helping them recognize, organize, and display their knowledge and skill to others (Bird & Little, 1985a). They ensure that new leaders work as successfully with colleagues as with students. And finally, they ensure that leaders have access to discretionary resources and are able to invent good strategies for using them.

A second challenge is to introduce a new role to an institution and an occupation. Leadership by teachers will require a more common pattern of teacher-to-teacher work in the daily operations of schools, as the basis on which teacher leadership comes to be found sensible and feasible. It will require shifts in authority relations in schools, in the bases for power and prestige. It will require changes in longstanding and firmly held conceptions of teaching, learning to teach, and teacher education.

NOTES

1. Descriptions of teachers' involvements in preservice teacher education can be found in Lanier, 1983, and in "Teacher Induction Programs and Research," the January–February 1986 issue of the *Journal of Teacher Education*. On teachers' involvement in teacher licensure, see Furtwengler, 1985, and the Connecticut State Department of Education, 1984. On teachers' involvement in teacher evaluation, see Wise et al., 1984.

2. The Office of Educational Research and Improvement (OERI) is preparing a summary of the experience of 55 "teacher incentive" planning grants, most of which were targeted to career ladders. The Career Ladder Clearinghouse of the Southern Regional Education Board has recently prepared an update on its earlier state-by-state review (Career Ladder Clearinghouse, 1986). Wagner (1985) provides an overview of the California Mentor Teacher Program. Other well-established programs have promoted special roles based on teachers' demonstrated knowledge and skill (see Kent, 1985). The most celebrated recent example of "career restructuring" is the "lead teacher" recommended by the Carnegie Forum in its report *A Nation Prepared* (1986). Following the Carnegie proposal, Devaney (1987) has prepared a discussion paper for use by local constituencies in deciding an approach to teacher leadership at the school and district level.

3. The following discussion is based on research conducted at the Center for Action Research, Inc., Boulder, Colorado, under Contract NIE-G-82-0020, and at the Far West Laboratory for Educational Research and Development, under Contract 400-83-003, both with the National Institute of Education, U.S. Department of Education. The views expressed herein are not necessarily the views of that agency.

In the first year of the instructional leadership study (Bird & Little, 1985b), case studies were completed in five schools (two districts). In the second year, surveys were completed in the five case-study schools and in three additional schools (four districts). The districts included a small city district, two large suburban districts, and a large urban district. In other related studies, the Professional Development Studies Group investigated the California Mentor Teacher Program (Bird, 1985), a countywide teacher advisor project (Little, 1985; Kent, 1985), and school-level instructional support teams (Little & Long, 1985). The studies described were conducted in partnership with my colleague, Tom Bird. The arguments developed here reflect his thinking in ways I am no longer able to untangle after 14 years of collaboration.

4. The survey was completed by 476 teachers and 22 administrators in eight schools. Return rates varied from 50% to 100%. (Six of the eight schools had return rates of 77% or above; in three schools, all teachers completed the survey).

5. The results that follow were obtained in a second survey in six schools. The survey was completed by 282 teachers and 14 administrators; return rates were above 70% in each of four schools, and 44% and 65% in the remaining two schools.

REFERENCES

Acheson, K. A., & Smith, S. C. (1986). *It is time for principals to share the responsibility for instructional leadership with others.* Eugene, OR: Oregon School Study Council, University of Oregon.

Arikado, M. S. (1976). Status congruence as it relates to team teacher satisfaction. *Journal of Educational Administration, 14*(1), 70–78.

Bennet, C. (1985). Paints, pots or promotion? Art teachers' attitudes toward their careers. In S. J. Ball & I. F. Goodson (Eds.), *Teachers' lives and careers* (pp. 120–137). London: Falmer Press.

Benveniste, G. (1987). *Professionalizing the organization.* San Francisco: Jossey-Bass.

Bird, T. (1985). *The mentor's dilemma.* San Francisco: Far West Laboratory for Educational Research and Development.

Bird, T., & Little, J. W. (1985a). *From teacher to leader: Training and support for instructional leadership by teachers.* San Francisco: Far West Laboratory for Educational Research and Development.

Bird, T., & Little, J. W. (1985b). *Instructional leadership in eight secondary schools.* Final report to the National Institute of Education, Contract NIE-G-82-0020. Boulder, CO: Center for Action Research.

Bird, T., & Little, J. W. (1986). How schools organize the teaching occupation. *Elementary School Journal, 86* (4), 493–511.

Career Ladder Clearinghouse. (1986). *1986—Incentive programs for teachers and administrators: How are they doing?* Atlanta: Southern Regional Education Board.

Carnegie Forum on Education and the Economy. (1986). *A nation prepared: Teachers for the twenty-first century.* New York: Author.

Cohen, E. (1981). Sociology looks at team teaching. *Research in Sociology of Education and Socialization, 2,* 163–193.

Connecticut State Department of Education. (1984). *The beginning year teacher support and assessment program.* Hartford, CT: Author.

Cuban, L. (1985). *How teachers taught.* New York: Longman.

Cusick, P. A. (1983). *The egalitarian ideal and the American high school: Studies of three schools.* New York: Longman.

Darling-Hammond, L. (1987). Schools for tomorrow's teachers. *Teachers College Record, 88* (3), 354–358.

Devaney, K. (1987). *The lead teacher: Ways to begin.* New York: Carnegie Forum on Education and the Economy.

Feiman-Nemser, S., & Floden, R. (1986). The cultures of teaching. In M. Wittrock (Ed.), *Handbook of research on teaching* (3rd ed.) (pp. 505–526). New York: Macmillan.

Furtwengler, C. (1985). Tennessee's career ladder plan: They said it couldn't be done. *Educational Leadership, 43*(3), 50–56.

Goodwin, L. A., & Lieberman, A. (1984, April). *Effective assister behavior: What they brought and what they learned.* Paper presented at the annual meeting of the American Educational Research Association, New Orleans.

Griffin, G. (1985). The school as a workplace and the master teacher concept. *Elementary School Journal, 86*(1), 1–16.

Hargreaves, A. (1984, October). Experience counts, theory doesn't: how teachers talk about their work. *Sociology of Education 1984, 57,* 244–254.

Johnson, R. (1976). *Teacher collaboration, principal influence, and decision-making in elementary schools* (Technical report No. 48). Stanford, CA: Stanford Center for Research and Development in Teaching, Stanford University.

Joyce, B., & Showers, B. (1981, April). *Teacher training research: Working hypotheses for program design and directions for future study.* A paper presented at the annual meeting of the American Educational Research Association, Los Angeles.

Kent, K. (1985). A successful program of teachers assisting teachers. *Educational Leadership, 43*(3), 30–33.

Klein, F. (1985). The master teacher as curriculum leader. *Elementary School Journal, 86*(1), 35–43.

Lanier, J. E. (1983). Tensions in teaching teachers the skills of pedagogy. In G. Griffin (Ed.), *Staff development: Eighty-second yearbook of the National Society for the Study of Education* (pp. 118–153). Chicago: University of Chicago Press.

Lipsitz, J. (1983). *Successful schools for young adolescents.* New Brunswick, NJ: Transaction Press.

Little, J. W. (1985). Teachers as teacher advisors: The delicacy of collegial leadership. *Educational Leadership, 43*(3), 34–36.

Little, J. W. (1987). Teachers as colleagues. In V. Koehler (Ed.), *Educator's handbook: A research perspective* (pp. 491–518). New York: Longman.

Little, J. W., & Bird, T. (1986). Instructional leadership "close to the class-room" in secondary schools. In W. Greenfield (Ed.), *Instructional leadership: Concepts, issues, and controversies* (pp. 118–138). Boston: Allyn and Bacon.

Little, J. W., & Long, C. (1985). *Cases in emerging leadership: The school-level instructional support team.* San Francisco: Far West Laboratory for Educational Research and Development.

Metz, M. H. (1978). *Classrooms and corridors: The crisis of authority in de-segregated secondary schools.* Berkeley: University of California Press.

Rosenholtz, S. (1985a). Effective schools: Interpreting the evidence. *American Journal of Education, 93,* 352–388.

Rosenholtz, S. (1985b). Political myths about education reform: Lessons from research on teaching. *Phi Delta Kappan, 66*(5), 349–355.

Rosenholtz, S. J., & Kyle, S. J. (1984). Teacher isolation: Barrier to profes-sionalism. *American Educator, 8*(4), 10–15.

Schlechty, P. (1984, April). *A school district revises the functions and re-wards of teaching.* Paper presented at the annual meeting of the American Educational Research Association, New Orleans.

Showers, B. (1983). *The transfer of training: the contributions of coaching.* Eugene, OR: Research and Development Center for Educational Policy and Management.

Soltis, J. (Ed.). (1987). *Reforming teacher education: The impact of the Holmes Group report.* New York: Teachers College Press.

Sykes, G. (1983). Public policy and the problem of teacher quality. In L. Shulman & G. Sykes (Eds.), *Handbook of teaching and policy* (pp. 97–125). New York: Longman.

Teacher induction programs and research. (1986). *Journal of Teacher Edu-cation, 37*(1), entire issue.

Wagner, L. (1985). Ambiguities and possibilities in California's Mentor Teacher Program. *Educational Leadership, 43*(3), 23–29.

Wise, A. E., Darling-Hammond, L., McLaughlin, M. W., & Bernstein, H. T. (1984). *Teacher evaluation: A study of effective practices* (R-3139-NIE). Santa Monica: The Rand Corporation.

Yee, S. M. (1986). *Teaching as a career: Promotion versus development.* Stanford, CA: Stanford University School of Education.

Zahorik, J. (1987). Teachers' collegial interaction: An exploratory study. *Elementary School Journal, 87*(4), 385–396.

PART II

Building Collaboration and Expanded Leadership Roles and Responsibilities

6

Restructuring Secondary Schools

HOLLY M. HOUSTON

My intention in writing this chapter is to uncover some of the critical phases in the process of restructuring schools. In developing this analysis, I have relied heavily on my own and my school colleagues' work within the Coalition of Essential Schools. The Coalition, established in 1984 with the philanthropic support of five foundations and the endorsement of several educational associations, is presently an alliance of some 45 schools in the United States and Canada.

The qualities of education and schooling that are featured here—those that influence the "structure" of the educational enterprise—are at once organizational, relational, and psychological. I analyze the role of school leaders, the issue of organizational scale, and ways in which the presence or absence of a system for checks and balances may influence the education of young people. I also explore how bureaucratic assumptions often influence the evaluation of teaching and learning and why the locus of responsibility for budget development and resource allocation is a critical factor in restructuring schools.

The restructuring of these various elements of organizational life in the Coalition has led to changes in the way adults relate to one another, to students, and to the curriculum. It has also led to changes in the way teachers define themselves as professionals. Perhaps a more accurate way of describing these phenomena would be to say that, to a significant degree, these favorable adjustments in the relational and psychological dimensions of school life are *both* the antecedents and consequences of change in the organizational design.

These topics are addressed under two headings. The first concerns the justification and evolution of these new structures; the second is an exploration of what is needed to sustain the structures once they have been established.

THE EVOLUTION OF NEW STRUCTURES

A New Philosophy and Its Implications

The common principles of the Coalition (see Appendix) focus our attention on a limited number of important features of schooling: the school's purpose should be to help students learn to use their minds well; the school's goal should be that each student master a limited number of essential skills and areas of knowledge; the academic and social goals of the school should apply to *all* students; teaching and learning should be personalized; the student is to be the worker and the teacher more of a coach; the diploma should be awarded on the basis of demonstrated competence; the school's norms should emphasize trust, decency, and unanxious expectation; the faculty should view themselves as generalists rather than specialists; and the budget should permit total teacher loads of no more than 80 pupils, while staff salaries remain (or become) competitive and total expenditures remain fairly constant (i.e., they are not to increase more than 10 percent beyond current cost-per-pupil). With these principles as a backdrop to the actual affairs of school-keeping, our colleagues in the Coalition have begun to craft programs that honor their own local histories and priorities as well as this general philosophy. A careful look at some of the implications of these nine principles helps to illuminate the salient structural features of these school programs.

Those implications of the Coalition's philosophy that will be analyzed here are significant—but they are not necessarily self-evident or predictable extensions of the common principles. For instance, one of the implications of this philosophy is that a particular kind of leadership for this effort will be needed in each school. If it is the principal who leads the faculty and community in analyzing and restructuring the school's program, he or she will need to devise ways of spending less time on noninstructional matters and more time planning and consulting with teachers and appealing to board members and other policy makers. Finding ways to refine the principal's job description or to enlarge the scholar-manager tier of the faculty will require imagination and a good deal of conviction about the school's priorities.

Another implication of the common principles is that teachers will need to deliberate long and hard about educational standards and methods of assessment if students are to be equipped to demonstrate their competence as a condition for promotion. Successful exhibitions of mastery will be a function of *both* carefully defined standards and personalization, and personalization (as described in principle 4) will necessitate radical changes in the staffing plans of most secondary schools. In order for the teacher-to-pupil ratio to hover around 1:80, new forms of teacher collaboration and new approaches to scheduling will have to emerge.

An additional implication of this philosophy evolves out of the expectation that costs should not exceed (by more than 10%) the present rate of expenditure in schools. Many practices and priorities that we take for granted (large athletic programs, extracurricular programs, purely vocational programs) will need to be reexamined. Ultimately some programs will need to be trimmed or entirely removed from the menu of school offerings. This "politics of subtraction" is bound to be challenging.

Two Essential Schools-in-the-Making

Thomas and Alva High Schools are actually composites of several essential schools-in-the-making whose students and faculty have permitted us to see both their planning and implementation phases from the inside. As such, these aggregate pictures of school structure and life are deliberate simplifications. Their complexities have been reduced in order that we may attend to what seem at this stage to be the most important indicators of successful or unsuccessful organizational overhaul.

Thomas High School. Thomas High is fairly large—1,780 students—and mixed in terms of ethnicity and the social class of students' families. Some students come from families who are considered among the city's social elite; others are new arrivals in this country and have, therefore, a more fractured social and economic identity. These are the extremes at Thomas High, and between them are the children of the middle class. The teachers, with one or two exceptions, are from this wide-ranging middle class—at least in part because of their middle-level economic status. Most of the teachers at Thomas High grew up within the region, coming from families, public schools, colleges, and universities that are rooted in a 30-mile radius of the school.

The school became associated with the Coalition in 1985 as a result of quiet urging by the district superintendent, who had been involved with some of the research leading up to the publication of *Horace's Compromise* (Sizer, 1984). At that time, the principal and superintendent decided to organize the Thomas Essential School as a separate entity within the larger comprehensive high school. With some funding from corporate foundations, the district was able to hire a central-office curriculum supervisor as the planner and administrator for the Essential School. Four teachers were to be hired, one in each of the "essential" subjects—English, social studies, science, and math—and approximately 100 students were to be recruited for the ninth grade. There were about seven months during which the newly designated coordinator of the Essential School could plan the program, hire staff, and recruit students.

Now in its second year of operation, the Thomas Essential School has already stabilized, and in some ways regressed. A collapsed history of the Essential School reveals that its anticipated growth to include tenth-graders did not materialize. The teachers describe their relationship with the surrounding comprehensive high school as tenuous at best; at times it is overtly hostile. There are few occasions for interaction or reasons for interdependence among the faculties of these two schools housed within the same building. Just as distressing is the fact that during their first year the teachers had thrown off the shackles of the six-period day in favor of a four-period schedule that included a common one-hour planning period/lunch, but today they have no common planning time and no hour-long lunch break. Their explanation for this particular regression is that the schedule of the larger school devoured their experiment, and they acknowledge that they should have been more vigilant in protecting it.

The principal of Thomas High School is a well-informed educator who supports the Coalition effort from a distance. The daily responsibility for running the Essential School program and making the dozens of (apparently minor) decisions that coalesce into policy is delegated to the Essential School coordinator. The principal, after all, has a large comprehensive high school to run: there are community groups to address, school board members to appease, discipline problems to deal with, attendance policies to review, a large two-story building to patrol, and athletic banquets to attend. As it is, she entrusts a number of assistant principals with responsibility for teacher evaluation and assorted supervisory duties that are mandated by state law. The Essential School coordinator is part of this group of middle-level administrators who share responsibility for evaluating teachers, though his primary responsibility is to the four teachers in the Essential School.

There have been many instructive events in the Thomas Essential School over the past 18 months. One of these occurred within the first month of the program. The math teacher found that the so-called ability levels of his 100 students ranged from the second grade (unable to do basic arithmetic operations) to beyond the algebra I that he had intended to teach. Since he was the only math teacher in the program, he decided to design his classes around the principles of individualized instruction. Every student was given his or her own assignment to do either alone or with classmates. The teacher's role was to compare completed homework and tests to the answer sheets filed in his bottom desk drawer and then to make an appropriate follow-up assignment. In theory this may appear to be a sound solution to the problems that arise when more than half the students in one's charge are not prepared for high school–level work, but in practice this amounts to doing 100 tutorials a day. It took this teacher about four weeks to admit to deep fatigue and frustration.

There was a second noteworthy occurrence after the close of the first semester. All four teachers in the Essential School had agreed in September that there would be a minimum score for passing in each subject. Those students who did not pass the first semester would (somehow) have to make up the missed or failed work in order to receive credit. The minimal score that was adopted as the standard was borrowed from the district's competency exam cutoff score: 75%.

By mid-December of that first year, more than half the students had failed to complete one or more classes. It is important to note, however, that the morale among students was high—in spite of the fact that many had thought the old rules (emphasizing mere attendance as a requisite for passing) would apply. But in addition to surprising many students, the teachers had cornered themselves in their effort to establish and uphold a standard. Now that the students had shown themselves to be all over the map in terms of achievement (not only in mathematics), and fully half of them had not met the minimal standard for passing, what could be done to make it possible for the teachers *and* their students to move on to the second semester—movement demanded by the lock-step pace of tradition?

In both situations the faculty of the Thomas Essential School responded to the problem by relying on the known and familiar: several students were released from the program on the grounds that they were not yet mature or responsible enough for it. Another strong urge was to admit a group of students whose ability levels were sufficiently homogeneous to make the teachers' job easier. As reasonable as these solutions may appear, they reveal deeper problems. One of these problems is that the small scale of Thomas Essential School does not permit much curricular flexibility. Nor does it allow for the checks and balances afforded by a larger faculty. Individual teachers, even teams of teachers, cannot be expected to be perfectly self-monitoring while in the midst of creating a new program. A wise group of persons is needed to ask questions that will force assumptions to be revealed early in the implementation process. "Seventy-five percent of *what*?" "How do your tests accord with the curriculum?" "What *is* the curriculum?" "Is individualized instruction the same as personalized education?" No one at Thomas High School had the role of friendly skeptic. The Essential School, like the surrounding comprehensive high school, was fueled by unexamined good will.

Alva High School.   Alva High is a little larger than Thomas. On most days the student population exceeds 2,100, but it can fluctuate so much from one month to the next that class size and composition are rarely fixed. Alva has a decidedly urban constituency, though by big city standards it "feels" suburban. In the 1950s and 1960s Alva was predominately white. During the 1970s Alva, like so many schools nationwide, came under a desegregation order. Today one-quarter of the students are black; about half are white; and the remaining quarter are Hispanic and Asian. In 1984, when a dozen teachers were asked why they wanted to affiliate with the Coalition of Essential Schools, most revealed that they had a memory of a better Alva High School that they wanted to stir back to reality. It was a collective memory for those teachers—who themselves reflected the racial mix of the student body. But for the principal, who was in her second year at the school, affiliation with the Coalition was a means for marshaling resources in a city school system that was renowned for its miserly unresponsiveness to initiative.

The dozen teachers who worked most closely with the principal during those early months of deliberation and planning called themselves "the dirty dozen." They met weekly and were granted considerable power over decisions pertinent to the Coalition project at Alva. At the end of that school year a vote was taken among the faculty to determine whether the school should go ahead with plans to join the Coalition. Out of 105 staff members, 76 voted in favor of affiliation; 23 were "on the fence" but would support the effort if the majority favored it; and 6 were in the "if Alva becomes part of the Coalition, I will ask for a transfer" category. An advisory committee, chaired by the principal and composed of parents, teachers, and two students, was formally established and by midsummer had outlined a plan for an experimental ninth-grade cluster of three teachers and 90 students that would begin operation in September.[1]

This single team of teachers and students has expanded to the point where now—midway through its second year of operation—the entire ninth grade at Alva is organized in groups of 75 to 100 pupils, each one served by a team of either 3 or 4 teachers. The issue of team size is a delicate one at Alva, because many teachers do not like teaching the "odd subject," which is what is required for teams composed of 3 teachers who must nonetheless teach 4 subjects. The 3 experimental cluster teachers had forewarned of the additional strain associated with teaching subjects that one has never before taught, in spite of one's dual certification. This warning, which really came in the form of advice during transitional team meetings last summer, is suggestive of the many ways in which the whole crew of ninth-grade teachers was able to benefit from the experience of those few who had made the maiden voyage the previous year. After the first half of this second year, several changes were made in the team configurations, and the school's administration continues to be responsive to the teachers' requests for modifications and guidance.

The principal of Alva High School is actively involved in policy decisions that affect the Essential School. Even if she were not disposed to be so involved it behooves her to be, since the Essential School now involves a quarter of the student body and will probably expand to include a portion of the tenth grade next year. The principal's other duties have not diminished, but she has devised a system of school governance that allows her to share some managerial responsibilities with members of the Essential School advisory committee and with those teachers who were among the original dirty dozen. Last summer, prior to the expansion of the Essential School program to include all ninth-grade teachers and students, one teacher was hired as the coordinator of the Essential School. This new coordinator has earned the respect of many teachers because of his administrative acumen, his wide acclaim as a drama coach, and his visible commitment to opening channels of communication. He has no formal supervisory duties, but has more time than the principal does to visit classes and talk to teachers about matters of teaching and learning. Jokingly, the principal refers to herself as the Queen Elizabeth of the Essential School that is marvelously governed by her prime minister. This description is apt, and the division of labor seems appropriate at this stage in the development of the Alva Essential School.

One very significant development at Alva resulted from the expansion of the Essential School program. This year there are enough ninth-grade history, English, science, and math teachers to constitute four small departments. Early in the fall the ninth-grade teachers began meeting as departments every other week or so. This form of mutual self-help complements the team meetings that take place informally (whenever there is a problem) and formally (about once a week). Another important feature of the Alva Essential School is that students can take two outside electives and are free to participate in extracurricular activities. What marks their Essential School experience as special is not so much the lean course of study as the fact that each student belongs to a distinct subgroup of the ninth grade. By all accounts, absences, tardies, and discipline problems are dramatically below the seasonal norm.

Analysis by Way of a Third Alternative: Edison High School

The experience of the teachers and students at both Thomas and Alva Essential Schools suggests that some structural features may be more promising than others. Looking back to the Coalition's common principles, we can again isolate their major implications and begin to assess the structural features of the programs at these two imaginary schools. The common principles suggest the need for genuine leadership from the principal and his or her staff; they emphasize the role of assessment as a guide for teachers and students; they imply a need for imaginative staffing plans; and they pose the question of what must be sacrificed if we are to realize this simplified structure without doubling our per-pupil expenditure. Paying close attention to these four issues—particularly the need for assessments of student learning that emphasize student exhibition of mastery, and staffing plans that will encourage collaboration and personalization—we can propose a design for an Essential School whose structural qualities are borrowed from the best of Thomas and Alva Essential Schools.

The design will reveal at least three important structural components. The *scale* of the restructured school is sufficiently large to permit flexibility in team assignments. There may be as many as 15 interdisciplinary teams, suggesting that teachers and students could be carefully matched. (This also implies that the "new" structure is now the norm and therefore is not threatened by a larger or more traditional framework for organizing school life.) In addition, there are expectations that a variety of people will assume *leadership responsibilities*, thus making organizational flexibility and accountability possible and likely. The department chairpersons would act as assessment teams and examiners, for instance, thus investing real responsibility and authority at the department level. And finally, this design has built into it a system of *checks and balances*. Departments and teams perform important balancing functions for one another, and they ensure that each teacher feels the pull of dual allegiance: The responsibility that the departments have for developing subject-specific tests (called performances) balances with the teams' responsibility to devise exhibitions that will encourage the integration of knowledge and skill across disciplines. Performances within courses are intended to focus students' and teachers' attention on essential questions and skills specific to a discipline; together the department chairpersons act as an assessment team, sharing responsibility for reviewing tests and advising individual teachers. Exhibitions are intended to bring about integration of skills and subject matter; the board of examiners is made up of department chairpersons and outside consultants.

At Edison Essential School, each *department* collaborates on decisions pertaining to:

Choice of subject matter within courses
Selection of resources
Essential questions, theories, and concepts
Essential skills
Design and review of performances

Departments should meet for one full week during the summer to devise and refine performances for the following fall semester; similarly, three to five days of meeting time should be reserved for teachers during the winter recess.

Each *team* of four teachers is responsible for 80 to 100 students, as well as for the:

Design and coordination of class schedules
Integration of knowledge and skill instruction
Design of exhibitions, subject to review by the board
   of examiners

WHAT SUSTAINS THE NEW STRUCTURE?

The structure of Edison Essential School is only as sturdy as the teachers there are responsible and competent. Teachers become competent by having had rigorous educations themselves and by

working under conditions that afford opportunities for frequent reflection and feedback on their professional practice. It is they who
establish and breathe life into an institutional mission, and in so doing
ensure that aims cohere and are intelligible to adults and adolescents. They are also the ones in whom trust should be placed for
managing resources within the school. These qualities of an able
teaching staff in any school are the result of careful recruitment,
thoughtful evaluation of teaching, continuous teacher education, and
decentralized budget management. Hence, these are the elements that
support the structure espoused by the Coalition: the *education of
teachers* (which includes their schooling and their introduction to
professional roles and responsibilities in particular schools); the *system used to evaluate teaching* (which should reveal the values of the
institution as opposed to reducing teaching to a series of techniques
that can be quickly "assessed" by occasional observation); and *decentralized responsibility for budget* development and resource allocation.

A Closer Look at Structural Supports

Consideration of some of these structural elements, in particular
teacher education and the evaluation of teaching, leads directly to the
issue of professional development over the entire lifespan of the educator. The novice—as in the case of the student teacher—often has
one foot in the university and one foot in the secondary school. This
can account for some valuable opportunities (as in the case of having
encouragement for reflection on one's practice), and it can account as
well for a deeply felt dissonance (in the sense that the institutional
norms of the high school are not usually synchronized with those of
the university, nor should they necessarily be). The veteran, on the
other hand, is squarely within one institution, and the norms at work
in the high school are a powerful, often univocal, influence on one's
expectations and aspirations. These features of professional life are
significant because they will influence how we go about ascribing
value to teaching. The evaluation of teaching is, after all, an interactive exercise. The way in which we offer suggestions or judgments to
a novice will differ from how we judge an experienced professional
(though in both cases we would look at student learning as the most
powerful indicator of successful teaching). The more significant difference between the two types of teachers, however, lies in our sense
of where responsibility should be placed for making judgments about
professional practice. We assert that the veteran teacher is a profes-

sional to the degree that he or she is a self-assessor and therefore self-correcting. This presupposes an enormous prior capacity for collaboration and an ability to learn from practice and trusted feedback. The task of the beginning teacher is to embark upon this course—to learn about and practice collaboration—so as to become responsibly experimental and self-correcting.

But much of what we aspire to in schools is bound to be either frustrated or short lived unless there is some consensus about institutional and professional aims. And this coherence needs to exist in more than just the adult mind; we must explore what it means to a 16-year-old to experience the school day, the rhythm of classes, and the (often perplexing) range of expectations that adults and peers in secondary schools present. The effects of this coherence (or incoherence) are deeply felt, although its essence and nature are often difficult to see or grasp—for both adults and teenagers. But this coherence matters, as anyone who has benefited from the seemingly transparent effect of well-articulated norms and expectations in a family, school, or office will affirm. One might go so far as to say that we do not have any way of knowing how we are doing unless we can glean or accurately manufacture some sense of what is expected. Our professional responsibility is to attend to this coherence.

And why do we insist that decentralization is fundamental to the support of this new structure of secondary schooling? The philosophy of the Coalition rests on this premise: "Schools are fragile places [that] gain their stability from often subtle accommodation to the needs, character, strengths and weaknesses of the communities in which they reside. The heart of fine education is the constructive confrontation of able teachers and willing pupils—a joining that cannot be mass produced. It emerges from deft and sensible adaptation, school by school, even classroom by classroom, and from a commitment to learning which best flourishes when students and teachers feel a strong sense of ownership of their particular school" (Sizer & Houston, 1987). Essential Schools are not to be designed and organized merely to serve the needs of bureaucratic efficiency. Instead, they are to be structured in such a way as to ensure that local ownership and accommodation are possible. Decision making about all varieties of resource allocation must, therefore, rest in the hands of those professionals and laypersons who have an interest in that school's community.

The sustenance of those structural elements characterized generally as "scale," "leadership," and a "system of checks and balances" is made possible in part by decentralized authority for budget development and resource allocation. "Decentralization" suggests that significant authority for hiring and program maintenance resides at the school site. By "budget development" we mean the attribution of value and priority among a field of competing interests. "Resource allocation" refers to decision making about everything from curriculum (what is and is not to be included in a course of study), to the purchase of resources (such as textbooks), to the identification of maximal and minimal teaching responsibilities (acceptable teacher-to-student ratios, class schedules, and so forth).

There is, of course, ample historical justification for just the opposite of what we are here advocating—that is, justification for the centralized management of school systems. From the late nineteenth century to the present, school systems have been modeled on a design promulgated by industry.[2] In these systems a premium is placed on efficiency and standardization, and this ethic has permeated all layers of schooling—right down to the organization of classrooms and curricula. States continue to mandate and prescribe curricula, textbooks, and minutes of instruction. Often they do so with an eye to minimum levels of compliance, but centralization has a way of transforming even enlightened statements about expectations into regulations that emasculate initiative.

The aim of secondary schooling, says the Coalition, is to help students learn to use their minds well. Each student is to master a limited number of essential skills and areas of knowledge. And these goals of the Essential School apply to all students—not just the privileged or gifted few. With this aim in full view, the teachers in the Essential School need to craft a program that will allow movement toward this goal. How they get there is largely up to them—as a collection of professionals. Hence decentralized responsibility for budget development becomes both a necessity and a possibility, given that these schools do not labor under the illusion that they are producing standardized products.

The Heart of the Matter: Evaluation of Teaching and Learning

What do we value in teaching? What do we theoretically expect of teachers, of schools, and of students? And what do our practices (perhaps unwittingly) reveal about our priorities? Whether we like it or not, education is a normative enterprise. Values lie at the heart of all decisions about curriculum, school organization, and teaching style. If values influence our judgments, how do we ensure that these judgments are uniformly fair without being narrowly prescriptive? On what basis does one judge idiosyncrasy?

Most educators—indeed most professionals of all stripes—prefer to dodge these questions by taking refuge behind seemingly objective solutions to problems that grow out of efforts to establish and uphold standards, to construct and score tests, or to assess professional, academic, artistic, or social competence. In our consideration of the evaluation of teaching, we wish to confront these difficult problems that arise out of the need to judge (rather than merely "score"), and so we begin by revealing our bias: in the Coalition we do not seek uniformity of practice on the part of teachers, but we do favor teaching that routinely puts the student in the role of "worker."

How do we know when the student is the worker? One framework for considering the conditions under which the student can be said to be the worker takes the form of three questions. In class, does each student know what he or she is expected to do? Would each student know how to proceed with assignments or tasks with some healthy degree of autonomy? Does each student know why this work is important? The ability to respond to these questions thoughtfully is a necessary but not sufficient indication that the student is equipped to be the worker. The teacher's role from this point is crucial, for the teacher must entice the student to perform by helping him or her either to overcome resistance or to follow through on good intentions with hard work.

If students show that they know *what* is expected of them, then we can infer that the teacher has provided clear directions. This delineation of aim might be achieved through such time-honored means as written and oral guidelines, visual displays, or by modeling a procedure for doing things, such as verifying polynomial equations. Clear directions could also take the form of a final exam presented at the *beginning* of the unit on polynomials that lays bare the expectations we have for student learning (Elbow, 1986).

Our students' response to the question of *how* they are to proceed with an assignment would ideally reveal a sense of where they might turn for help once they lose sight of the next step. This means that they would not begin the process of developing an oral report on Jonathan Edwards with perfect knowledge of all the steps that need to be followed in preparing such a presentation. Surely the problems inherent in such reporting must be allowed to reveal themselves if students are to grow and respond to challenges that they themselves perceive. The sign of a teacher who is "with it" is that he or she seizes the problematic moment as an opportunity for teaching and learning. Thus the question of "how are you going to proceed with the assignment?" should not yield a recipe-book response ("I have to do this and then do that"), but rather should reveal the existence of a roadmap on which there are checkpoints. These checkpoints exist for the benefit of the student as well as the teacher. There might, for example, be practice discussions of Edwards's work and life; rough drafts of essays submitted for preview; rehearsals of poetry recitations. The roadmap offers some general sense of direction—but it leaves room for learning, which always entails detours, rough spots, the occasional need for an aerial view of the surrounding territory, and some measure of surprise.

But it is when we ask students *why* they are supposed to do an assignment or learn mathematics that we move into the more sophisticated realm of reflection, socialization, and rationalization. Responses to the question of "why?" could range from the dull "I dunno," to the merely reactive "we have to do it," to the more insightful and bounded "we are reading about American writers so that we can talk to one another about their lives and their work . . . I am interested in the influence of the church in Puritan times . . . everyone seemed to belong to the same church . . . that is different from today . . . I am kind of shy, I want to get better at talking in front of people before I go to college." We would hope to find students capable of grasping the connectedness of the skills of inquiry and expression and the subjects they are studying as they proceed through secondary school so that they might allude to an expanding web of meaning when we ask "why are you doing this?" "This work matters because . . ." is the leitmotif we should listen for.

If we can agree that this is a desired effect of teaching—namely, that the student is an engaged and active learner[3]—the process of formerly ascribing value to the intentions and actions of the teacher is simplified. But in the Coalition we agree that students ought to be equipped not only as workers; they should also be prepared to exhibit their knowledge and know-how as a condition for promotion and graduation.

By considering the question of what we value in teaching within the context of the exhibition, we shift from a concern about the process of learning (which necessarily involves the student as a worker) to the product of this work—demonstrated competence. This is what we seek as a condition for promotion in place of credit hours: Can a student do what we, the adult professionals and our peers in schools and educational organizations across the country, deem essential for responsible entry to high school studies? for promotion to advanced high school studies? for entry into adulthood?

To make judgments about the effect of teaching on the basis of such mastery seems appropriate only if there is considerable support for a streamlined educational agenda that emphasizes competence in specifiable academic and social skills and areas of knowledge. This consensus is imperative if any progress is to be made toward actualizing the aim of the Essential School. Since these schools do not purport to be all things to all people in the manner of the comprehensive high school, they must be precise in drawing their boundaries of responsibility for teaching and learning.

In our mythical Edison Essential School, different groups of teachers are charged with responsibility for developing and reviewing two types of student achievement. One grouping of teachers is by academic department, another by team, and yet another is composed of all department chairpersons. The department of English, for example, would spend considerable time designing and reviewing student performances (subject-specific assessments of knowledge and skill). All English teachers would share a collective responsibility for ensuring that their quizzes, tests, exercises, and exams reflect the values of the department and of the larger institution. Such a department might place a great deal of emphasis on written and oral expression, and their various forms of student assessment should reflect that value. Another English department might favor knowledge of American literature and written expression as essential aims for student mastery. In each case the fact of the student performance would serve to focus teachers' and students' attention on what is essential. The performance would thus become as much the compass as it is the destination.

The interdisciplinary team members would retain their allegience to their respective departments but would, in addition, have a responsibility to ensure that their students sense the connectedness between the essential skills required in English and those required in history. Team members are to devise exhibitions that are occasions for the integration of knowledge and skills from across the curriculum. To do this the teams would need recommendations and counsel from the so-called board of examiners, made up of department chairpersons and outside experts. Thus the mission of the institution is reflected in a mutually reinforcing grid of team and department obligations for student achievement.

Evaluation of teaching under these conditions becomes an exercise in collaboration.[4] For instance, as a department member and as a team member I should share responsibility with others for helping students to learn to think, write, imagine, and so forth. I would work with my colleagues in planning and developing courses of study and various kinds of assessment. Such close association makes my strengths and weaknesses visible and encourages complementarity, as opposed to redundancy, among team members. In the course of each day I would be subject to evaluation because I would see or hear about alternative approaches to teaching. Under such conditions it would seem ludicrous to have an administrator stroll into my classroom with checklist in hand—prepared to "do" an evaluation of my teaching.[5] A more sophisticated set of professional responsibilities such as has been outlined demands a more refined system for the evaluation of teaching. Surely this evaluation of teaching would need to take broad contextual and developmental factors into consideration, and it would itself need to be primarily educational.[6]

CONCLUSIONS

These practices and structures that are emerging in the Coalition are attempts to organize school life with particular values in mind. To the degree that these structures permit adults and adolescents to learn to use their minds well and to participate in the formation of a fair and humane social environment, these new structures may be deemed appropriate or successful. We have seen some promising indicators of successful restructuring—as embodied in the design of Edison Essential School. These structural features can be summarized as follows.

1. The Essential School program may begin as a small-scale experiment, but for it to be fully institutionalized, it must gradually incorporate all grade levels and influence expectations throughout the school.
2. An effort to restructure schooling requires strong and diversified leadership. The school administration plays a pivotal role in reinforcing a new organizational design. The principal must be an exemplary manager-teacher, capable of articulating a vision and enlisting teachers, parents, and students in efforts to clarify aims and expectations. School counselors, deans, and assistant principals are particularly influential in matters pertaining to scheduling, discipline, and the evaluation of teaching. Department chairpersons would become increasingly visible as architects of the school's plan for exhibitions and performances. Teachers, working in transdisciplinary teams and as members of academic departments, must be encouraged to approach teaching as a collaborative venture. Everyone in the school, including parents, will

require training and reeducation in order to assume these new leadership roles.

3. A web of interlocking responsibilities for devising and implementing school policy must be established. This system of checks and balances should be employed for the development of long-term plans, the evaluation of student learning as displayed in performances and exhibitions, and in the design of budgets and staffing plans. The school is to be viewed as a network of interdependent people, each of whom bears special responsibility for students' learning.

These structural features do not themselves ensure that children will be challenged and delighted by schooling. Nor are they adequate for the task of reeducating our teaching force. But, just as present-day expectations are largely determined by the structures within which we are socialized and educated, alternative structures for schooling can profoundly influence our vision of the possible.

NOTES

1. One function of such a committee is to engage in what Matthew Miles calls "metaplanning": developing time tables, deciding on how planning and implementation will be linked, considering what data need to be collected for future decision making, and so forth. See Miles, 1978, especially Chapter 3, "Planning and Implementing New Schools: A General Framework."

2. See Elizabeth Vallance's (1986) thoughtful analysis of the "language of justification" that supported the shift toward centralization.

3. This outline of an approach to teaching and learning has some significant features in common with Applebee and Langer's concept of "instructional scaffolding." They outline five elements of successful instructional interaction: student ownership of the learning event; appropriateness of the instructional task; structured and supportive instruction; shared responsibility (or collaboration); and internalization (or transfer of control). Their research is in the area of literacy instruction, specifically reading and writing. Because they deemphasize the importance of "coverage" and approach the problem of literacy instruction from the perspective of teachers concerned with helping students to gain mastery over a symbol system that bears meaning, their work warrants closer attention. See Langer and Applebee, 1986.

4. See Judith Warren Little's (1981) elaboration on the "norm of collegiality" and the "norm of continuous improvement" and their relationship to organizational efficacy.

5. Michael Scriven (1981) makes an even stronger case against basing evaluation of teaching on sporadic classroom visits.

6. See Judith Warren Little's (1981) article on the relationship of sustained "staff development" to the improvement in teaching.

APPENDIX

The Common Principles of the Coalition of Essential Schools

1. The school should focus on helping adolescents to *learn to use their minds well*. Schools should not attempt to be "comprehensive" if such a claim is made at the expense of the school's central intellectual purpose.
2. The school's goals should be simple: that each student *master a limited number of essential skills and areas of knowledge*. While these skills and areas will, to varying degrees, reflect the traditional academic disciplines, the program's design should be shaped by the intellectual and imaginative powers and competencies that students need, rather than necessarily by "subjects" as conventionally defined. The aphorism "less is more" should dominate: curricular decisions should be guided by the aim of thorough student mastery and achievement rather than by an effort merely to cover content.
3. *The school's goals should apply to all students*, while the means to these goals will vary as those students themselves vary. School practice should be tailor-made to meet the needs of every group or class of adolescents.
4. *Teaching and learning should be personalized* to the maximum feasible extent. Efforts should be directed toward a goal that no teacher have direct responsibility for more than 80 students. To capitalize on this personalization, decisions about the details of the course of study, the use of students' and teachers' time, and the choice of teaching materials and specific pedagogies must be unreservedly placed in the hands of the principal and staff.
5. *The governing practical metaphor of the school should be student-as-worker*, rather than the more familiar metaphor of teacher-as-deliverer-of-instructional-services. Accordingly, a prominent pedagogy will be coaching, to provoke students to learn how to learn and thus to teach themselves.
6. Students entering secondary school studies are those who can show competence in language and elementary mathematics. Students of traditional high school age but not yet at appropriate levels of competence to enter secondary school studies will be provided

intensive remedial work to assist them quickly to meet these standards. *The diploma should be awarded upon a successful final demonstration of mastery* for graduation—an "exhibition." This exhibition by the student of his or her grasp of the central skills and knowledge of the school's program may be jointly administered by the faculty and by higher authorities. As the diploma is awarded when earned, the school's program proceeds with no strict age grading and with no system of credits earned by time spent in class. The emphasis is on the students' demonstration that they can do important things.

7. The tone of the school should explicitly and self-consciously stress values of *unanxious expectation* ("I won't threaten you but I expect much of you"), of *trust* (until abused), and of *decency* (the values of fairness, generosity, and tolerance). Incentives appropriate to the school's particular students and teachers should be emphasized, and parents should be treated as essential collaborators.

8. *The principal and teachers should perceive themselves as generalists* first (teachers and scholars in general education) and specialists second (experts in one particular discipline). Staff should expect multiple obligations (teacher-counselor-manager) and sense a commitment to the entire school.

9. Ultimate administrative and budget targets should include, in addition to *total student loads per teacher of eighty or fewer pupils, substantial time for collective planning by teachers, competitive salaries for staff, and an ultimate per-pupil cost not to exceed that at traditional schools by more than 10 percent.* To accomplish this, administrative plans may have to show the phased reduction or elimination of some services now provided students in many traditional comprehensive secondary schools.

REFERENCES

Adler, M. (1984). *The paideia proposal: An educational manifesto.* New York: Macmillan.

Cusick, P. (1983). *The egalitarian ideal and the American high school.* New York: Longman.

Elbow, P. (1986). *Embracing contraries: Explorations in learning and teaching.* New York: Oxford University Press.

Goodlad, J. (1984). *A place called school: Prospects for the future.* New York: McGraw-Hill.

Langer, J., & Applebee, A. (1986). Reading and writing instruction: Toward a theory of teaching and learning. *Review of Research in Education, 13,* 171–194.

Little, J. (1981, April). *The power of organizational setting: School norms and staff development.* Paper presented at the annual meeting of the American Educational Research Association, Los Angeles.

Miles, M. (1978). *Project on social architecture in education.* New York: Center for Public Policy Research.

Phenix, P. (1964). *Realms of meaning: A philosophy of the curriculum for general education.* New York: McGraw-Hill.

Powell, A., Farrar, E., & Cohen, D. (1985). *The shopping mall high school.* Boston: Houghton Mifflin.

Ryle, G. (1949). *The concept of mind.* London: Hutchinson and Company.

Scriven, M. (1981). Summative teacher evaluation. In J. Millman (Ed.), *Handbook of teacher education* (pp. 244–271). Beverly Hills: Sage Publications.

Sizer, T. (1984). *Horace's compromise: The dilemma of the American high school.* Boston: Houghton Mifflin.

Sizer, T., & Houston, H. (1987). "Prospectus" of the Coalition of Essential Schools. Providence, RI: Brown University.

Vallance, E. (1986). Hiding the hidden curriculum: An interpretation of the language of justification in nineteenth-century educational reform. *Curriculum Theory Network, 4* (1), 5–21.

7

School: A Community of Leaders

ROLAND S. BARTH

> One day—lying alone in the lawn on my back
> with only the drone of a distant train
> on some far off track,
> I saw before my eyes, 5,000 feet high or more,
> a sight—which to this day, I must say,
> I've seen nothing like before.
>
> The head goose—the leader of the V—
> suddenly veered out, leaving a vacancy
> which was promptly filled by the bird behind.
> The former leader then flew alongside,
> the formation continued growing wide—
> and he found a place at the back of the line.
>
> They never missed a beat.
>
> (Stromberg, 1982)

For many years I have been developing a personal vision of the school in which I would like to be principal or teacher. Not surprisingly, this is also the school I would like my daughters to attend. Mine is a personal vision, a conception of what might be, what could be, perhaps what should be, rather than a projection of what will be. I find the continuous exercise of vision-making to be engaging, fun, often useful, and above all, hopeful. Those of us who work in or near public schools need hope.

A few months ago I heard a teacher from Maine recite from memory an unusual and haunting poem, a portion of which appears above. In the poem, two important ideas emerge—leadership and community—which gave me a name for an element of my personal vision I had been struggling to clarify and articulate. It was not difficult to transform the metaphor "geese: a community of leaders" into "school: a community of leaders."

Like most of us, I have been reading some of the recent national reports. I find that the concept of a school as a community of leaders has become both fashionable and controversial. It appears that concern about the relationship between teacher and principal, engaged together in schoolwide decision making, will be with us for a good while. I hope so.

Unfortunately, well-intentioned efforts to involve teachers in decision making have exacerbated tensions between union and management, between teacher and principal. Teachers and their associations have responded with anger that it has taken so long to include them, suspicion that they are being tricked, and confidence that the revolution is now at hand.

The national professional principals associations have responded defensively to the idea that teachers might "lead" schools. So has the American Association of School Administrators, which recently issued a policy statement that cautiously "encourages schools and districts to establish formal procedures that will promote appropriate involvement of teachers in decision making." This would take place under the direction of a "strong, effective principal. Substituting a lead teacher or a committee of teachers for the principal is unacceptable" (Rodman, 1987, p. 9). Far from lead geese moving back from the head of the line to allow others a turn at leading, attempts to rearrange decision making within a school seems to be ruffling feathers.

For several years, thanks to mastery learning, the effective schools literature, and the concept of high expectations, most of us have been seeing and saying that "all children can learn." Initially many teachers, principals, parents, even children were skeptical. Now the belief that all children can learn is widespread, and the implications for instruction and students are profound.

When I was working to establish the Harvard Principals' Center six years ago, I based my efforts on different assumptions: every principal is very good at something; there are other principals who would like to know and to be able to do that; principals can convey their important craft knowledge about staff development, parent involvement, discipline, or managing the lunchroom to one another. In short, I believed that all principals can learn and that all principals can teach. Many were skeptical of these preposterous propositions. Some university people, superintendents, parents, teachers, students, and even principals might still take exception. Yet the convictions that principals have substantial professional knowledge of immense value to others in improving schools and that they can convey these insights to their colleagues are having profound implications for principals, for their professional development, and for the improvement of their schools—as the formation of principal centers around the world attests.

I would like to suggest another astonishing proposition: all teachers can lead. Skeptics might say "some teachers," or "a few," or even "many." But there is some important part of the life and work of the entire school that every teacher is good at, wants to become good at, and can become good at. A classroom teacher is no more "just a teacher" than Corazon Aquino is "just a housewife." Teachers harbor extraordinary leadership capabilities, and their leadership potential is a major untapped resource for improving our nation's schools. All teachers can lead. The world will come to accept that all teachers can lead, as many now accept that all children can learn and all principals can teach, if we can overcome the many impediments facing teachers and principals that block teachers' leading and if we can find conditions under which teachers will exercise that leadership.

As a principal, I used to think I shared leadership. I did. Or, I should say, I went as far as I could go or felt the school could go. But reflecting on my leadership a decade later, I see that I stopped well short of establishing a community of leaders. Leadership for me was delegating, giving away or sharing participation in important decisions to others so long as the curriculum, pupil achievement, staff development, and, of course, stability were not much altered. Now I see it differently. Rather, my vision for a school is a place whose very mission is to ensure that students, parents, teachers, and principals all become school leaders in some ways and at some times. Leadership is making happen what you believe in. Everyone deserves a chance. Schools can help all adults and youngsters who are part of them learn how to lead and enjoy the recognition, satisfaction, and influence that comes from serving the common interest as well as one's self-interest.

I would like to consider the idea of a school as a community of leaders by examining particularly what teachers and principals might do there.

TEACHERS AS LEADERS

Shortly after my arrival as principal of an elementary school, a veteran teacher sent me a memo indicating his intention of staying away from school until the "deplorable and illegal fire safety standards have been corrected." A challenge to the new authority? Perhaps. An unwelcome hassle from an unexpected quarter? Perhaps. And an opportunity? Perhaps.

In a long talk with the teacher, his energy and concern for the

safety of the children, as well as his anger, emerged. At the conclusion of the conversation I asked him if he would accept responsibility for the fire standards of the entire school and assume the position
of fire marshal—all of the responsibility. He was appropriately suspicious. The next day he agreed. I gave him the key to the fire-alarm
system and pledged my support for any plan he proposed. I asked that
he consult with me from time to time as his plan developed.

Somehow, in addition to his full-time teaching responsibilities,
he began to devise a most incredible school fire-safety system. He met
with each class and teacher and talked about the seriousness of fire
in a 50-year-old brick and wood building full of papers and people.
He held a drill for each class, established an exit route, and assessed
with teacher and students how the drill had gone, what could be improved, and how long it took to evacuate the building. Then he announced the first schoolwide fire drill. The fire chief from the city
attended and watched in wonder as 450 children and 30-some adults
cleared the building quickly, quietly, and in an orderly manner. He
informed the fire officials that he was concerned about how long it had
taken them and their equipment to reach the school. He told them that
once a year he would call a drill—and time the officials to see how
quickly they could respond!

Furthermore, he reasoned that in the event of a real fire, especially during the long New England winter, the population of the
school (many without shoes and coats) would have to stand in the
snow and freezing cold for an indeterminate time. This was unacceptable. He visited a nearby church and made arrangements with the
pastor to secure a key. During the next drill, the entire school filed
into predetermined pews of the church. I will never forget his sol-
emn assessment—from the altar—of the process.

Unusual lengths to go to for safety? A pathological obsession
about fires? Too much time spent off "the basics"? Most of us would
rather have our own children in a school that takes safety this seriously than the one that had been operating the previous year—or the
school in which I had tried to administer fire safety along with everything else.

When teachers are enlisted and empowered as school leaders,
everyone can win. Other teachers' concerns are frequently better
understood by one of their fellows than by someone who performs a
different job. Important schoolwide issues receive more care and attention when the adult responsible is responsible for no other major
areas. And the principal wins by recognizing that there is plenty of
leadership to go around. If the principal tries to do all of it, much of

it will be left undone by anyone. Leadership is not a zero-sum game in which one person gets some only when another loses some. The principal demonstrates leadership by entrusting some of it to others. And important needs of the teacher-leader may be met. In this case, the teacher's rapport with the faculty improved. He was dubbed "Sparky" and at an end-of-year faculty meeting awarded a shiny red fireman's hat (the kind about which 8-year-old boys dream at Christmas) on which was emblazoned "Chief." Recognition that he *was* chief. Of something. Other teachers can become chief of something, too. And were each of 30 teachers to become chief of something, a school would be well along the path toward becoming a community of leaders.

But many teachers and principals feel that teaching and leadership are mutually exclusive. One visitor to a school who was interested in leadership asked to shadow a teacher for a day. "I'm not a leader. I'm just a teacher. If you want to see leadership, go shadow the principal," said the teacher. To be a leader is equated with being an administrator. That all teachers lead within their classrooms does not seem to count. Leadership is perceived as happening among adults. It is commonly held that if you are a teacher the only way to become a leader is to leave teaching.

There may be few opportunities for teachers to offer schoolwide leadership. Others may not feel it possible. Yet for more teachers the question is, "Why would I want to lead anyway? Shut the door and leave me alone." As one principal put it, "Teachers in my building don't want more participation." Most teachers already feel overwhelmed and overworked. Teachers spend vast quantities of time and energy beyond their work hours correcting papers, repairing what happened today, and preparing for what may happen tomorrow. An opportunity for leadership is an opportunity to deplete more time and energy. Opportunities for teachers to run meetings and manage fire drills are peculiar opportunities, indeed. The would-be teacher-leader seeks fulfillment and satisfaction but more often encounters committee work, meetings, and conflict. Already bombarded with interpersonal overload, few teachers are eager to accept such "opportunities."

When others are deciding, teachers can resist, lobby, hold out, and in inventive ways attempt to influence a situation to their own advantage. When teachers work for the common good, they may lose a large measure of self-interest in the outcome. With leadership and responsibility comes the need to see others' points of view and act fairly in their eyes. Many teachers are not willing to make this trade.

And, as principals know, no decision pleases everyone. Any decision displeases someone. Why would teachers want to engender the wrath of their fellows? Let the principal do it. That is what he is paid for. And, given the distance in many places between union and management, why should a teacher do what an administrator is supposed to do, thereby lightening the load of the adversary and increasing one's own? As one teacher put it, "to go across" can be debilitating.

The rewards of leadership, then, so treasured in the eyes of teachers, are often illusory, no more immediate and satisfying for teachers than for principals. For most teachers, the school world is the world within the classroom: teaching. Because every teacher can lead clearly does not mean that every teacher wants to lead, should lead, should be expected or required to lead.

There is a touch of irony in the fact that those in history who have been most widely celebrated as teachers have also been leaders. Socrates, Plato, Jesus, Moses, Ghandi are all names synonymous with teaching and leading. But teacher leadership is clearly not a common contemporary condition. Why, then, did Sparky agree to serve as school fire marshal? Why, for that matter, would *any* teacher choose to engage in serious, sustained school leadership?

Public policy makers respond that opportunities for teachers to lead will attract more able people to the profession. And by engaging teachers in leadership activities, the very able, empowered, ennobled, and challenged will choose to *remain* in teaching.

Others argue that leadership opportunities will bring out the best in teachers; and the very best from teachers will bring out the very best in their students. Teacher leadership will raise pupil achievement. *Time for Results: The Governors' 1991 Report on Education* (National Governors' Association, 1986), for instance, offers less regulation of teachers if they will provide leadership at the school level and accept responsibility for student achievement.

The literature from successful businesses, from Japan to IBM, offers evidence that when workers participate in decision making their satisfaction and the quality of their work rises. Teacher-leaders, too, it is reasoned, will become more invested in the school and in its success. By sharing leadership, teachers will feel more ownership and commitment to the implementation of decisions. And by providing teachers with leadership opportunities, one accords them recognition. Therefore, they will work harder and better and longer. In short, research suggests that the greater the participation in decision making, the greater the productivity, job satisfaction, and organizational commitment.

That is why policy makers and businessmen would have teachers lead. But, given the reasons suggested above, why would any *teacher* want a hand in major school decisions? One teacher put it this way:

> What is the passion I have for education? The classroom experi-
> ence. That is what I love. On reflecting upon it I realized that I
> love my own experience; that which occurs within the walls of
> my room and with students I call mine. What happens in my
> room, I like to think, is quality learning. What happens outside
> my room has very little to do with me. And that, quite simply,
> is what's wrong with public schools.

Another teacher put it differently: "the concept of teacher-leader ought not to be such a difficult one to accept. After all, teachers are leaders in the classroom every day. There is no reason why the skills of the classroom cannot be transferred to areas of the school life outside the classroom." And another said,

> Teachers are leaders every day in dozens of ways. We provide
> educational direction and create the kind of educational envi-
> ronments we believe in for our students. We work with other
> teachers to create new curriculum or to consult on problems we
> have with students. We work with parents in reflecting on their
> children's development and by providing information about ac-
> ademic matters. We voice matters of concern for ourselves, our
> colleagues, our students and administrators, and frequently ini-
> tiate major programmatic changes in our schools.
>   To assert one's leadership as a teacher, often against forces
> of administrative resistance, takes commitment to an educa-
> tional ideal. It also requires the energy to combat one's own in-
> ertia caused by habit and overwork. And it requires a certain
> kind of courage to step outside of the small prescribed circle of
> traditional "teacher tasks," to declare through our actions that
> we care about and take responsibility for more than the mini-
> mum, more than what goes on in the four walls of our class-
> rooms.

Many teachers feel, then, that no matter how fulfilling, how important, and how successful the work within classrooms, there is more to teaching.

Other teachers become concerned about the whole school because they think "if only someone will." When "someone doesn't" for long enough, they become the "someone." They are propelled from classroom to school leadership by anger.

> I've thought about my own development as a school leader, it was clearly anger which pushed me out on the leadership "limb." Put another way, anger provided the adrenalin which made it possible for me to take the risk of assuming a leadership role. Moreover, beyond the initial "push," anger fueled the courage to persist in a leadership role which was often uncomfortable, unpleasant, and unfamiliar. For me, then, anger both precipitated and sustained my role as a faculty leader. Anger enabled me to find my voice and compelled me to speak out publicly. Speaking publicly, in turn, required that I channel my anger into constructive and articulate criticisms of and challenges to my principal's policies and decisions.

And many teachers want to lead for precisely the reasons others do not. They derive respect, if not acclaim, from other teachers for their efforts; they derive energy from leadership activities, which fuels, rather than depletes, their classroom activities; by leading, they find they can more fully understand the points of view of other teachers and administrators; they enjoy meetings and interactions with other adults as well as with children; they find they learn by leading, that leadership offers profound possibilities for one's professional development; and they aspire to distinguish themselves with respect to their peers.

In short, the opportunity to engage in school leadership is attractive for Sparky and other teachers because it offers possibilities for improving teaching conditions; it replaces the solitary authority of the principal with a collective authority; it provides a constructive format in which adults can interact that overcomes daily classroom isolation; it helps transform schools into contexts for adults' as well as children's learning.

THE PRINCIPAL AND A COMMUNITY OF LEADERS

Principals, by virtue of the authority of their position, are seen as school leaders. Recently I participated in a lengthy conversation about shared leadership with an elementary school principal and a junior high school principal.* We agreed on several assumptions about

*I am indebted to Richard Ackerman and Jeannie Nicholas.

teachers as leaders: all teachers have leadership tendencies; schools badly need teachers' leadership; teachers badly need to exercise that leadership; teachers' leadership has not been forthcoming; the principal has been at the center of both successes and failures of teachers' leadership; and principals who are most successful as leaders themselves are somehow able to enlist teachers in providing leadership for the entire school.

Guidelines for Principals

Once this common understanding was established, we began to examine how principals might facilitate an improvement in this situation. Specifically, we considered what principals can do to develop a community of leaders within a school, what they do that thwarts the development of teacher leadership, and what they do that makes the emergence of school leadership from teachers more likely. A set of guidelines emerged from this discussion.

Articulate the goal.   In order to move a school from where it is to where one's vision would have it be it is necessary to convey what the vision is. This is risky. Many principals may not be sure of what their vision is. They may not want to face faculty and parental dissonance that might surface if they shared their vision. They may not want to expose their thinking to the central office, which may not see the connection between, say, a community of leaders and minimum competence in three-place multiplication. Consequently, few administrators telegraph their vision to the school community, preferring to believe that "they'll figure it out." A community of leaders, involving teachers and students in school leadership, is more likely to occur when the principal only articulates this goal in meetings, conversations, newsletters, faculty memos, and community meetings.

Relinquish power.   There are short lists and long lists of the behaviors of "effective principals." They include continuous monitoring of performance, exercising strong leadership, and involving parents. One state has extracted 91 different behaviors of the successful principal. I have never seen on such a list the "ability to relinquish." And yet there are too many schoolwide responsibilities for any principal to handle. Most principals have in their bottom drawers a few marbles of authority that come with their appointment and even more that they earn over time. Some principals try to play these marbles alone. Others do not play at all, making few decisions themselves and allowing others to make even fewer. I think it best to have all the marbles played by as many players as possible. But many principals feel they already have too little power over a tottering building. To convey any to others is illogical. It is against human nature for us to relinquish power when we will probably be held accountable for what others do with it. One should accumulate and consolidate, not relinquish. This leads to the common belief that "I cannot leave my building." Perhaps the most important item in the list of characteristics of effective principals is the capacity to relinquish, so that the latent, creative powers of teachers may be released.

Empower and entrust.   It is important for a principal to relinquish decision-making authority to teachers. But the teacher will not become a leader of the school community if, when the going gets tough and the angry phone call comes from a parent, the principal violates the trust and reasserts authority over the issue. It takes only a few such incidents of undermining a teacher's leadership before teachers secede from the community of leaders. The principal must bet on a horse and have the courage and trust to stick with it and help it finish. To change the bet in the middle of the race is to create conditions under which everyone loses.

Involve teachers before decisions are made.   Commonly, when a problem, like inadequate fire safety, emerges, the principal quickly reaches a solution (bringing in the fire chief to lecture students and teachers) and then invites a teacher to "handle" the situation. This is an opportunity for maintenance, not leadership, which few teachers will embrace. The energy, the fun, the commitment around leadership come from brainstorming one's *own* solutions and then trying to implement them. For a community of leaders to develop, important problems need to be conveyed to teachers before, not after, the principal has played them out.

Carefully consider which responsibility goes to whom.   Wanting desperately to resolve a problem for the school and oneself, the principal often selects a responsible, trusted teacher who has successfully handled similar problems. But, by relying on the tried and proven teacher, the principal rewards competence with additional hard work. It will be only a matter of time before the overburdened teacher burns out, concluding that if one is going to *act* like an assistant principal one might as well be paid like an assistant principal, and leaves teaching. Other oft-chosen teachers will one day declare, "I'm drowning and I must return my attentions to the classroom. I'm sorry I can't do it."

The better match, as in Sparky's case, may be between an important school issue and a teacher who feels passionately about it. For one teacher, it is fire safety. For another, the supply closet. While another would favor reforming the science curriculum, finding both fire safety and the supply closet menial tasks, not leadership opportunities. Teacher leadership is less a matter of according trusted teachers responsibility for important issues than of ensuring that all teachers are given ownership of a responsibility about which they care deeply. One person's junk is another person's treasure.

Reliance upon a few proven teachers for schoolwide leadership also excludes the majority of untried teachers from the community of leaders, contributing to divisiveness and leaving little of a community. For Sparky, the opportunity to have the "key" had far more meaning than for other teachers who had been offered and accepted many keys. His inclusion expanded the community by one.

Too often the criterion for bestowal of the "key" of leadership is evidence that the person knows how to do it. Yet the innovative solutions come more often from teachers who do not know how to do it but want to learn how. This is where leadership and staff development intersect. The moment of greatest learning for any of us is when we are responsible for a problem that we care desperately to resolve. Then we need and seek out assistance. We are ready to learn. At this moment the principal has a responsibility and an opportunity to assist the teacher in developing leadership skills and finding success with responsibility. Mere delegation or "being kept informed" is not sufficient involvement on the principal's part for the development of a community of leaders. Unsuccessful leaders do not make a community of leaders. Most teachers, like most principals, need assistance in becoming successful school leaders. The principal who supports and teaches the beginning school leader assumes a burden of considerable time and patience. "It would be easier and quicker to handle it myself." Yet this is what is really meant by shared leadership. It is interactive, interdependent.

By turning for leadership to untried and perhaps untrusted teachers who express a passionate interest in an issue, as Sparky did, everyone can win. The overburdened teacher receives no further burden; the teacher who displays excitement about an issue is enlisted in the growing community of leaders. The teacher comes alive as an adult learner, as well as leader. And the principal wins. If this year the principal can help anoint, induct, and support the initial efforts of teacher-leaders, those efforts will be rewarded next year by a level of teacher independence that will require much less from the principal.

Share responsibility for failure.   If the principal conveys responsibility to a teacher for an important schoolwide issue and the teacher stumbles, the principal has several options. Principals can, of course, elect to shoulder all the responsibility themselves, but this is a needlessly lonely and self-punishing position. Alternatively, they can blame the teacher: "I entrusted leadership and authority for fire safety to Sparky and he blew it. Now I'll find someone who can do it better or I'll do it myself." This may protect the principal in the short run, but in the long run neither Sparky nor other teachers will choose to make attempts again. Without the principal's support, few teachers will take chances; thus no community of leaders will emerge. Fortunately, there is a third possibility: shared responsibility.

If the principal bets on this horse and it runs poorly, "we" are responsible, for together we have given our best efforts. Both teacher and principal have something of importance to them and the school that bonds them. Responsibility for failure is shared. Usually schools deal more kindly with mistakes made by a coalition of teacher and administrator than with those made by either alone. Additionally, the important issue is not whose fault it is but what happened, what can be learned from it, and how it might be done better next time. The principal who stands behind a teacher has hope for developing collegiality, staff development, and morale. There is much, then, to be gained by both teacher and principal from failing together.

Permit the teacher to enjoy responsibility for success.   Whereas it is important to the development of a community of leaders that failures be shared by teacher and principal, it is equally important that success reflect upon the teacher, not the principal. The principal has many occasions during the school day and year to be visible. Running the assembly, coming in over the loud speaker, sending notices to parents, meeting with the press about the National Merit Finalists. For the teacher there are few opportunities to expect and enjoy recognition from the school community. For the principal to co-opt or share the limelight is to reduce the recognition for the teacher and make less likely continuation of membership in the community of leaders.

Schoolwide success replenishes the teacher personally and professionally. I have seen classroom performance, morale, commitment to teaching, and relationships with colleagues all benefit from public recognition.

Additionally, teachers should enjoy the success because they have done most of the work. My part in the fire-safety plan took a fraction of the time Sparky put in. Mine were prime minutes, but there were few of them.

Principals, of course, have their own needs for success and recognition, which often impede the development of a community of
leaders. But in the long run, teacher success begets further teacher
leadership and success. The school improves. And the principal justly
comes in for ample credit as the one who pulled it off. Everyone wins.

Recognize that all teachers can lead.   Just as high expectations that
all children can learn have been associated with unexpected learning
on the part of children whose race, social class, and family background might not predict achievement, high expectations on the part
of principals that all teachers can be responsible, committed school
leaders make more likely the emergence of the leadership tendencies that all teachers possess.

How might principals' expectations for teachers as leaders be
raised and conveyed? Principals can articulate a community of leaders as a goal, look for and celebrate examples in other schools or in
one's own school.

Embedding in a principal's conception of leadership the idea that
all teachers can lead has a lot to do with the ways schools respond to
differences. Just as I would like to see our disdain for differences
among students replaced by the question, "how can we make use of
the differences for the powerful learning opportunity they hold," I
would like to see our disdain for differences among teachers and
compulsion for eliminating them replaced with the question, "how
can we deliberately make use of differences among teachers to provide leadership for the school?" The teacher interested in restoring
fire safety *is* different in many ways from the teacher who would turn
the library into a media center. Differences of philosophy, style, and
passion are remarkable sources for school leadership.

Be willing to say "I don't know how." The foregoing discussion about
principals helping teachers become citizens of a community of leaders implies that the principal knows how to do it but for a variety of
reasons would like teachers to do it. I probably could have handled
the problem of fire safety. Yet principals who always know how to do
it perpetuate what one referred to as "the burden of presumed competence." A principal is hired from among many candidates because
the selection committee supposes he or she knows how to do it.
Thereafter, for principals to admit they do not know how is a sign of
weakness at best, incompetence at worst. Many principals succumb
to the "burden of presumed competence" by pretending, sometimes
even *convincing* themselves, that they know how. This can kill the
development of a community of leaders. The invitation for a teacher

to take on fire safety may often be framed, then, as a veiled challenge to see if the teacher can do it as well as the principal. Competition on the part of the teacher to exceed the principal's knowledge and skills in turn engenders a wish on the part of the principal that the teacher fail. School leadership then becomes an occasion to renew the adversarial relationship that is often latent among teachers and principals.

Teachers know that principals do not know how to do it all. When a principal initiates conversations with "I don't know how," this declaration becomes a powerful invitation to teachers. It suggests that the principal and school need help and that the teacher can provide it. And it gives the teacher room to risk not knowing how either and perhaps to fail. Or the teacher can emerge a genuinely helpful leader of the school and friend and colleague of the principal. "I don't know how" is an attractive, disarming, and realistic invitation likely to be accepted and handled with responsibility.

Enhancing the Principal's Sense of Security: A Prerequisite

These suggestions for teacher and principal to move a school toward a community of leaders imply a level of personal security on the part of both principal and teacher. To publicly articulate a personal vision, relinquish control, empower and entrust teachers, involve teachers early, accord responsibility to untried and aspiring teacher-leaders, share responsibility for teacher failure, accord responsibility to teachers for success, and have confidence that all teachers can lead, a principal has to be a secure person willing to take risks. Security of the principal, above all else, is a precondition upon which development of a community of leaders rests. With some measure of personal security these ideas have plausability, without security they have little.

The security of principals might be influenced in several ways. During the preservice preparation of the aspiring principal, including certification requirements, university coursework, and peer interaction, the concept of a community of leaders might be introduced, so that candidates might become familiar and comfortable with this idea.

The manner in which principals are selected for the position tends to be a Byzantine process. Criteria are put forth and decisions made on the basis of a host of factors, usually determined within the school district. Seldom is personal security among them. Yet interview techniques, as well as written and oral instruments, exist that might help identify this important quality.

The third and perhaps most promising point of possible influence on principals' security occurs at the *inservice* level. Principals have as a context the school over which they preside, a sense of the faculty's and the student body's differences and strengths, and fellow principals with whom to explore the unfamiliar, perhaps threatening, idea of shared leadership.

But schools are organizations that suffer from scarce resources and limited recognition. Teachers compete with teachers; principals compete with principals; and teachers compete with principals for these precious commodities. For principals to feel sufficiently secure to share control with others, their own needs for recognition, success, and security must be acknowledged and addressed.

The Program Advisory Board of the Harvard Principals' Center (made up of 18 principals and 3 university faculty members) has selected shared leadership as a focus for activities in the belief that "shared leadership expands the possibilities for school improvement, increases commitment, complicates decision-making, and makes for more effective education for children" (*Principals' Center,* 1987).

Two-hour workshops—with titles such as "Building School Coalitions"; "A Nation Prepared: Teachers for the 21st Century"; "The Principal and the Conditions of Teaching"; "A Case for Shared Leadership: The Revolution that is Overdue"; "Who Owns the Curriculum"; "School Improvement Councils"; and "Working Together for Quality Education"—have occupied the attention of many principals as well as teachers. These discussions may not transform the insecure into the secure, but they have made the concept of school as a community of leaders more compelling and less risky. It remains to be seen what will happen back in the schools.

COMMUNITIES OF LEADERS

The vision of a school as a community of leaders is not a fantasy. The membership of the National Education Association (NEA), when it was founded in 1870, included not only teachers but also principals and superintendents, all banded together in the cause of good schools.

A century later, the NEA, now a teachers' organization, has joined with the NASSP, a secondary school principals' organization, to create *Ventures in Good Schooling* (1986), a document that seeks collaborative schools in which the professional autonomy of teachers and managerial authority of principals are harnessed. Among the recommendations of this effort are that principals involve faculty members in decision making; teachers participate in the school budgeting process and in evaluating principals' performance; principals seek teachers' advice on staffing needs and decisions; and principals and teachers jointly devise a schoolwide plan for instructional improvement and for recognizing student achievement. It is one promising step toward a community of leaders.

Several secondary schools, including Brookline and Andover High Schools in Massachusetts and Hanover High School in New Hampshire, have been working to create what they call "democratic schools." A town-meeting school government provides teachers and students a structure for participating in the major decisions confronting these schools. Teachers and students join with administrators in determining policies about such matters as smoking, pupil evaluation, and use of space, so long as decisions are not illegal or in violation of school board policy. The principal has one vote in the assembly but may veto its actions, subject to an override by a two-thirds vote of the whole. These assemblies are demonstrating that schools can not only teach about democracy, they can *be* democracies. In fact, these schools raise the question of whether it is possible for a school to teach democracy through nondemocratic means.

Alaskan small schools are places to watch. Their isolation makes them promising laboratories uncontaminated by the rest of the world for growing all sorts of unusual cultures. For instance, in Alaska, where one might routinely find K–12 schools staffed by three or four adults, many educators do not know that teachers are not supposed to be leaders. In many schools all teachers, whether called "teacher," "teaching-principal," or "principal," enjoy schoolwide leadership over issues from leaky roofs to parent involvement.

And many parochial schools thrive under what is often referred to as "servant leadership" on the part of the principal or headmaster. Principals, like parish priests, lead adults by serving adults. This invariably means involving teachers in important school decisions. It is impossible to serve teachers by excluding them.

Quaker schools, too, have traditionally worked with great success by creating for students and adults a culture of participatory leadership, similar to the leadership of Quaker meetings. They assume that *everyone* has an "inner light," something to offer the group if given the opportunity. And every member has something to learn from others. Members work together as equals, sharing ideas, planning, giving feedback, and supporting each other in new efforts. Leaders emerge in various ways at various times and then give way to other leaders.

The work and the leadership of the group is a responsibility and an opportunity for all, as one observer at a faculty meeting in a Massachusetts Friends school discovered:

> One teacher sat down in the large circle of staff with a box of tangled yarn which had been donated for art projects. The teacher quietly took a mass of the yarn and began winding it into a ball, while listening to and discussing staff issues. Soon the person on her left reached into the box and began unraveling and winding another ball of yarn. The person to her right did the same, and soon the yarn had spread around the circle, with *everyone* winding while participating in the meeting. No one had ever said a word about the yarn.

These examples suggest that it is possible for adults and students in schools to work and lead together, to everyone's benefit. A community of leaders, neither a new nor an imaginary concept, seems foreign only to the majority of public schools in this country.

CONCLUSION

> So that's how I found out how the goose can fly
>   from way up North to way down South
>   and back again.
>
> But he cannot do it alone, you see.
> It's something he can only do in Community.
>
> These days it's a popular notion,
>   and people swell with emotion and pride
>   to think of themselves on the eagle's side,
>
> Solitary
>   Self-sufficient
>   Strong
>
> But,
> We are what we are, that's something we cannot choose.
>
> And though many would wish to be seen as the eagle,
> I think God made us more like the goose.
>   (Stromberg, 1982)

The relationship between teacher and principal is coming under sharp scrutiny. Shared school leadership is a timely, volatile, and very promising issue for the improvement of schools, because public schools are strapped for adequate personnel resources at the same time that extraordinary personnel resources lay unacknowledged, untapped, and undeveloped within each school.

I have suggested a reconfiguration of the relationship between teacher and principal because the relationship among the adults who operate in a school affects the character and quality of the school and the accomplishments of its students more than any other factor. Students' needs will not be fully addressed until teachers and administrators together have worked out their own needs. Principals who faithfully monitor minimum competency, comply with districtwide curricula, carefully manage budgets, and carry out the school boards' and superintendents' policies frequently do so at the considerable expense of distancing themselves from teachers, stifling teachers' creative energies, and establishing adversarial rather than cooperative relationships with teachers.

Top-down, hierarchical relationships foster dependency. Teachers learn not to move without orders or permission from the principal; principals learn that they cannot leave "their" building, lest it disintegrate. Thus dependency immobilizes and distances teacher and principal when what they need to accomplish their important work is maximum mobility, responsibility, and cooperation.

A community of leaders offers independence, interdependence, and resourcefulness. While much of the current literature suggests that effective principals are the heroes of the organization, I suspect that more often effective principals enable others to provide strong leadership. The best principals are not heroes; they are hero-makers.

Few current indications suggest that public schools are heading toward communities of leaders. But the important issue is not what our schools *will* become but what they *might* become. There is a critical difference. The question of what *will be* implies the exercise of purely rational faculties, calling for trend analyses, projections, extrapolations, and probability curves. A view of what *could be* is not confined to these means. It requires intuition, creativity, morality, and vision along with reason. It extends inquiry from the realm of the probable to the realm of the possible. The realm of clear vision combined with the realm of clear reason offers inventive, promising, and powerful ideas.

A community of leaders is a vision of what might become a condition of the school culture, a part of the shared norms, beliefs, rituals, and actions of the school. And a community of leaders is far more than a piece of a professional school culture. Without shared leadership it is impossible for a professional culture in a school to exist. Professionalism and shared leadership are one and the same.

REFERENCES

California Commission on the Teaching Profession. (1985). *Who will teach our children?* Sacramento: Author.

Carnegie Corporation. (1986). *A nation prepared: Teachers for the 21st century.* New York: Author.

National Education Association & National Association of Secondary School Principals. (1986). *Ventures in good schooling.* Washington, DC: Authors.

National Governors' Association. (1986). *Time for results: The governors' 1991 report on education.* Washington, DC: National Governors' Association, Center for Policy Research and Analysis.

The Principals' Center spring calendar, January–May. (1987). Cambridge, MA: Harvard School of Education.

Rodman, B. (1987, February 25). Administration group outlines positions. *Education Week,* p. 9.

Stromberg, R. D. (1982). *The Goose.* Unpublished song.

8

Teacher Leadership: Ideology and Practice

ANN LIEBERMAN
ELLEN R. SAXL
MATTHEW B. MILES

The "second wave" of school reform has been characterized by much talk of restructuring schools and professionalizing teaching. Commission reports from business, education, and statewide policy groups are calling for major changes in the ways schools go about their work and the ways teachers are involved in their decision-making structure (Darling-Hammond, 1987). There is clearly an attempt to change the organizational culture of schools from one that fosters privatism and adversarial relationships between and among teachers and principals to one that encourages collegiality and commitment (Lieberman & Miller, 1984; Little, 1986; Lortie, 1975; Rosenholtz, in press). On the political level, some states and school districts are creating new roles and new structures in an attempt to change the social relations of the people who do the work at the school level. The leap from report to reality, however, is a difficult one, for there are few precedents, few models, and no guidelines. We are literally learning by doing. What is needed, then, is a beginning description of this work and some understanding of the people involved—what they know and do, what the dynamics of their interactions look like—as these new forms come into being. What are these new structures? What can we learn about the meaning of these new roles for teachers? What is teacher leadership? What actually happens when teacher-leaders help other teachers? Our purpose here is to understand some of these new roles and begin to answer some of the questions now being raised as we look at a particular group of successful teacher-leaders in a major metropolitan area. We consciously use the term *teacher-leaders* to suggest that there is not only a set of skills that are teacherlike, but a way of thinking and acting that is sensitive to teachers, to teaching, and to the school culture.

THE SKILLS OF TEACHER-LEADERS

From 1983 to 1985 we had a unique opportunity to study 17 former teachers who played leadership roles in a variety of schools in a large eastern city (see Miles, Saxl, & Lieberman, in press). (We have continued to work with some of them for an additional two years.) Within that time, we were able to collect a great deal of information about who these people were, what they had learned in their new roles, what they did in the context of their school, and even, in their own words, their view of being teacher-leaders. The 17 teacher-leaders worked in three different programs, and all were considered successful in the work they did within their schools. The criteria for success varied, depending on the context, all the way from creating a healthy climate, to making organizational change, to raising achievement scores.

The programs represented three different approaches to working with school people. The first was based on the "effective schools research," the second had as its major strategy the formation of a large school site committee with a broad constituent group, and the third utilized an organic approach to working with teachers on a one-to-one as well as a group basis—providing support and expanded leadership roles for teachers. Despite the differences in strategy, we looked to see if there was a core of skills that was common to these people in their roles as teacher-leaders. (Skills to us meant knowing how to do something rather than knowing that something was appropriate to do. Our focus was on the *capabilities* of these people to activate strategies for change.) We reasoned that, as leaders, these people had to have or develop both process and content skills and that they had to be able to adapt to different contexts and different situations. It is important to note that although these people were very experienced, they learned from both their new role and the context of their particular program.

First, it was necessary to separate out what these teacher-leaders knew when they came to the job from what they had learned while on the job. This gave us not only a sense of the possible criteria that were used in choosing these leaders, but what their new learnings had been as they worked to create these new roles and structures. Ultimately, we were looking for what skills would be teachable to new teacher-leaders in the future.

Entry Characteristics

We found that these leaders had a broad range of skills, abilities, and experience, which included teaching children at several grade levels as well as adults. They were truly "master teachers." In addition, many had been involved in *curriculum development* in the past, as well as having held positions that enabled them to teach new curriculum to others. Their enthusiasm for learning was made manifest by an impressive array of *academic pursuits* and accomplishments. They held many academic degrees, as well as having attended a broad spectrum of courses, conferences, and workshops on topics as diverse as conflict resolution, teacher effectiveness, and adult development. They came to their work knowledgeable about schools, the change process, and how to work with adults. Most had held positions in which they had gained experience in *administrative and organizational skills* and had learned something about the complexity of school cultures. They were knowledgeable about community concerns as well as schools, some having served as school board members, community organizers, and in a variety of support positions in schools.

These leaders were risktakers, willing to promote new ideas that might seem difficult or threatening to their colleagues. Their *interpersonal skills*—they knew how to be strong, yet caring and compassionate—helped them legitimate their positions in their schools amidst often hostile and resistant staffs.

On-the-Job Learning

In spite of this impressive array of skills and abilities, it was significant that these leaders had so much to learn to cope with their new positions. Where before, working in a variety of roles, they had been sensitive to individual personalities and perspectives, now they had to be aware of the interests of teachers, principals, and the community as a whole. These new conditions made it necessary for them to seek new ways of working, which, in turn, led them to find new sets of learnings. They found that what had worked in more narrowly defined positions would not work in the pursuit of a larger, common vision.

Learning about the school culture.   Without exception, these leaders learned about the school culture as if it were a new experience for them. They saw how isolated teachers were in their classrooms and what this isolation did to them. They realized how hard it would be to create a structure to involve them, to build trust within the staff, and to cut through the dailiness of their work lives. They were confronted with the egalitarian ethic held by most teachers—the belief that teachers are all alike, differing only in length of service, age, grade level, or subject matter, rather than function, skill, advanced knowledge, role, or responsibility (Lortie, 1975). They saw that, while some principals understood the need for teacher involvement in their own growth and for allocating time during the school day for reflection and adult interaction, other principals pressed for "outcomes"— with or without a structure or process for teachers to learn being in place. In some schools, they saw literally no one supporting anyone. It came as no surprise then that some of these leaders said that the school climate and the administrator's style were the two most critical components of the school culture.

New skills and abilities.   All of these leaders learned a variety of techniques for gaining acceptance by teachers and principals. They learned to break into the everyday activities and provide hands-on experiences to get teachers interested. They provided new environments and activities in which people could communicate with one another and learned how to facilitate both group and individual learning and involvement. They learned to be part of the system, but not get co-opted by it—a difficult but essential ability. They struggled with the collegial/expert dichotomy, one that clearly contradicts the egalitarian ethic that was being disrupted. In working with adults, they tried hard to listen more and suggest less and to resist jumping in with too many solutions. In spite of a high self-regard, several reported that they had not realized how much they did not know (Goodwin & Lieberman, 1986).

These new leadership roles tend to expose the powerful infantalizing effects on teachers of the existing structure of most schools. It is not that no one is in charge, or that people are inherently distrustful, but that the structure itself makes it difficult for adults to behave as adults. Rather than work collectively on their problems, everyone must struggle alone. This ubiquitous isolation dramatizes what "restructuring schools" means. New organizational forms enabling people to work together are certainly necessary, but in order for them to be established, the teachers must be organized, mobilized, led, and nurtured, with the principal's support, participation, and concern and the support and concern of all who share in the life of the school.

Self-learning.   In addition to the techniques, skills, abilities, and new understandings that these leaders learned in their schools, they strongly expressed the feeling that they had learned a great deal about themselves as well. Many spoke of a new confidence that they felt in their own abilities. Some thought that they had acquired a more complex view of how to work with people. One said, "I can't believe I have learned to motivate, to lead, to inspire, to encourage, to support, and yes, even to manipulate." Assuming leadership in schools, then, may provide the means for greatly expanding one's own repertoire. Providing and facilitating for other people in the school offers opportunities for learning how to work with others, how to channel one's time, how to develop one's own abilities—to stretch both intellectually and personally.

It is paradoxical that, although teachers spend most of their time facilitating for student learning, they themselves have few people facilitating for them and understanding their needs to be recognized, encouraged, helped, supported, and engaged in professional learning. Perhaps this is what we mean by "professionalizing" teaching and "restructuring the work environment" of teachers. Maybe the opportunities for participating in the leadership of schools, and the structures created as a result, are the means to break the isolation of teachers and engage them in collective efforts to deal with what surely are large and complex problems.

BUILDING COLLEAGUESHIP—A COMPLICATED PROCESS

Researchers have found the building of collegiality to be essential to the creation of a more professional culture in schools (Little, 1986; Rosenholtz, in press). They have also documented that norms of collaboration are built through the interactions created by the principal's facilitation of collegial work. In Little's now-classic study, she describes how these norms were built as daily routines of isolation were replaced by talking, critiquing, and working together. In Rosenholtz's study, schools were differentiated as being of two kinds—"collaborative" or "isolated." In "collaborative settings" teachers perceived the principal to be supportive, concerned with treating any problems as collective schoolwide opportunities for learning; in "isolated settings" teachers and principals were alienated, with teachers feeling that any requests they made threatened the principal's feelings of self-esteem.

Since our study focused on the introduction of a new role that expanded the structure of leadership in a school, we were looking for the kinds of skills, abilities, and approaches that these leaders utilized in building collegiality in schools. In our search to understand how these teacher-leaders worked, we created sets of clusters, each cluster representing different skills, abilities, and approaches to building collegiality among the faculty. Although their contexts and styles were different, the similarity of the ways these leaders worked has added to our understanding of the complexities involved in changing a school culture when the leadership team is expanded beyond the principal.

The clusters were drawn from 18 different skills that were manifested by these leaders (Saxl, Miles, & Lieberman, in press). They include:

Building trust and rapport
Organizational diagnosis
Dealing with the process
Using resources
Managing the work
Building skill and confidence in others

Building Trust and Rapport

A very important cluster, this set of skills appears early in the development of the work of all teacher-leaders. We found that these leaders did a variety of things to gain the trust of the people in their buildings and that, even when the person was previously known to all the teachers, the same kind of work was still necessary. Because these leaders, in every case, did not have a teaching load, they were immediately suspect: "How come this person doesn't have a class load like me? What are they supposed to be doing anyhow?" Thus the first problem to be faced was how to clarify the expectations of their role for the teachers in the school.

To begin with, the leaders had to figure out for themselves what they could realistically do in the school. Then, they tried to explain to the teachers what they were going to do, describing in a broad way why they were there and what might be the effects of their work. In some ways, perhaps, it is like the beginning of school, where the students want to know what kind of teacher this is, what will be expected of them, and what will go on in the classroom. The relationship here is similar, in that these expectations are negotiated over time, but different, in that the adult culture in schools is not kind to newcomers, especially those of their own rank. The image and the reality of a new role (a teacher without a class) is not the norm, and it is often easier to use a new person as the source of one's frustrations rather than to accept her or him as a helper, go-between, or leader of a different kind.

Just as in the teacher/class relationship, the leader must come to be seen by the teachers as legitimate and credible. They try to accomplish this by finding various ways to demonstrate their expertise and value to the teachers. For some, it is giving a make-or-break workshop—one that they know will either give them immediate credibility if it is successful or set them back for months if it fails. For others, it means becoming a "gofer" and providing resources: going to the library, bringing new materials, keeping the coffee pot going and the cookie jar filled. Somehow they have to do enough to show the staff that they are "good"—experts and helpers, important enough to belong in "their" school. It is at this point that these leaders must learn to deal with *addressing resistance*, for they are coming into a social system with well-developed formal and informal ties. Sometimes this resistance is based on old disappointments and unfulfilled promises from past years. Other times a newcomer takes the brunt of all kinds of existing tensions in a school, caused by everything from lack of adequate communication to complaints about space, resources, time, and so forth.

Engaging in open supportive communication is part of building trust. These leaders found ways of working with teachers and proving to them that they were capable of being open without betraying trust—that they were there for the staff in a helping, nonevaluative way. As they worked with the teachers, they began to *build a support group*, people who came to see that they could work together, struggle collectively, and feel comfortable working as a group rather than alone. For many leaders this meant finding teachers who could be experts in their own right, teachers who could teach other teachers things that they had learned. In the process of facilitating for others, the leaders began to *develop shared influence* and shared leadership. The idea that there are problems common to teachers and problems in a school that can be addressed collectively began to take hold, and teacher-leaders began to build a set of *productive working relationships.*

The abilities mentioned above appear to be necessary to the building of trust and rapport, which are the foundation for building collegiality in a school. Regardless of the size or complexity of the school, the age or experience of the staff, or the differences in the programmatic thrust, the same kinds of skills were used to legitimate the leadership role.

Organizational Diagnosis

This set of skills—an understanding of the school culture and the ability to diagnose it—is crucial if a leader is to have the basis for knowing how and where to intervene to mobilize people to take action and begin to work together. Leaders did this in very different ways. Some people had an intuitive awareness of the formal and informal relationships in a school, while others consciously worked out strategies to help them collect data to help them better understand the school social system.

Depending on the specifics of the program, the methods of collection ranged from a formal needs assessment that asked teachers what they would find useful, to an informal collection of information about the principal, curriculum, resources, and so on. However it was accomplished, some initial *data collection* gave teacher-leaders a beginning awareness of the school environment. All were involved in picking up cues from staff, bulletin boards, teachers rooms, principals, parents—anyone who could provide information.

In the beginning . . . I had to overcome my own personality— the tendency to move too quickly and speak out.

When you are a teacher, you only know your classroom problems. Now I look at the whole system. . . . When I was in the classroom, I controlled it; the higher you go, the less control you have.

As we can see, collecting information while being conscious of one's self within the larger system was a strategic part of the teacher-leaders' way of working. Either as an insider or as one who came to a school with a leadership role, these people came to form some kind of a *conceptual scheme* in their minds—a map of what the school looked like, who one might work with, where the trouble spots were, who was open to thinking about working on schoolwide problems. As they collected information about the school by being there, hanging around, talking to people, and so on, they began to get enough information to *make a diagnosis*.

If action and change were what their diagnosis called for, these

leaders had to find ways to engage key school people with their observations, to *share the diagnosis* with them to see if it was theirs as
well. This series of steps, not always consciously thought out, formed
the basis for action plans for the school. We begin to see a process:
understanding the school, collecting information about the people and
how they work, constructing a valid picture of the organization, sharing the picture with others and planning a strategy for action.

Dealing with the Process

Critical to the work of teacher-leaders were their understanding
of and skill in managing the change process. Since this meant, among
other things, promoting *collaborative relationships* in schools where
people had little experience in working together, it involved the use
of *conflict mediation* and *confrontation skills.* They soon learned from
the realities of their work that, when one tries to get people to work
together where they have previously worked alone, conflicts arise, and
that their job was to find the means to deal with them. As they worked
in their schools, building and modeling collaborative work, they were
called upon to weave their way through the strands of the school culture. This involved many types of interactions with teachers, staff
members, and administrators.

The relations with the principal varied according to the style of
the principal and the structures for collaboration that were being created. When the structure called for working as a team and the principal had been used to working alone, the teacher-leader had to show
the principal the benefits to the school of shared decision making.
Where a teacher center had been created, the principal had to learn
to give support for teachers to work independently without feeling
that the existence of this room threatened her or his perceived role as
"instructional leader." The tact, skill, and understanding of the
teacher-leader was crucial to the involvement of the principal in supporting these new modes of collaboration.

Sometimes the school was in conflict from the start: "The first
mission was to bring teachers together to talk to each other. There was
a general distrust of the administration by the teachers." Sometimes
the job entailed helping the faculty work through conflicts. "At committee meetings, many conflicts come up. He helps us talk them
out. . . . We ventilate and direct our energy in a specific way."

Collaboration does not come as a natural consequence of working in a school. It must be taught, learned, nurtured, and supported
until it replaces working privately. There were times when these

teacher-leaders were the ones who had to confront negative information and give feedback where it was appropriate. Where conflicts
appeared as a result of personal incompatibilities or differing interests, their job was not merely to smooth them over, as had often been
the case in the past, but to find areas of agreement based on a larger
view of the school and its problems.

They worked hard to *solve these problems* by making decisions
collaboratively. This was a key skill: Who will do what, how will we
do it, when will we make it happen, and how will we come to agree?
They found that it took more than a vote to build consensus. It was
always necessary to be alert to discontent and to practice and work on
being open, communicating together, and finding ways to bring people, as individuals, to think of themselves as part of the group with
group concerns.

Using Resources

The fourth cluster of skills involved the use of resources. This
refers to people, ideas, materials, and equipment—all part of the
school, but often not utilized in the pursuit of collective goals. The
teacher-leaders found themselves engaged in providing material
things for teachers that helped to link them to the outside world.

> I'm a reader. I need follow-up materials from the literature to
> find out about good ideas.

> They needed a lot of resources.

> I would attend conventions, day and weekend seminars and
> collect handouts.

> I keep on tops of things. What texts are good?

They did workshops for teachers, demonstrated techniques, and provided follow-up. They also looked inside the school to plug people
in to what was already there and, where appropriate, to link people
together.

In the process of finding resources and using existing staff to help,
these teacher-leaders also began to build a *resource network,* which
included developing active linkages between teachers and other
members of the school community. It was not just knowing where or
who to go to for help, but choosing the right person or right thing at

the right time. Matching local needs and capabilities became the key skill.

Finally, it was necessary to help people make good use of the resources. Just getting the "stuff" there was not enough. The leaders had to perform a brokerage function and then follow-up to see that the resources were being used. As we observed, this cluster of skills is part of a complicated process: from finding people and materials, both inside and outside the school, to building networks with these resources, to seeing that whoever, whatever, and wherever they were, they were available and utilized.

Managing the Work

The teacher-leaders worked hard to maintain a balance between the process of getting people to work on collective problems and providing the content or substance around which they worked. Managing this work required a subtle blend of skills, including managing time, setting priorities for work, delegating tasks and authority, taking initiative, monitoring progress, and coordinating the many strands of work taking place in their schools. (It should be noted that these leaders differed in the amount of time they spent in a school. Some spent four days a week in one school, while others spent one day a week in four schools.)

Administrative/organizational skills, although part of their qualifications, were far more complex in these roles than the teacher-leaders had faced before. Time was a persistent problem. How much time does one spend with people having difficulties, or getting resources, or making arrangements for workshops, or demonstrating, or troubleshooting? This proved to be a formidable task, with the successful teacher-leaders we studied gaining great skill in allocating their time as they became experienced in their role.

Managing and controlling skills were needed to organize and manage the work. The teacher-leaders had to learn to move from thought to action. Some used charts to keep track of their activities; some did not. But all of them had to learn how to mobilize the staff and coordinate the many activities, while walking the fine line between exerting influence and "overmanaging" the process of change.

Although contexts differed, these leaders shared the skill of being proactive, that is, having a bias for action. This included modeling specific new techniques as well as promoting a general vision of more productive ways of working. Maintaining momentum in their work, without usurping the authority or the prerogatives of other leadership in the school, required them to take initiative while negotiating their way through the delicate yet tough relationships between and among teachers and principal.

Building Skill and Confidence in Others

The last cluster of skills involved the continuous monitoring and *individual diagnosis* of teachers' communication needs and concerns, while attending to the general organizational health of the school. Working for several years in the same schools, these leaders tried to make normative the notions that it was both legitimate to have technical assistance and necessary to have in place some structure for problem solving. They were attempting to socialize a whole staff to have individual teachers look at themselves critically and take action on their own behalf, while continuing to build supportive structures to better carry out the work as a whole.

They tried to involve as many people as possible in leadership roles by institutionalizing a process or mechanism for dealing with improvement goals, at the same time trying to make sure that constructive changes occurred that would be visible to the whole school. They were concerned with building a support network for the school community, based on commitment and involvement, that was sensitive to individual teachers and other members of the community and, at the same time, promoted organizational change. This required constant vigilance: building networks for support, continuously recognizing and rewarding positive individual efforts that improved the school, helping to create short-term goals, and always working to institutionalize individual and collective efforts at improvement so that they would become "built into the walls."

TEACHER-LEADERS IN THE CONTEXT OF THEIR SCHOOLS

The skill clusters we have been describing are based on interview and observational data from the 17 teacher-leaders we studied from 1983 to 1985. We can get another view, perhaps more integrated and dynamic, by being there, by seeing these people in their own contexts. We did several case studies of these teacher-leaders in 1985 and 1986. The following summary of two of them will help round out the picture we have drawn thus far (Miles, Saxl, James, & Lieberman, 1986).

Urban High School

Urban High is a large comprehensive high school that also serves as the special education center for the entire area. It is in a blighted area in a large urban city. There are 3,500 students in the school, 62 percent Hispanic and 30 percent black. Achievement is low overall. The majority of the students (2,000) are enrolled in general education. Reading, math, and writing scores are low. The principal is young, energetic, and extremely receptive to innovative ideas and any means to improve the school. He is very concerned with raising the level of instruction and increasing the professionalism of teachers through staff development and increased teacher control of the curriculum.

In March 1985, a teacher center opened in the school. Brenda C., a former English teacher at Urban, became the teacher-specialist—a full-time teacher-leader hired to run the teacher center and work with the staff. Because the school was in the process of reorganizing from departments to clusters, experienced teachers were becoming the coordinators or heads of special projects, causing them to leave teaching and move to these new positions. (Given the harsh conditions of the school context—crime, purse snatchings, noise, pitted chalkboards, lack of necessary supplies, prisonlike rooms, and other difficult teaching conditions—it is not hard to see why teachers would want these positions.) When they left new teachers replaced them.

Brenda wanted to do three things during her first year: improve morale, facilitate communication between the various groups in the school, and encourage the staff to utilize the center for professional growth. Subtle resistance plagued her efforts in the beginning. There was the natural resistance to being "improved," as well as the notion that being a high school teacher—a subject-matter specialist—somehow made one already expert.

She began, during her first month, by just offering free coffee and refreshments to the teachers. (The principal had supplied a large room and the coffee.) She spent a great deal of time and money (her own) buying materials that would be of interest to the teachers. She tried hard to get materials that would engender self-help as much as possible, attempting to be sensitive to the sensibilities of her peers. She spoke at department meetings to advertise the availability of these materials to the teachers.

Little by little the teachers began to come to the center. At first they came only for coffee. Brenda wrote personal notes to people to encourage them to come back and to participate in other activities. To enhance communication, she formed a site committee made up of representatives from the various cluster groups. (Finding a common meeting time for everyone was impossible, so staggered meetings went on during the day.)

With encouragement from the director of the teacher center consortium, Brenda helped create a workshop, given after school was over in June, to teach teachers about the latest research on classroom management, mastery learning, and learning styles. The workshop was planned in such a way that the teachers had an obligation to attempt one or more of the ideas in their classrooms in the fall. In this way, Brenda hoped to begin to build a core group of teachers, encourage professional development in the center, and work on greater communication among the teachers.

The impact of these efforts, and others, has been to draw more and more teachers to the center. They read the bulletin boards, look at materials, use the machines, plan lessons, talk together, and work with Brenda. Informally, teachers come for afterschool courses from other schools, which indicates that the center is reaching out to a larger network in the district.

Teachers from the site committee have been instrumental in disseminating information about the center to other teachers. New teachers have talked about being offered nonjudgmental assistance by Brenda in the center. Experienced teachers have spoken about the amenities that make their life easier: a quiet place to work, rexograph machines, and new materials and supplies. All of this has greatly increased the morale of the staff. (An indication of the center's growing popularity was the success of a party for the staff that was given at the end of June. Almost all the teachers came—a highly unusual occurrence.)

Brenda, who has been a teacher at Urban High for 23 years and knows the social system of her school as an insider, has been using this knowledge to create an "oasis in the desert." We see the special role that a teacher in a leadership position can play—encouraged and supported by a sensitive principal—as she gently and cautiously plans for and takes on the function of building morale and professionalism among the staff. She helps alleviate the tensions of a large, experienced staff trying to deal with the tremendous problems that exist in a school in a depressed community. She builds trust among the faculty, recognizing not only the classical resistance to new ideas, but also the special nature of high school teachers (subject-matter specialists with advanced degrees who have their own special reasons to resist being "improved"). Although just a beginning, Brenda's leadership has begun to fill in the tremendous gap between a professional environment and the bare level of subsistence in a complex, difficult high school.

Parkridge Elementary School

At Parkridge Elementary School, Andrea G., a teacher-leader who came from another part of the city, also runs a teacher center. She has been at her school for four years. Her school has always been known as the showcase school of the district. It is a school with 1,500 children. The ethnic mix of the neighborhood has changed over time from Jewish and Italian to Hispanic and black, with a small percentage of Caucasian children.

The school has many fine teachers, many of whom have been there since the 1960s, when additional resources were given to particular schools, including this one, to help with their special problems. These teachers were attracted to the school because of the supply of specialists and the support they would be given. They came because they felt it would be a good place to teach. To this day, the school is still quite special for the area, but it is manifesting problems that are eroding the quality of the program. (Because of the positive reputation of the school, many parents want to send their children there; as a result, the school is suffering from serious overcrowding.) The principal is known to be a real "professional." He is very hard working and the school is remarkably stable. The principal has been there for fifteen years, which is almost unheard of in this area.

Andrea, unlike Brenda, came from the outside to work at Parkview, but, like Brenda, she, too, had the problem of legitimating her presence to the teaching staff. Because the staff was large, and because many had been there for a long time, there were numerous cliques among the teachers. There was also a group of eight new teachers who had taken over classrooms with little preparation for the job. (There was a massive teacher shortage in this city at the time.) An all-day kindergarten program had just been implemented, and the district had called for the school to involve the parents in working with their children at home.

In looking over this situation and figuring out her goals for the year, Andrea decided that the new teachers would be a focus for her work. She also decided to take on the responsibility for working with the parents of the kindergarten children to facilitate better understanding of what the school was doing and what the parents could do to reinforce student learning. In addition, she continued to maintain the teacher center—although it was a small, crowded room, teachers would know that at least there was a place to come where they could give and get help, put their feet up, and share some hot soup from the corner deli.

Everyone speaks of Andrea as the "glue" of the school: "She has made the school a family. Everyone feels a sense of gratitude and loyalty to her." Because she is a very giving person, her mere presence and her way of working fill a great void in this large, three-story building. Her first words are always, "How can I help you?" An hour and a half with her illustrates the point.

> On this day Andrea arrives at the center at 8:15 A.M. She is immediately involved in a "major" problem. One of the teachers, who has a refrigerator in his room, is complaining that because people leave food in it his room smells, thus disturbing him and the students. Andrea gets into the conversation to try to sort out who is responsible for cleaning the refrigerator and what needs to be done to get it cleaned. (This may seem like an insignificant problem, but no problem is insignificant. The message to the teachers is that all problems can be worked on in the center.)
>
> Andrea goes downstairs to the auditorium. She is due to hold a meeting there to teach parents how to provide for reading-readiness activities for their children. When she gets there she finds someone else is rehearsing a play.
>
> Instead of complaining that the auditorium was reserved for her, she quickly negotiates with the teacher to use his room and runs to the front door to alert the parent sitting there to tell the parents what room to go to. Stopping off at the photocopy room to see that the materials are being run off for the parents, she finds a paraprofessional having trouble with the photocopy machine and also with someone in the office. Andrea helps her fix the machine and then intervenes to ease the problem with the staff person. She then makes her way to the new room, where several parents are waiting, and quickly makes arrangements for one of the parents to translate for one who does not understand English.

In this one-hour period, Andrea has already made four interventions that do not go unnoticed. She has helped a teacher (with the smelly refrigerator), changed her room (by negotiating with the teacher in the auditorium), helped the paraprofessional with the photocopy machine (and a small problem with an office person), and provided for a translator (so that her work with the parents could go on in two languages). Such sensitivity does not go unnoticed, even in a faculty of this size. As a matter of fact, it turns out to be a mode of leadership that is felt by everyone. The principal is extremely respectful of Andrea's good work with the faculty. The supervisors find her presence welcome, since she helps them with their work without overstepping her authority. The specialists know that Andrea and the teacher center can support their work and also help them deliver services. And the new teachers come to the center because they know they can get help and support from both Andrea and other teachers who serve as a support group for them.

THE TEACHER-LEADER AS LEARNER

From this initial look at teacher-leaders, we see that they are not only making learning possible for others but, in important ways, are learning a great deal themselves. Stepping out of the confines of the classroom forces these teacher-leaders to forge a new identity in the school, think differently about their colleagues, change their style of work in a school, and find new ways to organize staff participation. As we have documented, it is an extremely complicated process, one that is intellectually challenging and exciting as well as stressful and problematic. Changing the nature of an occupation turns out to have the possibilities for both "high gain and high strain" (Little, Chapter 5 of this volume). The gain is mostly in the personal and professional learnings of the leaders themselves: the technical learnings about teachers, instruction, and curriculum; the social learnings about schools as social systems, including how to build collegiality and manipulate the system to help teachers do a better job; the personal learnings about their own professional competence as they learn new skills and abilities and find new approaches to being a leader among their peers; and even, in some cases, the satisfaction of learning how to create structures that alter the culture of the school.

But the strain is there, too. Building trust among teachers, who have long felt that they have little or no voice in choosing what is best for their students or themselves, is not easy. Initial hostility and resistance is always there, and it is hard not to take some of it personally. (What works with students does not necessarily work with adults.) Dilemmas of being a colleague and also being an "expert" are not easily negotiated. Being nonjudgmental and helping are often in conflict with making value judgments that affect the priorities for one's work. Listening to teachers—rather than giving advice—and working with them *on their terms* is sometimes in conflict with personal style. Learning to negotiate from a position of leadership—in a school where there is little precedent for teacher leadership—without threatening those in existing administrative positions takes skill, courage, and nerve. Teacher-leaders have to learn that these tensions and dilemmas are an inevitable part of the drive to professionalize schools and of the change process itself.

THE TEACHER-LEADER AS PROFESSIONAL MODEL

Part of the ideology developed in these new roles is the belief that there are different ways to structure schools and different means to work with teachers and other members of the school community. This involves such characteristic themes as:

Placing a nonjudgmental value on providing assistance
Modeling collegiality as a mode of work
Enhancing teachers' self-esteem
Using different approaches to assistance
Building networks of human and material resources for the school
  community
Creating support groups for school members
Making provisions for continuous learning and support for teach-
  ers at the school site
Encouraging others to take leadership with their peers

We are only beginning to understand the nature and impact of these new roles in schools and the subtleties of fashioning new ways of working with the school community. From studying these teacher-leaders, we see that some sort of team, teacher center, or site committee—a structural change—appears necessary to the creation of collegial norms in a school. More cooperative work, increased interaction across department lines, and support groups for new teachers require new modes of collaboration to replace the existing isolated conditions prevailing in most schools.

What we have, then, is a new leadership role that can help in the creation of new collaborative structures. It appears that a combination of these new roles and structures is necessary to professionalize the school culture and to bring a measure of recognition and respect to teachers—who may be, in the final analysis, the best teachers of teachers as well as children.

REFERENCES

Darling-Hammond, L. (1987). Schools for tomorrow's teachers. *Teachers College Record, 88*(3), 354–358.

Goodwin, A., & Lieberman, A. (1986, April). Effective assistance personal behavior: What they brought and what they learned. Paper presented at the annual meeting of the American Educational Research Association, San Francisco.

Lieberman, A., & Miller, L. (1984). *Teachers: Their world and their work.* Alexandria, VA: Association for Supervision and Curriculum Development.

Little, J. W. (1986). Seductive images and organizational realities in professional development. In A. Lieberman (Ed.), *Rethinking school improvement: Research, craft, and concept* (pp. 26–44). New York: Teachers College Press.

Lortie, D. (1975). *School teacher.* Chicago: University of Chicago Press.

Miles, M., Saxl, E., James, J., & Lieberman, A. (1986). *New York City Teacher Center Consortium evaluation report.* Unpublished technical report.

Miles, M., Saxl, E., & Lieberman, A. (in press). What skills do educational "change agents" need? An empirical view. *Curriculum Inquiry.*

Rosenholtz, S. J. (in press). *Teacher's workplace: A social-organizational analysis.* New York: Longman.

Saxl, E. R., Miles, M. B., & Lieberman, A. (in press). *ACE—Assisting change in education.* Alexandria, VA: Association for Supervision and Curriculum Development.

9

Unlikely Beginnings:
The District Office as a Starting Point
for Developing a Professional Culture
for Teaching

LYNNE MILLER

The current discussion among public school educators about improving schools and creating a professional culture for teaching focuses almost exclusively on the individual school. And within the individual school, the principal is assigned the role of instructional leader (Edmonds, 1979; Brookover, Giglcotti, Henderson, & Schnieder, 1973). According to this view, it is the principal who creates the conditions for teachers to become better instructors and it is the principal who lays the groundwork for and nurtures the changing professional culture of the school.

While I do not want to argue against the power of the principal and the unique potential of the person in that position to influence the environment of teaching and learning, I do want to challenge the notion that the principal's office is the only, or even the best, place to start to build a new professional culture. I want to argue that we can find starting points in some of the most unlikely places as long as we are willing to suspend business as usual and create opportunities for teachers to use their knowledge and talents. In this chapter, I will present a case for using the district central office—in particular, the office of curriculum and instruction—as an arena in which the transformation of the teacher culture can be initiated and encouraged.

It is obvious to anyone who has ever worked in a school that the district central office is, indeed, an unlikely starting point for professionalizing teaching. At best, the central office is characterized as a "foggy bottom" and its denizens as bureaucrats caring more about procedural correctness than professional activism. Removed from the realities of schools and classrooms, central-office administrators are more often than not viewed as people who left education behind when they moved "downtown"—hardly candidates for providing leadership in instructional matters.

Such was the state of things when I moved from building-level administration into the position of assistant superintendent of curriculum in a midsized (22,000 student population) city in 1982. In five years' time, things have changed. A cadre of central-office staff in the curriculum division found that by altering the way we function, we could affect the way teachers function and that, in so doing, we could lay the foundation for the development of a professional culture in the schools of our district. We organized our divisional activities so that teachers took an active role in (1) curriculum writing, (2) staff development, (3) practicum-oriented research, and (4) coordination of the district program. In the pages that follow I discuss each of these activities and their implications for the development of a professional culture.

CURRICULUM WRITING

As central-office staff, we worked to encourage the active engagement of teachers in a variety of projects centered on the production of curriculum materials and guides. The teachers involved in these projects focused their energies on developing better programs and experiences for children in classrooms. While the major and tangible products of these efforts were curriculum guides, I believe that something else was produced—something less tangible, though no less durable. A new professional culture, with norms and values that differed markedly from business as usual, began to grow and flourish.

Organizing to Write

The process we use for curriculum writing is quite simple. Teachers volunteer to work on a specific project. The union contract guarantees an hourly stipend for such work. The groups form immediately after school ends in June, and they work through the summer until the project is complete. The groups subdivide into smaller workgroups, each led by a teacher selected by the group members. In an opening meeting for all teachers involved, general expectations are set. The workgroups then meet on their own, sometimes in each others' living rooms, other times in classrooms, other times in formal meeting rooms. They have access to secretarial services, copying machines, a professional library, and a variety of staff resources. If they desire, they may request special consultants to assist in the work. The group leaders meet regularly with the central-office staff assigned to the project. These meetings are for the purpose of presenting progress reports and raising any issues or concerns that are emerging. As the project nears completion, the groups meet as a whole and present their work to each other for feedback and revision. The central-office staffperson does a final edit on the volume and oversees its preparation for publication. All final products carry the subtitle *Prepared for and by the Teachers of the South Bend Community School Corporation.* Before school begins, the new curriculum is presented to the appropriate teachers in an inservice program designed by the curriculum writers. Throughout the year, teachers meet regularly to discuss the curriculum and to suggest revisions where necessary. These revisions are important in providing updates on the curriculum materials.

Pioneering the Process

A discussion of our first major curriculum project elucidates what comes from this process. In 1984, Governor Orr initiated legislation in Indiana for Project Primetime. The objective of Primetime was to provide incentives, in the form of faculty salaries, to school districts to reduce class size in first grade to a ratio of 18:1. Our district, like many others, adopted Primetime enthusiastically. Unlike other districts, however, we did not see reduced class size as the panacea for primary education. We saw the need to rethink and redo the curriculum and instructional program as well. We decided to use Primetime as the key to unlock the primary curriculum, to place language development at the center of all learning, and to develop a unified approach to the first-grade curriculum. A Primetime committee was formed, composed of 20 teachers who volunteered to work over the summer. Pioneers in the process, these first-grade teachers quickly divided into four groups: language arts and reading, mathematics, science, and social studies. They combed their basements, their file cabinets, and their attics for appropriate material. They met with the producer of our educational radio station, the central-office coordinators in all subject areas, and outside reading consultants. The result was an astounding array of materials and approaches to teaching first grade, all compiled in a volume entitled *First-Grade Primetime Digest.* In the introduction to the *Digest,* teachers wrote,

The point of view of the *Digest* is clear: First grade instruction relies on a developmental approach, with a focus on language skills.
The Primetime curriculum is a language-centered and integrated
program which, when supported by reduced class size, should lead
to increased learning by:
>   Individual attention to student needs
>   Close monitoring of student progress
>   Appropriate grouping for instruction
>   On-going communication with parents (SBCSC, 1984)

Among items presented were: reading guidelines (placement procedures, pacing and mastery guidelines, remediation and enrichment
units), a total reorganization of the sequence of math topics, options
for teaching social studies and science without a textbook, the development of radio programs and listening activities, and storytelling as
the basis for instruction. The *Digest* was enthusiastically received by
the other first-grade teachers and by principals. A formal evaluation
of the Primetime program found that 75% of teachers attributed the
success of Primetime to an improved curriculum and that over 90%
of the teachers depended on the *Digest* as a guide for teaching.

Expanding Our Efforts

The next year, we implemented Primetime in second grade. This
time, second-grade teachers engaged in the curriculum-writing process. Building upon the work of their first-grade colleagues, these
teachers took the mission of making language development the center of the curriculum even more seriously. They developed a "whole-
language" approach to teaching science, using children's literature as
the basis for instruction. They also created a new interdisciplinary
unit in life sciences, combining instruction in science, health, and
social studies; they wrote their own radio scripts to accompany to
units.
   In the course of discussing the reading program, the second-grade
teachers noted some inconsistency between what they were saying
and what the first-grade *Digest* had presented. In a series of intensive and intellectually charged meetings, the second-grade reading
workgroup met with their first-grade counterparts to discuss their approaches to reading and, ultimately, to hammer out a reading philosophy and to develop guidelines for the entire elementary program,
grades K–6. These discussions were far-ranging, touching on the appropriateness of teaching phonics, alternative strategies for teaching
reading, the importance of comprehension skills, the pros and cons

of a basal reading series, the use of "whole-language" and "language-experience" approaches, the uses and abuses of mastery learning, the integration of reading and writing, and the best approaches for grouping students and organizing a total school reading program. Perhaps the comments of two teachers best sum up the power of these sessions (these and all subsequent teacher quotes are from teachers in the South Bend Community School Corporation):

> It's like I'm back in graduate school, only this time the problems are real and I'm the one with the answer, not my professor.

> For the first time in a long time, I'm using my brain. I'm debating reading topics with fellow teachers and suddenly I feel we're all very smart people.

This level of discourse has become common in all of our curriculum-writing projects. Projects have been initiated at all grade levels and in a wide range of disciplines. Included among them are a fourth-grade social studies unit on local history; advance placement courses in English, math, and science; a middle school basic-skills program; guidelines for elementary mathematics; advanced-level courses in foreign languages; and a computer literacy curriculum.

Changing Roles: Teachers as Collaborators

In all instances of curriculum writing, as teachers work in small groups over time, they come to view themselves as colleagues engaged in a common enterprise. They draw on their experiences, pool practical knowledge acquired over many years, and reach consensus on what works in classrooms. The isolation and privatization of practice (Lieberman & Miller, 1978) that characterizes teaching is replaced by collective action and collegiality. Long accustomed to deriving their rewards almost exclusively from children (Lieberman & Miller, 1978), teachers find in their peers an additional source of feedback and encouragement. Instead of working from textbooks and curriculum guides written by someone else, teachers as curriculum writers become authors of published works, copywrited volumes, which are disseminated throughout the district and—ultimately— throughout the state.

By relinquishing control of the curriculum-development process, central-office administrators place themselves in a unique position to provide the opportunity for teachers to assume leadership. Once teachers "try on" leadership, they find that it fits them like a glove. As teachers become leaders, they come to view themselves as serious theoreticians as well as capable practitioners, as contributors to a collaborative process as well as individuals in classrooms, and as major decision makers in the educational process as well as implementers of programs. They come to value themselves and they come to value each other; and in so doing, they transform the professional culture in which they work.

TEACHER-LED STAFF DEVELOPMENT

Closely related to curriculum writing is the arrangement of staff development activities that place classroom teachers at center stage as the designers, presenters, and evaluators of a wide range of inservice programs. Our first attempts at teacher-led staff development were more the result of serendipity than of intentional planning. Early on, teachers working on curriculum-writing projects saw the need to organize ways to introduce the teaching staff to the new materials, recommended procedures, and effective strategies included in the digests and guides that were being produced in the district. Bereft of funds, they had to seek internal experts. And they found they were plentiful.

Getting Started

Our first teacher-led program involved the creation of instructional games for use in Primetime classrooms. Ms. F, a kindergarten teacher working with developmentally delayed students, was known throughout the district for her inventiveness in the classroom. The first-grade teachers who had worked on the curriculum digests identified her as an ideal presenter for a workshop in using games to teach language skills. Ms. F did not disappoint them in her workshop. The teachers who attended quickly spread the word about the workshop's relevance to classroom teachers, the array of materials that were introduced, and the bravura performance of Ms. F.

Another workshop followed soon after. This one was led by Mrs. O, a first-grade teacher who had helped lead the discussions of reading instruction that occurred during the Primetime curriculum-writing project. Mrs. O was enlisted by her fellow teachers to develop a workshop on planning and organizing the classroom for effective reading instruction. Again, the session was applauded by the teachers present. Mrs. O was entreated to run an additional session to accommodate teachers who heard of the success of the first workshop and who wanted to learn from her.

Building a Tradition

From such rudimentary beginnings, we recognized that a new tradition was taking root in our district. As a complement to writing curricula, teachers began to plan activities for staff to ensure the implementation of their programs. We saw the need to provide room for the tradition to develop. We created a central-office position for a staff-development specialist. Rather than advertising the job as an administrative one, we designed it as a special assignment for a teacher on leave from the classroom. Mrs. H, an elementary teacher with more than 25 years experience and the chief orchestrator of our initial Primetime staff-development efforts, was appointed to the job. Mrs. H brought to her work a widely held reputation as an effective classroom teacher and curriculum innovator. These attributes guaranteed immediate credibility and ensured that a teacher's point of view on staff development would be represented.

In the three years of Mrs. H's tenure, teacher-led staff development has become commonplace. Over 90% of our scheduled inservice presentations are currently led by teachers. For example, cadres of teachers organized to visit schools and present workshops on the use of math manipulatives; teachers with effective discipline plans have led workshops and offered coaching on "assertive discipline"; our computer-literate staff have introduced other teachers to the uses of technology in teaching. Teacher response to peer-led staff development has been very positive. Our teachers report:

> I especially enjoyed the examples of materials actually used in classrooms. The ideas the teachers shared with us were practical for me.

> The topics discussed were targeted for real needs. The presentations were full of helpful information. The two teachers who led this session had a wealth of ideas for us.

> I learned how to handle word-recognition problems and how to prepare better lesson plans. I also learned that it's okay to share what knowledge or experience I have with other teachers and feel good about it.

Perhaps our most ambitious staff-development effort to date has been in the area of writing instruction. We sent two of our teachers to a three-week seminar, sponsored by the National Writing Project. Upon their return to the district, they became full-time writing consultants as part of a two-year districtwide writing-development program. Ms. B, an English teacher with experience in both middle and high schools, and Ms. F, a second-grade teacher in an inner-city school, have been working together for a year and have devised and implemented a wide range of writing-awareness activities for their colleagues. These activities include: traditional workshops, support groups, demonstration lessons in teachers' classrooms, and week-long summer seminars in the theory and practice of teacher writing. Slowly, our two writing consultants are teaching other teachers how to structure writing experiences, and, more importantly, how to share their successes with their co-workers in their buildings.

Changing Roles: Teachers as Experts

As with curriculum writing, there is nothing complicated about providing opportunities for teachers to lead staff-development programs. Such an approach, however, sends very powerful messages to teachers in the district. It proclaims that professional knowledge is not a commodity to be contracted from distant and degreed consultants but can be found locally in classrooms throughout the district. It implies that the skills of teaching children are transferable to teaching adults, that conceptualization, organization, explanation, and presentation are endemic to the act of teaching and are valuable and adaptable skills that make teaching a highly complicated and learned craft. And finally, it demystifies expertise. When teachers see familiar and accessible colleagues acknowledged as experts, they can begin to reevaluate their own experience and learn to value what they themselves know and are able to do.

PRACTICE-ORIENTED RESEARCH

We began organizing teachers in our district to do research shortly after we implemented the Primetime curriculum for first grade. The notion of school-based research is certainly not new, nor is it unique to our setting. "Action research" has its roots in Columbia University's Teachers College in the 1950s (Corey, 1953). More recently, Interactive Research and Development on Teaching (IR&DT) has spread from California and Vermont (Tikunoff, Ward, & Griffin, 1975) to a variety of locations. Our own approach differed from "action research" and IR&DT in that it did not depend on a collaboration with the professional research community. Our approach was more "homegrown." It placed teachers at the center of research design and implementation.

Designing an Evaluation Study

It took us little time to identify our problem; it was one we had already ourselves created. We wanted to know what the effects of Primetime were on the district. We convened a Primetime Oversight Committee in the fall to accompany our inauguration of the program. Composed of four teachers, three elementary principals, and three central-office staff, the committee assumed as its task the development of an evaluation design for Primetime. Our first task was to define research questions. We came up with four major questions that we wanted answered:

1. What are teacher, principal, and parent perception of Primetime?
2. How are Primetime classes organized for instruction? What happens in a Primetime classroom?
3. What are the effects of Primetime on student achievement?
4. What are viewed as the major strengths and weaknesses of Primetime?

In order to answer the four questions, we worked as a group to develop a variety of measures. To uncover perceptions of the program, we developed three survey questionnaires, a 37-item teacher survey, a 33-item principal survey, and a 12-item parent survey. We worked with our data-processing center to design a format for writing the questions and retrieving the data. Our questions about classroom instruction and general organization were, we felt, best addressed through direct observation. We designed an observation instrument that allowed us to record how teachers allocated time, how they grouped students, how much they used direct instruction as opposed to worksheets and workbooks, and how they used the materials provided them through the *Digest*. In addition, we were interested in recording the number of students who were engaged in learning activities (time on task) at intervals during the observation. We felt we could understand the effects of Primetime on student achievement by comparing standardized test results for current Primetime first-graders and for those students who were in first grade the previous year. We realized this was an imperfect measure, but it could provide information about general trends in achievement. Finally, we used open-ended interviews as well as the survey data to define the strengths and weaknesses of the program.

Observing Peers

The observational component of our study is worthy of some elaboration. The teachers' association initially opposed any observation as part of the evaluation. To their minds, observation was synonymous with evaluation of teacher performance, and they saw that as the purview of the principal under conditions spelled out in the negotiated agreement. The teachers on the committee met with the association leadership and worked out a compromise: only teachers who volunteered would be observed, and the observations would be paired peer observations. The compromise became an effective research strategy. And it had unintended benefits as well. Teachers who were involved in the observation commented on how much they enjoyed visiting another teacher's classroom and how much they were looking forward to being visited themselves.

> I learned so much from watching Dee in action. She is such a gifted teacher. I've never seen anyone teach before and it was a wonderful experience. I was a little nervous about her visiting my classroom the next week, but when we sat down to talk afterwards, I was delighted about her perceptions of my class and I think she was happy to hear what I saw in hers. This was so much more than something for an evaluation. It was a real sharing for me, the highlight of my year.

Seeing Results

The final evaluation of the program was compiled in a volume and presented to the board of school trustees. The results of the study were persuasive in the board's decision to implement Primetime in second grade the next year. The evaluation of Primetime-2 was completed during the following year, and its results were even more impressive. The concept was extended to third grade and, just recently, to kindergarten. Teachers involved in the project learned that they were capable of producing a study that carried real weight in decision making. They worked productively and professionally in a collaborative effort in an arena that would have at one time seemed threatening and intimidating.

There are many other examples of practice-oriented research going on in our district. High school English teachers are studying disaggregated standardized test scores to see whether their curriculum is effective with different groups of students. Industrial-arts teachers are evaluating the outcomes of a new technology curriculum that has been piloted in two schools. Foreign-language teachers are assessing the benefits of an exploratory program in the middle school as opposed to a traditional mastery approach. Teachers of gifted students are completing a comparative study of the effects of self-contained versus mainstreamed approaches for highly capable students. Kindergarten teachers have surveyed the literature in early childhood education to make recommendations about entry date for kindergartners, assessment instruments for readiness, and the relative strengths and weaknesses of developmental and academic approaches to the curriculum. The list goes on.

Changing Roles: Teachers as Researchers

What is most revealing about teacher-designed and teacher-implemented research and evaluation is that it places teachers in new roles so naturally and so easily. There is little discontinuity for the teachers involved as they move from their individual classrooms to their research groups, for they bring their concerns about their work with them and they make those concerns the focus for collective study and analysis. Through active engagement in research, teachers leave a world dominated by what has been called the "practicality ethic" (Doyle & Ponder, 1977) and enter the realm of ideas. "To be practical means to concentrate on products and not processes; to draw on experience, rather than research; to be short-range and not predictive in thinking or planning" (Lieberman & Miller, 1984, p. 7). Teachers who engage in research learn to value process, to draw on empirical knowledge, to become long-range and predictive, to depend on analysis rather than experience and intuition. And they learn, as in curriculum writing and peer staff development, to work with other teachers in groups, to recognize their own expertise and that of their peers; and to challenge the notions that being a teacher is somehow short of being a professional and that teaching is less than a profession.

CURRICULUM COORDINATION

One of the results of collaborative work involving central-office administrators and teachers is that the distinctions between the two roles become blurred. After four years of building the tradition of teacher leadership in a wide range of curricular areas, we felt we were ready to experiment with a new configuration of personnel in the curriculum division. The retirement of our full-time language-arts coordinator for grades K–12 provided the opportunity to introduce the concept of "teacher/consultants," staff who spend part of their day in classrooms as teachers and part of their day working out of the central office as curriculum facilitators.

Our first consultants divided the position of the retired language-arts consultant between them. Mrs. T, a second-grade teacher who had overseen the development of the K–6 reading guidelines, became the elementary language-arts consultant. She taught a kindergarten section in the afternoon and did district-level work in the morning. Ms. C, a high school English department head and recipient of the state's coveted "Teacher of the Year" award, had an opposite schedule. She taught two classes in the morning and spent the rest of the day in a coordinating role. Both brought to the central office a freshness and vitality that were totally disarming. More importantly, they offered a perspective and a "reality principle" that had long been lacking.

Teaching Teachers

The elementary consultant was quick to recognize a need that had received little attention in the past: she understood the importance of providing for the successful induction of new teachers into the district. She seized the opportunity to, in her words, "show first year teachers how to do it right," how to organize their classrooms for reading, how to accommodate student needs and interests, and how to take advantage of the wide array of resources and materials that were available. She managed to visit every new teacher by the end of the first month of school. Because she taught in the afternoon, she was able to visit these teachers in the morning, when most of them actually taught reading. Based on the visits, she was able to structure two formal workshops in which she could deal with common concerns. She continued to visit classrooms through the year; she knew that personal contact was the crucial variable in her program to teach new teachers to "do it right." The response of the first-year teachers was enthusiastic:

I've moved around a lot, and this is the first time that anyone
took the time to show me the ropes. Mrs. T made it very clear
to me what the district expected in the teaching of reading. Before I have always had to figure that out for myself.

Mrs. T was extremely helpful. She was not judgmental. She
came across as someone like me who was more knowledgeable
and experienced and who was there to help.

Because of Mrs. T, I learned to do things the right way from
the beginning. She helped me understand the philosophy of
the school district and how I could manage my classroom. She
made it clear that she—and the school corporation—takes the
teacher of reading seriously.

In the course of her visits to new teachers, Mrs. T found that
many of the veteran teachers took advantage of her presence in the
building to ask her questions and to seek assistance. Because she was
an actual classroom teacher, Mrs. T carried none of the baggage of an
administrator. She was not there to evaluate people; she was there to
assist in programs. Over time, Mrs. T made inroads into the most re-
calcitrant of classrooms and buildings. She was invited by individual
teachers, groups of teachers, and principals to help in the identification and resolution of problems associated with reading. In six months
in the position, Mrs. T worked to ensure the successful implementation of our reading program and experienced a high rate of success.

Establishing Communication

Ms. C's approach was different, just as secondary teachers and
elementary teachers are different. She performed the usual tasks of a
curriculum coordinator—holding monthly department-head meetings, following through on textbook purchases, overseeing curriculum-writing projects. Gradually she "won over" the high school and
middle school teachers, who were not as accustomed to teacher leadership and who had many more reservations about the replacement
of "their" coordinator with a teacher. Ms. C's first triumph was in
opening discussion between the middle school and high school English teachers. The two groups had been at odds for some time about
the scope and sequence of the English program. The middle school,
according to the high school teachers, was long on philosophy and
short on curriculum; it was strong in affective areas and less strong in

content. The middle school teachers, on the other hand, viewed the high school teachers as judgmental, having unrealistic expectations for entering high school students. While on paper it looked as though there was articulation between the two levels, it was obvious to the teachers that the situation cried out for improvement.

Ms. C did something that had not been done before: she brought the two groups together. First they met within the five high school feeder districts; then they met on the district level. These meetings were not easy; in the course of often-heated discussions, some of the problems that middle school teachers confronted were uncovered. For instance, there was a dearth of materials and textbooks at the middle school level. While the high school bookrooms were filled with novels and quality reading materials, the middle school teachers were limited by having one classroom set of books for each five classes they taught. History explained some of the problems. When the middle school was established seven years previously, teachers had not been involved in textbook selection and order requests. This condition persisted, a fine example of "benign neglect." What is so curious about this situation is that for seven years teachers had been talking about it among themselves, but at no time did word of their concern and their frustration reach their colleagues in the high school or the offices "downtown." Once the problem was identified, it was solved through the budget office. Teachers developed the purchase orders they needed; the materials will be placed during the next academic year.

Making a Difference

The two examples of teacher consultancy presented above are not intended to deprecate the good work that had been done by our full-time language-arts coordinator. The person who had filled that job enjoyed a reputation for being extremely supportive of teachers. The point of the discussion is to show that when teachers occupy such a position, they see it differently, they see themselves differently, they identify problems earlier, and they reach solutions collaboratively.

The idea of teacher/consultants has taken hold in our district. It has the full support of the teachers' association and is provided for in our negotiated agreement. We now have teachers working in this role in the areas of foreign language, industrial arts, business, and computer education. As our full-time curriculum administrators retire or assume new job responsibilities, their positions will be filled by consultants. As the two examples discussed above show, teacher/

1982). Dr. Robinson (the superintendent of CMS) was aware of this research, and local experience was consistent with the general findings. Thus we were in agreement that the teaching profession would, in the future, be facing what Linda Darling-Hammond (1984) called "an impending crisis."

A second point upon which Dr. Robinson and I were in agreement was that the quality of teacher education, and especially the quality of continuing education, left much to be desired. Furthermore, neither of us saw much prospect that institutions of higher education would take the lead in reforming teacher education. Indeed, my initial contact with Dr. Robinson centered around creating a multiagency group (later referred to as the Metrolina Education Consortium), which was specifically aimed at developing more job-embedded and work-related continuing education for teachers and administrators (see Schlechty et al., 1983).

Given these common views, however, Dr. Robinson and I tended to emphasize different operational elements as the critical leverage points for dealing with the problems we perceived. For Dr. Robinson the solution was to find some way to get the taxpayers to provide more money for teachers' salaries and to find a means to force university professors from the "ivory towers" and into the real world of the public schools. I generally agreed with Dr. Robinson's assessment, but my concerns were less programmatically focused. It was, and is, my view that the impending crisis in teaching could not be avoided unless there was a fundamental restructuring of the teaching occupation and unless the locus of responsibility for the continuing education of teachers and administrators was altered in fundamental ways.

THE MERIT-PAY COMMITTEE

In June of 1981, Dr. Robinson appointed a committee to study the issue of merit pay. This committee was comprised of teacher-leaders, business leaders, parents, administrators, and a representative of the board of education. I became chairperson of this committee in September of 1981. It was the work of this committee that served as the initial impetus to what became known as the Charlotte-Mecklenburg Teacher Career Development Program.

The initial charge of this committee was to study the possibility of implementing a system of merit pay in the Charlotte-Mecklenburg schools and to make recommendations to the superintendent regarding this matter. In keeping with this charge, the committee reviewed numerous documents, research reports, and position papers related to merit pay. Based on this study, the committee concluded that there is no existing system of merit pay that will work in schools. Furthermore, the committee found that teachers generally so distrusted the idea of merit pay that any effort to install it would likely do more harm than good. In a letter dated December 4, 1981, the chairman of the merit-pay committee informed the superintendent of the committee's views. The following excerpts from this letter indicate the sentiment of the committee as of December 1981:

1. There is no existing system of merit pay in schools that can provide a model for CMS. Indeed, there is more evidence to support the assertion that merit pay has had harmful and disruptive effects than that it has had positive effects.
2. In spite of these facts, there is strong evidence that some form of merit pay will be imposed on CMS and every other school system in the state in the near future.
3. If CMS is to escape the negative consequences that are likely to flow from such a state mandated program, the system has two options: a) prepare a strong statement, based upon available evidence against merit pay and resist the imposition with logic and political power, or b) endeavor to capture the momentum created by the present state-wide concern with teacher evaluation and merit pay to create a comprehensive system of incentives and evaluation that is logical and that would work if it were implemented.
4. The members of the committee have indicated that they will commit themselves to working on the latter task if they are assured that this is your intent. If, however, your intent is for us to review existing alternatives and make recommendations, our work is basically completed, for we see nothing in alternatives worth recommending. Furthermore, we do not believe that the alternatives that the state will provide will be any better than those we have already reviewed.

The committee was particularly concerned that merit-pay plans tend implicitly to punish the many by rewarding only a few. There was also concern that the basis of these rewards often becomes arbitrary and capricious. Given the public sentiment for merit pay, the committee was especially concerned that the Charlotte-Mecklenburg schools might unintentionally become participants in an ill-advised effort that would have negative and punitive effects on teachers, many of whom already felt that they were not appreciated for doing so much, for so many, for so little.

The superintendent accepted the committee's recommendation and asked the members to proceed to develop an evaluation, staffing, and incentive plan that would promote continuing professional development and encourage outstanding performance among all professional employees. Furthermore, it was agreed that positive reward for quality service and fairness in evaluation should be the paramount values upon which the system would be based.

Given this new and expanded charge, the committee ceased viewing itself as a merit-pay committee. Rather than merit pay, the committee became concerned with developing a comprehensive system of evaluation, staffing, and rewards designed to improve systematically the overall quality of instruction in the school system. Thus it should be understood that the committee was not recommending a merit-pay plan. *Rather, the committee was recommending a comprehensive system of evaluation, training, and rewards that would open new possibilities for all professional employees.*

A PERCEIVED THREAT

As chairman of the merit-pay committee, I quickly discovered that my concerns with restructuring teaching and improving teacher education would not be adequate to produce action. For action to occur, other definitions of the problem would need to be taken into account.

The teacher members of the committee were unanimous in their belief that teachers were not paid enough. (At that time, 1981, teachers had not received a pay raise for two years.) They also agreed that teachers did not occupy positions of respect in the community and that they lacked parental support. The teacher members of the committee also expressed concern about administrators' lack of sensitivity (though, interestingly, all spoke of Dr. Robinson in the most flattering terms). One of the more outspoken members of the committee summarized the sentiment when he spoke of "dumb ass" principals.

Also present in the group was some sentiment for the notion that teachers generally were not sufficiently accountable, that low performers were too easily tolerated, and that higher performers were not rewarded. The solution, according to one member of the group, was simple: merit pay based on test scores.

As the committee report indicates, these views were eventually negotiated, though not without considerable tension and distress. The dynamics of this process would in themselves be worthy of a case study, but a description of these dynamics would be distracting here.

What is critical are the strategies that were employed to refocus the group's attention away from those things that divided them and toward those things that united them.

Picking up on Dr. Robinson's assertion that it was unlikely that teachers would receive many more across-the-board pay raises unless "the way we do business is changed," and picking up also on the growing sentiment in the state legislature for making teachers "more accountable" (e.g., a statewide evaluation system had just been installed), I led the group to acknowledge that it was likely that some form of change in the way teachers were paid and evaluated was almost certain to occur in the near future. I then suggested that there were two choices—either we could create a system we could believe in or someone from the outside would create one for us. This strategy apparently had an impact on the committee members, for it subsequently showed up in public remarks made by teacher-leaders in explaining to their constituencies why they supported the initial committee report and subsequent activity. Furthermore, this theme was consistently reiterated during the 1983–1984 school year when detailed operational plans were being developed (see below) and large numbers of teachers were being invited to participate. Thus a degree of unity of purpose was generated by focusing on perceived threats from the outside (the legislature and the State Department of Public Instruction).

A COMMON VISION

Outside threats can unite groups *against* something, but outside threats do not generate action *for* something. Thus while the outside threat served to reduce resistance to change, it did not create commitment to change. Commitment to change requires a refocusing of attention away from present dilemmas (e.g., teachers who are underpaid, principals who are ham-fisted in their evaluations, and parents who are unsupportive) and an orientation toward future solutions. Commitment to change also requires an affirmation of the dignity, worth, and competence of those who are being asked to change, while at the same time indicating that the values held by those being asked to change will be threatened unless change does occur. Articulation of the conclusions from the research conducted by Vance and myself (see above) regarding the impending crisis in teaching served to focus attention on the future; it also served to threaten values that needed to be threatened if change was to occur.

Specifically, from the outset, I was aware that the line of research that Vance and I were pursuing could be used in ways that were unflattering to the teaching corps. It was not, however, my intent to be, as one militant national leader called me, a teacher basher. Neither was it my intent to suggest that test scores (SAT, NTE, or any others) predicted teacher effectiveness or teacher quality. From the beginning, our argument was that test scores were a proxy for occupational opportunity; in our test-oriented society, people who test well have more opportunity to do well, economically speaking.

Given the recent history of educational reform, the arguments regarding the changing demographics of the teaching workforce are now well understood, but in 1981 this was not the case. What Vance and I reported in 1981, 1982, and 1983 was newsworthy and noteworthy. Given the tendency of the press to sensationalize (e.g., one North Carolina paper acknowledged the initial study by Vance and myself with the headline, "North Carolina Teachers Getting Dumber"), I had numerous opportunities locally and nationally to articulate my views regarding the coming crisis in teaching.

One of the more interesting accidents in this endeavor was that, as a result of prior experience in CMS, I had developed a warm personal relationship with the president of the American Federation of Teachers as well as numerous other influential teachers in the school system. Thus when local public discussion occurred concerning the controversial studies by Vance and myself, I had access to numerous persons who could assure tolerant, if not enthusiastic, audiences. Over time, first inside the merit-pay study committee itself and later within the school system and the community at large, it became known and understood that the implications of the research by Vance and myself were less important to the present scene than to the future (e.g., who will replace our competent veterans?).

By fastening on the future, present teachers could affirm their own worth while at the same time being honestly distressed about the quality of teachers in the future. Consequently, it became possible for teachers, at least many teachers, to endorse changes that brought them considerable personal discomfort precisely because they felt that resistance to change might condemn the schools they valued to a declining future. This endorsement is illustrated by two quotations from teacher-leaders in endorsing the initial plans. One said, "I think it's like when my grandmother planted a walnut tree. She knew that she would never see it bear walnuts, but she planted it for her children and grandchildren." Another teacher said, "It looks to me like we've got to create a system in which some of us couldn't survive just to make sure that those who replace us are as good as we are."

The solution posed by the CMS Teacher Career Development Program was a complex one. It did not, therefore, lend itself to simple explanations and short news releases. Indeed, even now there are persons employed in the Charlotte-Mecklenburg system who are less than fully knowledgeable regarding what was and is intended. It is not possible to describe fully all of the activity that occurred to address this issue without producing a burdensome and overdetailed account. However, I will generally describe the strategies used.

First, both the superintendent and I availed ourselves of every opportunity afforded to appear on local television or to meet the press. We gave the press detailed background briefings and provided media representatives with all the documents we produced. We treated media representatives as friends and allies and assisted them by providing "quotable quotes." In talking with the media, we dealt more with the problems to which the Teacher Career Development Program was addressed than to specific solutions. The problems could be reduced to simple and understandable terms, whereas the solutions were more complex.

Second, the superintendent and I relied heavily on metaphors and analogies and had a knack for phrase making. We used these skills. We spoke of the school as a workplace and of teachers as executives and of the need to compete for executive talent. I consciously sought ways to express complex ideas with simple phrases or slogans.

For example, one of the early criticisms of the Teacher Career Development Program was that it did not "get rid of bad teachers." After several tries at giving a developmental argument and finding myself sounding professorial and theoretical, I came up with the statement "Getting rid of bad teachers does not get good teachers into the classroom." Perhaps these statements were not profound, but they did communicate.

The result was that we got extensive press and media coverage, favorable editorial support when it was needed, knowledgeable in-depth articles, and warm public response. Evidence that this strategy worked can be found in the fact that local taxes were raised, primarily to support the implementation of the Teacher Career Development Program, and that all ten candidates running for the five seats in the board of education election were publicly committed to continuing support of the Teacher Career Development Program.

Communication of problems and solutions to audiences external to the school system undoubtedly had an impact on internal audiences, because teachers and administrators read and watched the same media as the general public. Furthermore, external communication, which was essential if the program was to have the community support and financial backing it needed, required a great deal of time both from the superintendent and from myself. (More will be said about this topic in the next section.) However, internal communication was even more difficult and time consuming. As with external communication, it is not possible to provide a detailed description of all the tactics that were employed, but it is possible to describe the general tactics.

To the extent possible, existing communication mechanisms were used to convey information. However, it was recognized that these mechanisms were designed primarily to send messages rather than to receive input. Therefore, we created a separate system to receive reactions and input. Each school established a liaison committee. Additionally, an advisory/steering committee was established. Through a federal grant, it was possible to hire six liaison teachers whose sole responsibility was to maintain contact with the building-level liaison committees for the purpose of receiving feedback and criticism concerning the plans being made and actions being taken. I met on a regular basis with the advisory/steering committee and on a less frequent basis with representatives of the school-based liaison committees. Teachers were encouraged to call my office and were assured of a 24-hour response time. Question-and-answer sheets were regularly prepared and distributed. Insofar as possible, we endeavored to communicate complex information on a face-to-face basis (management by wandering around rather than management by memo).

In spite of these intensive efforts, there was, and continues to be, a considerable amount of misinformation and confusion regarding what was being planned, what was being done, what was going to be planned, and what was going to be done. Indeed, some of the confusion partly was due to the planning mechanism, which was predicated on norms of collegiality and participatory decision making. This mechanism was generally at odds with the prevailing culture of schools, where decisions were made from the top down with little real input from those who were required to implement them.[2]

Consequently, when preliminary planning documents were distributed to teachers and administrators and when changes were made in them based on feedback and criticism received from the field, these changes were often criticized as an indication that "nobody knows where they are going or what they want to do." Even more perplexing was that outdated documents and abandoned ideas frequently became the focus and rallying point for resistance to the plan. For example, one of the planning documents distributed during the summer of 1982 suggested the possibility of refraining from paying a local salary supplement to beginning teachers as a means of financing increased supplements to persons who advanced on the career ladder. This document clearly stated that it was not the intention to take the salary supplement from any presently employed teachers. Rather, newly employed teachers might receive less supplement. Based on reactions from teachers and on a subsequent analysis of the impact of such a change on recruiting new teachers, this idea was abandoned. However, in May 1983 critics of the plan referred to this early proposal as evidence that what was planned was to "take away the local teachers' supplement."

Given these reactions, and there were numerous similar ones, it is small wonder that public organizations often abandon participatory management in favor of small clustered planning groups that develop *the* plan and then work mightily to impose it from the top down. A participatory management strategy, especially in schools, requires that those in charge of the management process be willing to accept such criticisms. One of the costs of public planning is that one must plan in public.

In summary, the basic strategies employed in identifying and negotiating the problem, as well as in articulating and creating the solutions in CMS, can be stated as follows:

1. A means of developing unity of purpose was identified. In the CMS case, this means was an external threat —(i.e., the threat of a solution proposed from outside as a result of the lack of solutions from within).
2. A means of focusing attention away from the immediate situation and toward the future was developed, and a means was created to affirm the need and desirability of change without attacking the dignity and worth of those whose present practices and conditions would be affected. Even more, a means was created to demonstrate that the values embraced by current teachers and administrators were more likely to be threatened if the status quo was retained than if the pain of change was endured.
3. Efforts were made to communicate the problem(s) and solution(s) in the simplest and most easily communicated terms. Change was accepted as a political process, not simply a technical process.
4. The act of planning was consistently associated with the act of implementation. Indeed, involving teachers and administrators in the planning process was viewed as training for smooth and continuous implementation.

5. Every effort was made to communicate complex information through face-to-face dialogue, and emphasis was given to getting accurate information back into the management system as well as sending information out from the management system.

There can be little doubt that these strategies worked imperfectly. There remains considerable confusion regarding the nature and purpose of the CMS Teacher Career Development Program, even inside the Charlotte-Mecklenburg school system itself. Part of this inadequacy may be attributable to the strategies themselves. However, much more is attributable to the fact that the resources available simply made it impossible to do all that could be done with the strategies suggested. For example, providing six liaison teachers to work with building-level liaison committees appears to be a major investment until one realizes that there are 103 schools in the Charlotte-Mecklenburg system and only limited funds for providing released time for liaison committee members.

In spite of shortcomings, the fact remains that, at present, the CMS Teacher Career Development Program is continuing to evolve and has avoided much of the controversy surrounding programs implemented in many other places. Part of this relative success may be attributable to the fact that at least as much attention was given to identifying the problem and negotiating that problem in the larger environment as was given to identifying and selling the solution(s). Change calls for painful alterations of habit. Change is exhilarating, but it is also difficult. Exhilaration can sustain a fad, but compelling reasons are the basis for enduring change. Exhilaration has its basis in the immediate satisfactions of the present. Compelling reasons have their basis in anticipating the future.

CREATING A CHANGE SYSTEM

Given the functions that must be fulfilled to bring about change (i.e., conceptualizing the problems and issues; developing awareness of the problems and issues; gaining access to accurate feedback regarding the definition of the problem, the proposed solution, and the effects of actions taken; and, finally, carrying out actions necessary to assure the implementation of the solution), it is essential that individuals be identified to carry out these functions and that roles be created to assure that these functions are properly managed. By definition, change creates new roles and new responsibilities. It is, therefore, necessary to identify the talent that will be needed to carry out the new roles and responsibilities and to identify the resources that will be necessary to support that talent.

It has been my observation that it is the failure to recognize and/or the failure to come to grips with the complexities that are involved in creating change that has led to the demise of many change efforts, especially in schools. More specifically, change is a developmental activity. It requires a system to invest in the long run. The act of invention is not sufficient. Neither can change promise immediate results. It requires the application of different norms and rules, and, most of all, it requires a great deal of tolerance for ambiguity and the prospect of failure.

School systems, like most public organizations, are predicated on the assumption of program maintenance and certainty. Budgets are categorical and drawn up on an annual basis. As in most bureaucracies, job descriptions are precise and constraining. Doing things is more important than studying things, and acting is more valued than thinking. Since planning and implementing change require an upfront investment in an uncertain future, it is little wonder that public schools are so maladroit at them.

One of the reasons I accepted the superintendent's appointment as chairperson of the merit-pay study committee was that I saw in this appointment the possibility of addressing a fundamental issue of concern to me. I had no notion at that time where my involvement would lead me. Indeed, in the summer and fall of 1981, my intentions were to complete the research project that I had under way in Charlotte, assure the managerial stability of the Metrolina Education Consortium (it was then that I was serving as acting director of this organization), and return to the University of North Carolina at Chapel Hill in July 1982. For me, the assignment to the merit-pay study committee was simply a mechanism to help me clarify my thinking on the merit-pay issue and perhaps a means to gather further insight about a school system I had been studying intensely.

The result was substantially different from the one I anticipated. By November 1981, I was convinced that this committee could become a major force for change within the Charlotte-Mecklenburg school system and perhaps a catalyst for change elsewhere as well. By December 1981, when the superintendent agreed to charge the committee with the responsibility of creating an alternative to merit pay, I was convinced that a major social invention was possible and I was committed to playing a leadership role in this invention.

Given my view of the change process as articulated earlier (Schlechty, 1978), I saw my first task as playing the role of conceptualizer. Someone had to make sense out of this mess, and I was in a position to do so. However, based on prior experience, especially in Virginia Beach, I knew that the kind of change I was becoming committed to would require that I build a change system. It was not enough to have a good idea. It was more important to have support for that idea and to have people who were capable of assuring that the idea could be moved from a conceptual to an operational level. Therefore, I began intuitively, and sometimes consciously, to build a "skunk works" (an organization put together by cannibalizing other projects), though at the time I was not familiar with the term. Initially, the members of this skunk works were some members of the merit-pay study committee, some other staff from the Charlotte-Mecklenburg schools whom I had met as a result of my prior experiences in the school system, and Dr. Anne Joslin, who had worked with me in a variety of roles.

As is apparent from earlier descriptions, much of my emotional energy from 1975 through 1981 had been spent in developing ideas regarding the conditions of teaching, the conditions of teacher education, and what it would take to alter the undesirable consequences of these conditions. In addition to conceptualization, I had attempted to discipline my ideas with facts (e.g., Vance & Schlechty, 1982; Schlechty & Whitford, 1983; Schlechty & Vance, 1981). My research experience had convinced me that theory works in practice. My experience with the merit-pay study committee as well as subsequent experiences gave me an opportunity to see whether practice works in theory.

These matters aside, in January 1982 I began to give the activity of the merit-pay study committee central attention. Just as described in the textbooks on modern management, I began to cannibalize. First, I diverted my own time and energy to thinking about the problems that the committee was confronting. I used a secretary assigned to the consortium to prepare written materials and increasingly called on Dr. Joslin to help me think through the procedural and conceptual issues presented by the committee's work. In addition to playing the role of conceptualizer, I was thrust into the role of propagandist, or creator of awareness of the problem, by the publicity that my research on teacher quality had received. As the project emerged, I continued to serve in these two roles, though increasingly responsibility for both roles began to be shared. More important, perhaps, is the fact that while I was the obvious focal point for the conceptualization of the problem and its solution, I was frequently, in fact, nothing more than the instrument through which the conceptualizations of others were articulated. It is apparent, for example, that much of my thinking regarding the quality of teachers is from Waller (1932/1961) and Lortie (1975). Similarly, many of my ideas regarding the management of change are attributable to Gross (1979), and much of my thinking about evaluation and authority has been influenced by Dornbusch and Scott (1975) as well as others.

What is not so apparent is that many of the breakthrough notions that made it possible to proceed with the planning and implementation of the Teacher Career Development Program came from sources other than those commonly associated with the academy. For example, as much as I would like to take the credit for the notion that teachers should be viewed as executives or as much as this notion may be viewed as having come from David Berliner, who first and independently articulated it in a public forum in 1983, I must acknowledge that it was Royce Angel, a manager at Southern Bell and a member of the merit-pay study committee, who first suggested that we could never develop a workable plan until we thought of teachers as executives rather than production-line workers. The notion of teachers as executives has so guided the CMS plan that properly locating its origin is significant to the CMS story. Similarly, it was Olin Flowe (the local AFT president) who suggested the idea of inventing a new system in which present employees could volunteer to participate and new employees would be required to participate, as opposed to changing the rules midstream and creating needless pockets of resistance. I could go on listing similar contributions from others, but the point is that my position as committee chair and later as unofficial and then official special assistant to the superintendent gave the CMS project a clear intellectual center. There was a person to whom ideas could be attached, blame assigned, and sometimes credit given. Thus the project could have intellectual cohesiveness, especially in its formative stages. However, my role as conceptualizer and early propagandist was not without its drawbacks, both for me and for the long-term health of the project. As long as the project was identified as my idea and I was its primary spokesperson, the project did not belong to the system; it belonged to me, and I was an outsider even though I was also an insider. Both the superintendent and I recognized this problem as early as June 1982, and we consciously developed a strategy for shifting the identity of the project from me to him and subsequently from him to the board of education and the school system. It was in this act that the first conscious moves were made to develop the change system that served to sustain the planning and implementation of the CMS project.

Specifically, during the summer of 1982, the superintendent and I had numerous conversations regarding the implications of the merit-pay study committee's report and what it would take to move forward the program recommended by this committee. Two factors emerged as critical.

First, if a change as fundamental as the one suggested by the merit-pay study committee were to be effectively implemented, it would need active endorsement and active involvement from the superintendent. Passive assent or even approval would not be enough. In bureaucracies, leaders can delegate almost any responsibility or authority that they have except one, and that is moral authority. The Teacher Career Development Program required the moral authority of the office of the superintendent. Consequently, the superintendent and I agreed that he would serve as the primary spokesperson for informing the local business community and the board of education about the project. Not only did he communicate with these groups more effectively than I, but they perceived him to be a more effective and important communicator.[3]

In arriving at this decision, it was understood that I would continue to have heavy responsibility for communication with professional staff in the system and with representatives of the press and television. Dr. Robinson also made it explicitly clear that, for the time being, he did not want anyone other than himself or me to attempt to explain the proposal to any group. The operational reason for this decision was to cut down on confusion and mixed messages. The implementation of this decision also served clearly to shift the intellectual/conceptual center of the project to the office of the superintendent. And, in fact, the superintendent and the deputy superintendent began to play increasingly important roles in conceptualizing the details of the project. From September to December 1982, Dr. Joslin and I met with the superintendent and the deputy superintendent for three hours each week in order to work through various conceptual, logistical, and tactical issues related to the program.

Second, it was recognized that the management of a change process as complex as the one envisioned by the Teacher Career Development Program would require the full-time attention and energy of at least one person. I, therefore, agreed that should a decision to proceed become firm, I would find a way to give full attention to the project. In the meantime, the work I would do on the project would continue to be done as an add-on. Thus by early September 1982 we had begun to establish a role structure that included a clear locus for conceptualization and direction (i.e., the role of conceptualizer), clear assignments for "propaganda," and clear understandings regarding the need for resources and personnel to support actual implementation.

In addition to clearly establishing and defining the conceptualization, propagandist, and implementation roles, two additional roles were encouraged to emerge: those of informant and knowledgeable critic.

An informant is not a spy or a turncoat. Rather, an informant is a person who provides the anthropological researcher with inside information that makes it possible to gain insights into the tacit understandings of a culture or a group. Those who manage change processes necessarily occupy perceived power positions. If they are responsible and ethical, they need a clear and accurate image of how their work is affecting the lives of others and how it is perceived. Such data are difficult to get precisely, because change is threatening and those who are threatened tend to conceal what they know, think they know, or fear they know. Unfortunately, change managers are prone to act on the assumption that what people tell them in meetings and in official communications is what is really going on. Consequently, pockets of resistance develop around issues that could have easily been put to rest had the change managers been aware of them before a crisis arose. In my view, developing and nurturing the role of informant is critical to the management of change.

Initially, I relied on individual principals and teachers that I had worked with in the past to fulfill the informant function. I regularly called these persons, met with them in informal settings, or accompanied them to social events. I was open regarding my motives, but I also honestly enjoyed the company of each one. I tried to select informants who were plugged into a variety of networks in the school system. (Given my prior work in the school system, I had an image of some of these key networks.) I also tried to select informants who had different perceptions of and different ways of reporting reality. For example, some informants were quite literal. They could report accurately and precisely what was said in a given meeting. Others were metaphorical and interpretive. These latter types often distorted facts, but they provided a feel for events.

The role of informed critic is easy to define but difficult to develop. The informed critic is a person who is marginally committed to the change effort but is constantly looking for things that "just won't work."

One of the dangers of managing change is that the leader of the change will surround him- or herself with sycophants and true believers and avoid those who present unpleasant analyses. The acceptance of such information can, however, help to offset the possibility of ca-tastrophe. In the CMS situation, I carefully nurtured relationships with a few individuals whom I knew to be thoughtful but who tended to be skeptical regarding the prospect of any real change ever occurring. Such persons can find flaws in the most tightly reasoned argument and the most elegant design. They are invaluable.

As indicated above, the role structure that I have described was initially established as a skunk works. As the project emerged, espe-cially after May 1983, when a formal advisory/steering committee was established with instructions to proceed with detailed planning, this structure became more formalized and institutionalized. For exam-ple, in January 1984 I assumed the office of special assistant to the superintendent, thereby officially symbolizing the locus of the con-ceptual role as well as locating responsibility for continuing planning and implementation. Funding for this position was provided by the University of North Carolina at Chapel Hill and the school system. Later, partial funding was provided by a U.S. Department of Educa-tion grant. Simultaneously, the University of North Carolina at Char-lotte agreed to support Dr. Joslin as program coordinator. The establishment of the advisory/steering committee and the school-based liaison committees formalized the roles of informant and in-formed critic. Subsequently, funding from the U.S. Department of Education and the National Institute of Education made it possible to hire a group of liaison teachers and research assistants, who en-hanced even more the capacity to gather data about what was going on, how events were perceived, and how people felt about these events.

As should be apparent, considerable time, energy, and money were expended in developing a planning and implementation role structure. Furthermore, these investments were made up front and long before operational implementation. What started as a skunk works became an operating program. So far as can be determined, the establishment of this front-loaded planning and implementation structure is unique in the public school reform movement, though it is commonplace in the business world.

In spite of the conscious creation of such a structure, the CMS project confronted and continues to confront many of the problems typical of a change effort. There was and is considerable confusion regarding the nature and direction of the project. Some teachers and administrators who initially resisted the basic concepts underlying the program, continue to resist. However, the CMS Teacher Career De-velopment Program has not experienced some of the operational difficulties that have been experienced in other localities and states. It is my belief (I emphasize the word *belief*) that had CMS been in a position to commit more resources to this change structure and if those resources had been committed earlier, many of the problems experienced in the planning and early implementation stages could have been avoided. For example, had the time and money been available to provide specific training for the building-level liaison teams, the quality of information received from those teams could have been improved, or so I believe. Similarly, if the position of liaison teacher could have been retained during the 1984–1985 school year, when operational implementation began, communication problems could have been ameliorated, if not avoided. Unfortunately, when confronted with a choice of providing funds to enhance actual implementation roles (e.g., providing training for beginning teachers, experienced teachers, and observer/evaluators) as opposed to providing funds for the information-seeking roles, it was apparent that there just were not enough developmental resources available.

In my view, if the CMS Teacher Career Development Program continues to evolve and becomes institutionalized, as now appears to be the case, and if the project is successful, the basis for that success is largely embedded in the investments that were made in creating the necessary change support system prior to actual implementation. If, on the other hand, the project fails to survive or the change that was envisioned becomes overwhelmed by the maintenance needs of the system, it will in part be due to the fact that not enough was invested up front soon enough, as well as to the fact that the resource needs of operational implementation distracted attention from the need to maintain a commitment to supporting the change role structure.

PLANNING FOR INSTITUTIONALIZATION

Linear thinking suggests that institutionalization is the last thing that occurs in the change process. Naivete regarding issues of institutionalization is nowhere more clearly illustrated than in the frequent requests from funding agencies for assurances that the project being funded will, if successful, be continued after the initial funding cycle has ended. The fact is that by the time most projects end, the funds that were provided to support change have already been diverted to maintaining present programs (see Schlechty & Whitford, 1983). As Sarason (1972) has observed, the patterned regularities of schools overwhelm change efforts. Part of the reason for this is that *those who manage change do not address problems of institution-*

alization until it is too late. Put differently, once an organization is committed to testing an idea, technology, or strategy, it is essential that planners ask themselves several questions: (1) "Suppose what we're about really works and we want to continue it. What changes would need to occur in the structure of our organization or in the way we do business?" (2) "What would it take to bring the changes about?" (3) "How much would the changes cost?" (4) "How likely is it that these changes can be brought about?" And, even more important, (5) "Are there structural, organizational, or cultural changes that simply must occur in order to make the system being installed viable?" and (6) "At what point should these changes be in place and how long will it take to get them in place?" For example, the Teacher Career Development Program is based on the assumption of an intensive period of induction and the corollary assumption that a teacher should not receive tenure until the capacity to perform in outstanding ways over a sustained period of time has been demonstrated. It is also assumed that tenure should be a reward, as opposed to the denial of tenure being a punishment. Consequently, it was clear that for this system to work there would have to be some fundamental changes in the tenure law in North Carolina.

At the same time, the superintendent held the view that the level of community support necessary to secure the required funding base would require that community leaders be convinced that this project was not "business as usual." Suggested changes in the tenure law are sufficiently controversial to symbolize that something very different is going on. Consequently, the superintendent decided that he would not proceed with detailed planning and implementation until he was assured that the tenure law could be changed in ways that were supportive of the concepts contained in the June 1982 comittee report.

As indicated earlier, I assumed the position of special assistant to the superintendent in January 1983. The board of education had formally authorized the superintendent to proceed with the planning and implementation of the Teacher Career Development Program as outlined by the merit-pay committee. However, this endorsement took an interesting form, for it was embedded in a board motion authorizing the superintendent to ask the North Carolina legislature for permission to grant tenure on a variable base (after 3, 4, 5, or 6 years), as opposed to the then-current practice of granting tenure with the first contract after the third year of successful service. From the superintendent's perspective, the issue was symbolic as well as critical. As he put the matter, "If we can't get this little change, then we might as well give up on the whole thing. If people can't understand the need to change the tenure law, they sure won't understand all the other changes we're going to ask them to support."

The superintendent's commitment to the position that some antecedent structural changes had to occur before one could proceed with the substantive changes suggested by the Teacher Career Development Program was a critical strategic decision, and it had a number of unanticipated consequences. (At least, we did not anticipate them.)

First, this decision delayed proactive planning for the implementation of the Teacher Career Development Program for a number of months. In January 1983 I had presented the superintendent with a detailed timeline that called for establishing a planning committee in early March. The superintendent insisted that there was no need to establish a planning committee until we knew what the legislature would do. (The legislature acted favorably on the local bill on May 20; the first meeting of the planning committee was held on May 25.)

Second, the controversial nature of the proposed change in the tenure law generated a great deal of media interest regarding the reasons that the Teacher Career Development Program would require a change in the tenure law. This provided numerous opportunities for the superintendent and me to present increasingly detailed descriptions of the nature of the proposed changes and, consequently, increase local awareness of what was intended.

Third, because the tenure battle occurred primarily at the state level, it heightened awareness of the program throughout the state and eventually developed new allies and new opponents for the plan. For example, many local teacher-leaders were actively lobbying for passage of the tenure bill while state-level education leaders were lobbying against it. Eventually, the legislative process involved active support from nearly every local legislator, the governor of North Carolina, the State Superintendent of Public Instruction, and influential business leaders.

Fourth, by the time that the legislative process had been completed, the CMS project had ceased to be a local initiative. It was designated as a statewide pilot program. As such, the project was well positioned to gain access to resources that later became available as a result of subsequent reform legislation.

Fifth, as the Teacher Career Development Program began to gain increased visibility locally and at the state level, it began to gain visibility nationally as well, and here serendipity became an important factor. Just as the tenure battle was giving the Teacher Career Development Program local visibility, the Tennessee plan was being conceptualized. Both Dr. Robinson and I were invited to become involved in the Tennessee deliberations, and consequently we became connected with a network of reform-minded governors and state legislators.

Finally, again by chance, at precisely the time that we were gaining state visibility, two national reports, *A Nation at Risk* and *Education and Economic Development*, were released. These reports served not only to encourage legislators to view the Charlotte initiative more positively, but also to focus national attention on a project that envisioned doing many of the things these reform proposals suggested should be done. The national visibility served to build community pride and enhance the perception that this project really was quite important. For example, my office began to receive newspaper clippings and magazine articles from nationally oriented publications that contained favorable comments regarding what was going on in Charlotte. Such publicity heightened the perception that the Teacher Career Development Program was a significant event in the life of the community, and people increasingly expressed the sentiment that, "We don't dare let this thing fail now because we're in the national limelight."

Detailed descriptions of the political activities that occurred between January and May 1983 with regard to the Teacher Career Development Program would require more space than can be allotted here. *What is important, however, is that the superintendent's intuitive sense that "you don't change things without changing them" and his willingness to insist on prior commitments to some of the most critical and controversial structural changes that would be required for the proposed program to be installed probably enhanced the prospects of success for the program.* It certainly increased community interest, knowledge, and pride.

What is equally important to understand is that if the legislature had not acted favorably, if local teachers had not been supportive, if the local community had not responded affirmatively, if, in other words, the conditions supportive of change had not been present, the events of the spring of 1983 would have made that clear. Given such data, the superintendent would have been in a position to abandon the program having made only minor investments, and he could have done so with little jeopardy to the moral authority of his office.

The superintendent's insistence on confronting some of the most controversial structural implications of the Teacher Career Development Program was a highly visible strategy aimed at assuring institutionalization. There were other less visible strategies as well. Most particularly, there were strategies developed to assure continuity of leadership for the program and to assure that program development responsibilities increasingly were assigned to operative units within the school system rather than retained as the exclusive purview of a separate person or office. Conceptually, the strategy was relatively simple. *The structure that was designed to assure effective initiation and early implementation of the program, namely the office of the special assistant to the superintendent, was maintained as a temporary position.* There were several reasons for this. First, one of the major barriers to change is that those who occupy positions of leadership in the initiation of a change effort frequently are dependent on the continuation of the project to maintain their status. Indeed, their occupational futures are sometimes determined by their ability to create a permanent position for themselves. The unfortunate consequence is that this creates a condition in which the leader of a change effort sometimes becomes more interested in building an empire than in making the hard decisions necessary for instituting fundamental reform.

Second, to bring about change of the magnitude suggested by the CMS project, the person charged with responsibility for managing the change has to have extraordinary authority. To create a permanent position with such power and authority or to create a position that would threaten to become permanent would have been extremely threatening to the present power figures in the system and would have created unneeded resistance.

Finally, if change is to be institutionalized, it requires the redefinition of existing roles and sometimes the addition of new roles. When new roles are added, some of the problems of role overload associated with role redefinition can be avoided in the short run, but the addition of new roles simply to avoid the pain of redefinition frequently results in an increasingly top-heavy organization rather than an increasingly responsive system. Given those facts, the office of special assistant to the superintendent maintained an ad hoc quality throughout my tenure (January 1983 to January 1985). Persons who were employed by that office (e.g., liaison teachers and, later, observer/evaluators) understood that their assignments were short term and special. At the same time, I nurtured and developed persons who could assume leadership responsibilities once I departed from the scene. For example, the person who presently occupies the office of director of the Teacher Career Development Program was formerly employed as an observer/evaluator.[4]

There were, of course, a number of problems in implementing this strategy (i.e., developing the temporary structure).

First, it caused the special assistant to the superintendent (myself) and the project coordinator (Dr. Joslin) considerable personal inconvenience. Because of the impermanence, neither felt justified in taking up permanent domicile in Charlotte, so they had to commute, one from Chapel Hill and one from Wilmington, North Carolina.[5]

Second, in spite of the fact that the position of special assistant to the superintendent was designed to be temporary, there were many in the system who assumed that this was a ruse and that eventually I would be appointed as an associate superintendent and move my family to Charlotte. Thus, while the temporary nature of the office ameliorated rivalry, it did not completely dispose of this issue. As one middle-level manager reportedly said, "Phil is Jay's fair-haired boy" (Jay being the superintendent, Dr. Robinson).

Third, once actual implementation began to occur and demands began to be placed on other offices to support training activity, provide budgets, and coordinate specific programs, the ambiguous nature of the position of the special assistant to the superintendent in the organization of the school system made it difficult to command the resources necessary to do the job. On the one hand, because the office was established to provide leadership and direction to the implementation of the Teacher Career Development Program, many assumed that it was my responsibility to do the implementation. However, having no staff and no resources made that a bit difficult. On the other hand, because no one in the system other than observer/evaluators and liaison teachers reported to me, I was not perceived to be in a position to make administrative requests to persons who ran semi-autonomous departments. Eventually, this dilemma was resolved by the superintendent when he informed all of the involved parties that, "When Phil asks you for help, you just think I'm asking you for help. You don't give a person the responsibility for this kind of job without giving him the authority to do it."

Perhaps the most critical move in providing for the institutionalization of the program involved redefining the roles of the area superintendents and their staffs so that these persons would have the primary responsibilities for managing implementation tasks.

Operationally, each area superintendent is responsible for administrative services to one of five service areas. Two area superintendents served on the advisory/steering committee. Prior to March 1984, however, the area superintendents, as a group, were relatively uninformed and unconcerned about the program. In fact, as late as March 1984 many teachers and administrators assumed, according to comments and interviews, that the program would not get off the ground. As one said, "This, too, shall pass."

Based on prior observations in the school system, I was convinced that gaining the active support of area superintendents was a key to the success of the program. However, their day-to-day demands of managing their units made it difficult to get their attention. For example, between August 1983 and April 1984 I asked several times to be placed on the agenda of the area superintendents' meeting. The deputy superintendent, who conducted these meetings, was personally supportive of the Teacher Career Development Program, but the program was always placed last on the agenda and, frequently, this item was never reached. However, in March 1984 a number of events occurred that raised the Teacher Career Development Program higher in the priorities of the area superintendents. First, procedures were initiated for selecting the first group of career candidates and for selecting observer/evaluators. Second, serious planning for the summer training of the career candidates commenced, and many members of the executive council (made up of area superintendents as well as assistant and associate superintendents) became involved in this planning. Third, the superintendent became aware that the centrality of his commitment to the Teacher Career Development Program was not clear to his executive staff. Consequently, he made a number of presentations, one of them on local television. In these presentations he said, "This school system has five priorities—first, the implementation of the Teacher Career Development Program; second, the implementation of the Teacher Career Development Program; third, the implementation of the Teacher Career Development Program; fourth, the implementation of the Teacher Career Development Program; and fifth, everything else."

By late April 1984, the program was the first item on the executive council's agenda. Throughout the summer and fall of 1984, its concerns dominated the attention of the Executive Council. The first operational evidence of the central role of area superintendents and their staffs was in August 1984, when these persons had responsibility for developing a two-and-one-half-day training session for all administrators in the system regarding the details of the Teacher Career Development Program as it existed at that time. This training session was supported by the staff-development department and the communications department, which had created training manuals and operational-procedures notebooks. Currently, the bulk of the day-today management of the Teacher Career Development Program has been assigned to area superintendents, though the activity continues to be coordinated from the director's office.

As outside observers have indicated (e.g., McLaughlin et al., 1986), there are numerous difficulties still present in the CMS Teacher Career Development Program. There is slippage, uneven response, and continuing change of direction. As the superintendent recently noted, there is the constant threat that paperwork will overwhelm the program. If, however, early attention had not been given to issues related to institutionalization, it is unlikely that a project this complex ever would have moved from planning to implementation. Furthermore, if the superintendent had not established the implementation of this program as a high priority and thus created the condition of some short-term role overload, it is doubtful that the system could have supported this massive effort. Change produces tension. People must learn to do new things, but, equally important, they must learn to stop doing the same old things. It is clear that the Teacher Career Development Program and the superintendent's commitment to it have caused many persons to learn to do some new things. It is not yet clear, however, whether many persons have learned *not* to do some things they used to do. Unless old learnings can be abandoned, role overload will persist and, eventually, old habits will overwhelm new ideas.

In conclusion, it is my view that the success of the CMS program to date is partially attributable to early attention to the problems of institutionalization. If the program fails, it may be because we failed to understand the importance of deinstitutionalizing old ways of doing things. That is, new habits (and institutionalized change is a new habit) can only replace old habits (i.e., the status quo) when as much attention is given to unlearning old ways of doing things as is given to learning new ways of doing things.

THE SIGNIFICANCE OF AUTHORITY

Change, if it is significant, requires a reassignment of responsibility and authority. Significant change, therefore, cannot occur until and unless those who have the legitimate right to assign authority indicate their willingness to reassign it. The more widespread and fundamental the change, the higher in the organization one must go to find the appropriate legitimizing authority base. Given the nature of the CMS Teacher Career Development Program, there was only one authority base that could assure its success, and that was the office of the superintendent.

Given the previous discussion, it should be apparent that the superintendent played a central role in the planning and implementation of the CMS Teacher Career Development Program. He mastered the intricacies of the plan and contributed to its development. He obviously was committed to it. What is interesting is that it was not until March 1984, long after the tenure battle and long after detailed planning had occurred, that key decision makers inside the school system understood the seriousness of the direction in which the superintendent intended to lead. Indeed, the superintendent was somewhat taken aback when he realized that, in spite of his numerous public speeches and political actions, and in spite of board statements and newspaper accounts, there were many in the system, including many in relatively high-level positions, who continued to assume that "this, too, shall pass." In part, this skeptical view is attributable to the perception that fads come and go, but the system goes on. One informant referred to change as the *three*-year locust.

Persistently, throughout the planning and early implementation stages, individuals sought confirmation of their perceptions of the impermanence of intentions—some saw the temporary nature of my assignment as evidence of a short-term commitment and evidence for their view that when I left the project would be abandoned. Others speculated on the superintendent's retirement date. Still others came to view this project as a calculated move on the part of the superintendent and myself to further our personal careers and political ambitions. Even public statements by board members that this project belonged to the system and would outlast any individual did not offset all the skepticism or reassure all the cynics.

As the early chapter discussions should surely indicate, the CMS program developed a wide range of strategies to assure that sufficient authority was visible and present. The strategy that was missing, however, is one that was not thought of; that is, how does one assure permanence as well as power? It may in fact be that a part of the source of resistance to change is the perception that schools are fickle organizations. Change requires considerable expenditure of personal energy. Those who are willing to expend such energy have the right to expect that the commitments made will be honored in the long run. Developing strategies to assure the permanence of change while the change is occurring strikes me as one of the most difficult problems confronting managers of change. Perhaps my departure from CMS, which was preplanned, and the fact that the program has continued will function as such a strategy. If so, it will be a fortuitous event, for my leaving was not calculated to assure permanence, even though it may do so. Everett Wilson (1966) has suggested that one never knows whether a new role has been created until the first occupant of the role is replaced by a second and the patterns of behavior persist. Perhaps a similar statement could be made regarding the assessment of permanence. As long as a change depends on the presence of individual personalities, it is not a change; it is a social movement.

JOINING PLANNING AND IMPLEMENTATION: THE CASE FOR PARTICIPATORY MANAGEMENT

One of the persistent questions asked regarding the CMS project is, "When did you begin implementation?" A second question is, "How long did you spend in planning?" The nature of these questions indicates that most educators separate planning from implementation so much so that an honest answer creates confusion, for the honest answer to the first question is "sometime around 1981," and the honest answer to the second question is, "the planning is still going on." The answer that individuals want is that we began planning with the merit-pay study committee and we began implementation in the summer of 1984.

Many who argue for participatory management do so on the basis that it increases ownership and commitment. These arguments are valid, but equally valid is the proposition that participatory planning also reduces training needs and communication costs. Persons who are involved in the planning of change have an idea about what is expected of them when the change is implemented. Furthermore, when they are involved, they know what is going on. As noted earlier, participatory management is not without problems. It creates both confusion and clarity of communication. It would have been much easier had the superintendent and I simply gathered together a few individuals, developed a plan, and hired a public-relations firm to do a slick presentation of what we were about. Many of the existing reform efforts, especially those initiated at the state level, have proceeded very much in this direction. There is no way to demonstrate empirically that the effort in Charlotte to join planning and implementation in the context of a participatory management system is in any way superior to the more traditional American planning mode. It will be a decade before it is known whether any of the reform efforts that have been initiated in the last four or five years will endure. I am, however, prepared to assert that one of the greatest strengths of the Charlotte-Mecklenburg initiative resided in the joining of planning and implementation within the context of participatory management.

One of the greatest weaknesses of the CMS program was the failure to commit enough energy and resources to the development and nurturance of structures that were supportive of this strategy. The failure to develop these structures was not an oversight. The superintendent saw such structures as important, as did I. The problem is that school systems, like other public organizations, have great maintenance needs and little developmental capital. Time, energy, and money spent on planning is seen as wasted time, energy, and money, and many apparently prefer to waste their time, energy, and money on implementation. That is, without entrepreneurial effort on my part (e.g., procuring developmental grants and university support) and without conscious championing on the superintendent's part (e.g., a great deal of tolerance for such cannibalizing activity as co-opting secretaries and other staff), there would have been few developmental resources available to CMS.

The unfortunate fact is that the resources we were able to procure were inadequate to the task, and if the long-term outcome of this project is in doubt, I am personally convinced that the doubt has its origins in the lack of developmental resources. We did what we could with what we had.

STRATEGY AND TACTICS

During the 1960s and early 1970s, largely in response to a variety of federal initiatives, educators became oriented toward stating project objectives in behavioral terms. Picking up on the business concept of management by results, educators began to think in terms of management by behavioral results. Emphasis on results and a corollary emphasis on measurable results is, in our view, a desirable orientation. Unfortunately, the educational assumption that the only measurable results are behavioral results distracts attention from results themselves. The result of a round of golf is a score. One need only observe a single golf match to observe that there are a variety of ways of behaving that will result in a score of 100. Indeed, one need only follow a group of professional golfers to discover that there are a variety of forms of behavior that can lead to a score of 68. Watching a person swing a golf club will tell you how he or she swings. It will not tell you how he or she will score.

The point of this little foray into the world of objectives and the world of golf is that processes (and here *behavior* is defined as a process or evidence of a process) and tactics (defined as how a specific job is done) are not the same as results (here defined as goals or strategic objectives).

As another illustration, early in World War II, the Allied leadership defined a strategic objective of the war as "the unconditional surrender of Germany." In stating the objective in this fashion and by vigorously upholding this objective in practice, the Allies undoubtedly prolonged the war. There is considerable evidence that it was the fear of the consequences of unconditional surrender that sustained the support for Hilter long after it was apparent that the German armies were going to lose battle after battle on every front. Conversely, the public statement of the grand strategy served to focus the attention of the Allies on the need to concentrate resources to assure total victory. In Viet Nam and even in Korea, the strategic objective was neither clear nor compelling. "Stopping the Communists" is too amorphous a goal.

The function of goals, or strategic objectives, is to provide a framework for orienting action, to give meaning to action, and to provide a basis for evaluating the meaning of action. Tactics and behavior or specific programs and agendas can change, depending on their results. If, however, a change is to occur (e.g., a world in which the Nazi regime has no sway), then the strategic goals must be clear and relatively immutable. From the outset, an effort was made to assure that the goals of the CMS project were clear. In spite of popular opinion, it was not the goal of the program to implement a career ladder. A career ladder was a simple tactic. Neither was the goal of the project to develop a believable evaluation system. Evaluation was, and is, simply a tactic. The goal of the CMS Teacher Career Development Program was, and is, to develop, maintain, and retain individuals who are capable of and committed to outstanding performance in the classroom.

Such a focus made it relatively easy to deal with questions like, "How is the Career Development Program going to get rid of incompetent teachers?" The answer is, "That is not its purpose." The purpose is to develop and retain outstanding teachers. The present system has the capacity to rid itself of incompetence if those who manage it have the will to do so.

A clear focus on the goal also makes it possible to change tactics. For example, during the early stages of implementing the project, it became clear that the procedures for documenting performance were discouraging rather than encouraging many teachers. These procedures were examined and discarded, not because the standards were perceived to be too high, but because the paperwork was perceived to be too burdensome. Some new tactic had to be invented that assured high standards while avoiding distracting teachers from their task. Among other things, it became clear that this new tactic would include helping new teachers to understand that documenting performance did not mean producing new documents. Rather, it meant keeping a file of artifacts (e.g., tests given, materials produced). The objective was to have a database for assessing performance, and the performance being assessed was not the ability to document performance.

A variety of strategies were employed to assure goal clarity. First, it was essential that key leaders in the system achieve consensus regarding the nature of the goals. Thus there were regular and intensive meetings of the superintendent, the deputy superintendent, the special assistant to the superintendent, and the project coordinator. Slogans and catch phrases were developed to signify goal intent (e.g., "We're not interested in simply identifying good teachers"; "Getting rid of bad teachers does not get good teachers into the classroom"; "All we expect is that outstanding teachers continue to behave as they now behave and that all other teachers behave like outstanding teachers"; "Document for success, not for failure"; "If you can't document success, there must be a failure"; "Evaluations must be evaluated"; "We must be like Caesar's wife—not only must we be virtuous, we must appear to be virtuous"; and "We're building an airplane while we're flying it").

One-on-one communication was encouraged and fostered, but most important, perhaps, was the superintendent's decision that no one be permitted to speak for the project or try to explain it until he and/or the special assistant to the superintendent determined that the person was knowledgeable.

In spite of careful attention to assuring clarity of strategic goals, there was, and is, considerable confusion regarding these goals. Part of this confusion is attributable to normal communication problems in a large organization, but another part has to do with the culture of schools themselves. Put directly, in schools mastery of tactics and processes is more valued than is mastery of goals and direction. Thus change of tactics was often seen as changing the rules and evidence that "nobody knows where they're going." For example, during the early implementation, when it became clear that many career candidates were becoming discouraged by paperwork, fundamental changes were made in the requirements for the action growth plans and training sessions were held to clarify further the intentions of the program design. Some teachers appreciated the changes, but others were resistant. One said, "Do you mean that after I've done all this work, you've changed the rules?" It would have done little good to tell this teacher that what she had done in the first place was not within the rules. The fact is that this teacher (and there were many others) simply did not understand the strategic goal, and communication of strategic goals is one of the most important functions of leadership. In this case, and in many others, the leadership failed.

Given the personalistic nature of this account, I accept the possibility that the failure of leadership was often due to my own limitations. There are, however, a number of additional conditions that must be taken into account that might be instructive to those who manage change. First, because of limited resources and lack of experience (we were on the cutting edge of ignorance), we simply did not know what teachers would need to know in order to understand what was intended. During the second year of implementation (1985–1986), the training for experienced teachers was redesigned and more attention was given to the intentions of the action growth plan than was the case the first year.

Second, we vastly underestimated the power of bureaucratic habit and prior experience. For example, the only prior experience most teachers had with documenting performance involved the competition for "Teacher of the Year." This competition called on them to produce *new* documentation.

Finally, immediate concerns with short-term tasks and expectations (e.g., "How do I apply, who will evaluate me, and who will know?") frequently caused teachers to tune out discussions of long-term goals and the problems of implementation. Given the culture of schools, where certainty is valued, risk taking is discouraged, and public scrutiny is avoided, it is not surprising that many misunderstood the program's intentions.

In conclusion, it remains to be seen whether the CMS program will continue to pursue the goals for which it was initially designed. Goal displacement is a likely prospect. As of now, the signals are mixed. Some of our informants indicate that the growth and development orientation remains intact, though the results are spotty. Most informants indicate that how it is going really depends upon the principal: if the principal understands the program, it works fine. If the principal does not understand the program (as perceived by the informants), as one said, "It's a damn bureaucratic mess." Other informants see the goals are shifting from developing and sustaining outstanding teachers to identifying and rewarding a few who are deemed to be outstanding. Goal displacement is not uncommon in programs as complex as this one. It will be interesting to observe whether the efforts initiated in the early stages to assure goal clarity are effective. A definitive assessment at this time is impossible.

THE NEED FOR ACTION

Consistent with the notion that planning and implementation cannot be separated is the related notion that in managing change, action often precedes understanding. Indeed, it is the willingness to act that generates the momentum that sustains continuing planning and implementation. Plans that are made outside the action arena and plans that are not acted on before they are finished are likely to be plans and nothing more, or so we argue.

Indeed, it appears that it is difficult, if not impossible, to enlist individuals in the planning process until individuals perceive that what is being planned is likely to affect them. For example, between 1982 and the spring of 1984, it was difficult to gain from the administrators on the advisory/steering committee the sustained commitment that was needed for participation in the development of the plan. Indeed, one of the complaints of teachers on the committee was that administrators were too frequently absent from meetings and were not taking the planning seriously. In fact, administrators (other than the superintendent and deputy superintendent) generally provided little input to the planning process until concrete actions were taken to begin implementation. It was at this point that central-office administrators and building principals began to spend a great deal of time developing "operational plans."

Perhaps the clearest illustration of action preceding understanding is found in the unintended consequences of pursuing legislation regarding the granting of tenure. It was not our purpose to use this as a vehicle to inform the public of the details of the Teacher Career Development Program, yet it served that function. Looking back, it is easy to see that some symbolic vehicle was needed to fasten the public's attention on the significance of the program, but the invention of this symbol occurred through the accident of action.

CONCLUSIONS

The Teacher Career Development Program is continuing to be implemented in Charlotte. It is continuing to evolve and change.

Thus, what is described here is really what the Career Development Program was rather than what it is. I left Charlotte in January 1985 and have returned only occasionally. The superintendent left Charlotte in June 1986 to take a position with the University of North Carolina.

Some have suggested that any reasonable explanation of the events leading to the implementation of the Teacher Career Development Program should be based primarily on an understanding of the unique combination that some perceive Dr. Robinson and I represented. If, in fact, a personalistic explanation is appropriate, the next five years will verify that this is so. It is, however, my belief that while individual personalities may have made unique contributions, what is most unique, and perhaps at the same time most generalizable, is that the CMS Teacher Career Development Program was a theoretically guided effort to bring about change in schools.

NOTES

1. The reader who desires a detailed description of the CMS program should consult Schlechty, Joslin, Leak, & Hanes, 1984. I will not provide such a description here, since my purpose is to address the more general topic of leadership and management of change rather than to describe a specific change effort.

2. The Charlotte-Mecklenburg schools rely heavily on a participatory management approach within the upper hierarchies of the organization. The Office of the Superintendent is perceived by teachers as being responsive to teachers. However, building principals and teachers who were interviewed in earlier research studies had consistently indicated that they felt relatively powerless to shape decisions made at the top, and, in fact, most indicated that they did not feel they were heard. Thus, at the bottom of the organization, the norms were perceived to be those of top-down management even though the superintendent was personally viewed as responsive. That is, most teachers and administrators in the school system evidenced a great deal of trust for the leader (i.e., the superintendent) but considerably less trust for the system that he led. Therefore, planning and implementation for the CMS Teacher Career Development Program took place in a context in which the idea of participatory management was almost as alien as it is in a less responsive structure.

3. As an illustration of how important perceptions are, board reaction to the initial committee report was that it was too theoretical and professorial. After the board received the first report, the merit-pay study committee ceased to function, and I began operating as a member of Dr. Robinson's staff. Dr. Robinson asked me to author a second report, which was submitted to the board in August. Dr. Robinson submitted the report. The board found this report much more clear and understandable. As one board member put the

matter, "I knew once the old pro put his hand to it, we'd get something we could understand." Admittedly, the second report provided more detail and was presented in a different format, but the substance was the same, and it certainly was prepared by the same author.

4. It is important to understand that the office of director is not an institutionalized version of the office of special assistant to the superintendent. As special assistant to the superintendent, I reported directly to the superintendent, and I had the express and public consent to speak for the superintendent in regard to the Teacher Career Development Program. The director of the Teacher Career Development Program reports to the deputy superintendent and is, therefore, embedded in the organization in a way that is substantially different from the position I occupied. The director's job is primarily one of coordination and management. The Superintendent expressly told me that he did not want me, as special assistant to the superintendent, to get bogged down in the details of day-to-day management even though I would be criticized for not doing so. His words were, "You're the special assistant to the superintendent; you're not an assistant superintendent."

5. To assure the reader that the idea of a temporary planning structure is not a convenient post hoc explanation, the following quotation from the NIE proposal, written in March 1983, is presented below:

"Unfortunately, the developmental stage of the CMS project provides neither the P.I. nor the project coordinator with the kind of security they now have in their present circumstances. Furthermore, a temporary move (e.g., 2–3 years) would cost either or both the P.I. and the project coordinator $10,000–$15,000 more per year than they now are making (e.g., moving costs, increased interest rates) to say nothing of personal inconvenience to their families. The result is that temporary moves are out, and permanent jobs should not be assured in such a developmental project. Thus, there will be some very large and unconventional travel costs" (Schlechty & Joslin, 1983).

REFERENCES

Berliner, D. (1983, September). Executive functions of teaching. *Instructor*, pp. 18–33, 36, 38, 40.

Darling-Hammond, L. (1984). *Beyond the commission reports: The coming crisis in teaching.* Washington, DC: The Rand Corporation.

Dornbusch, S. M., & Scott, W. R. (1975). *Evaluation and the exercise of authority.* San Francisco: Jossey-Bass.

Drucker, P. (1973). *Management: Tasks, responsibilities, and practices.* New York: Harper & Row.

Garrou, T. (1980). *Implementing the "new social studies" curriculum: A case study.* Unpublished doctoral dissertation, University of North Carolina, Chapel Hill.

Gross, N. (1979). Basic issues in the management of educational change efforts. In R. E. Herriott & N. Gross (Eds.), *The dynamics of planned educational change* (pp. 20–46). Berkeley, CA: McCutchan Publishing.

Grove, A. (1983). *High output management.* Westminster, MD: Random House.

Joslin, A. (1982). *The effect of school context on the implementation of an innovation: A case study.* Unpublished doctoral dissertation, University of North Carolina, Chapel Hill.

Justice, B. (1978). *The impact of selected structural characteristics of schools upon teacher response to innovative social studies.* Unpublished doctoral dissertation, University of North Carolina, Chapel Hill.

Lortie, D. (1975). *Schoolteacher: A sociological study.* Chicago: University of Chicago Press.

McLaughlin, W. B., Pfeifer, S., Swanson-Owens, D., & Yee, S. (1986). Why teachers don't teach. *Phi Delta Kappan, 67*(6), 420–426.

Sarason, S. B. (1972). *The culture of the school and the problems of change.* Boston: Allyn & Bacon.

Schlechty, P. (1978). *Reassigning authority and responsibility in teacher education.* Paper presented to Deans' Workshop, Lake of the Ozarks.

Schlechty, P., Crowell, D. Whitford, B., & Joslin, A. (1983). *Understanding and managing staff development in an urban school system.* Final report to the National Institute of Education (400-79-0056), Washington, DC.

Schlechty, P., & Joslin, A. (1983). *Planning and implementing an alternative teacher career structure: A case study.* Proposal to the National Institute of Education, Washington, DC.

Schlechty, P., Joslin, A., Leak, S., & Hanes, R. (1984). The Charlotte-Mecklenburg Teacher Career Development Program. *Educational Leadership, 42*(4), 4–8.

Schlechty, P., & Vance, V. (1981). Do academically able teachers leave education? The North Carolina case. *Phi Delta Kappan, 63*(2), 106–112.

Schlechty, P., & Vance, V. (1983). Institutional responsibility to the quality/quantity issues in teaching. *Phi Delta Kappan, 65*(2), 94–101.

Schlechty, P., & Whitford, B. (1983). The organizational context of school systems and the functions of staff development. In G. A. Griffin (Ed.), *Staff development: Eighty-second yearbook of the National Society for the Study of Education* (Part II). Chicago: University of Chicago Press.

Vance, V., & Schlechty, P. (1982). The distribution of academic ability in the teaching force: Policy implications. *Phi Delta Kappan, 64*(1), 2–27.

Waller, W. (1961). *The sociology of teaching.* New York: Wiley. (Original work published 1932)

Whitford, B. L. (1981). *Organizational analysis of the implementation of an innovation: A case study.* Unpublished doctoral dissertation, University of North Carolina, Chapel Hill.

Wilson, E. (1966). *Sociology: Rules, roles, and relationships.* Homewood, IL: Dorsey Press.

Afterword

HARRY JUDGE

An afterword that is also a view from abroad must satisfy a number of difficult conditions. First, like all decent postscripts, it must be brief and its message as clear as possible. Second, it must add some information to the body of the text already devoured by the eager reader. Third, it must offer some new cross-national perspective on the key themes emerging from that text.

It is not clear to me that an observer writing in Oxford, England, is necessarily well qualified to meet these various conditions. My excuse (apart from politely responding to an invitation) is that the active interest shown in my work by the Ford Foundation—and especially by Edward Meade, Jr.—has enabled me to follow the fascinating changes within the United States in public attitudes toward teaching, teachers, and teacher education, which have been so remarkable a feature of the 1980s and to which the writers in this particular volume have made so distinguished a contribution. It is, perhaps, easier for an occasional but privileged visitor like myself to appreciate the scale and scope of these changes than it is for those who are deeply involved in the battle for change. Moreover, in reflecting on the levers of and obstacles to reform, a European is bound to be aware of those very American assumptions and practices that condition the nature of the reform movement (if, indeed, there is such a thing) in 50 very distinctive states.

How is the culture of schools changed? More immediately, how can a professional culture be built in schools? And how does that effort relate to the dominant dynamics of reform and to the public and professional politics that shape them? A consideration of the European case underscores the particular opportunities as well as the particular problems inherent in American efforts to generate national changes in the culture of teaching. I do not say that things are any easier, and still less that they are better, in the antique traditions of Europe: only that they are different. I do say that, for the purpose of this preliminary comparison, Britain is now very much a European country.

Three examples of such differences (between the British, standing as the epitome of the European, and the American tradition) may be helpful. First, in Britain now, as in France or Sweden, the authority of the central government is paramount. Local educational enterprise is a function of national legislation and leans heavily upon financial support delivered by the national government and legislature. When the British government wishes to change the nature of teacher education it can now do so by administrative definition and by exerting its direct influence through a Council for the Accreditation of Teacher Education appointed by itself. When it wishes to modify the structure of teachers' careers and the pattern of their professional responsibilities, it can do so by abolishing the preexisting negotiating machinery and substituting for it principles and conditions of its own design.

These things have not, of course, always been so in Britain, and I have no interest at this point in examining their virtues or their vices. The fact is that Britain is becoming a more European country, and wide powers that have long existed in law are now being used in practice to develop an overtly national system of education and to play down the gentler charms of partnership, devolution, and diversity. Teacher education and the configuration of teachers' careers and responsibilities are the two major determinants of the professional culture of schools.

In Europe, they are controlled by national government. In the United States, they are not.

A second potent difference relates to the deep-grained European habit of conceiving of two different cultures of schooling: one, of relatively low status, for the commonalty of people; the other, drawing high status, from an association with higher education and the education of middle-class students. The effects on the professionalization of some teachers are profound: witness in France the surviving distinction of title between the *instituteur* and the *professeur*, and all that it implies. The twin forces of democratization and modernization have, of course, softened these once-rigid distinctions: and not least in Britain, with the introduction over the past two decades of the comprehensive high school. Nevertheless, even in Britain, two traditions of teacher culture survive—the one predominantly associated with the university, and the other not.

In Europe, history has deposited two cultures of teaching and of teacher education. In the United States, it has not.

A similar distinction is reflected within higher education itself. By American standards, access to postsecondary education is still severely restricted in Europe, and restricted by the policies of national government rather than by the flexible disciplines of the marketplace. Proportionately three times as many American as British high school graduates gain access to college or university. These are the ranks from which future teachers are inevitably drawn.

In Europe, public school teachers are drawn from a preselected minority of the population and educated within an elitist system. In the United States, they are not.

A view from abroad suggests that it may in some ways be exceptionally difficult to build professional cultures in the generality of American schools. The power to change these schools is limited and dispersed. The traditions of schooling are open and populist rather than professional. Teachers are not differentiated by professional rank and status and are drawn, indiscriminately it is sometimes implied, from a wide segment of society. Put less negatively, this means that European traditions may permit the illusion of professional status and professional culture for a minority of teachers and a minority of schools. The challenge of books like this is the much more bracing one of raising the quality of all schools and all teachers.

That is a remarkable challenge. Nor is it clear to me precisely where it has been issued, and why. It seems to have emerged with surprising suddenness. In *A Nation at Risk*, and other hortatory reports pouring off the presses in the early 1980s, there were relatively few references to teachers or to their necessary professionalization. Former habits of thought persisted: educational improvement would be stimulated by more rigorous testing, by closer attention to basics, by raising standards of graduation from high school, by increasing time on task, by extending the school year, by ejecting bad teachers and making the rest more accountable, by restoring discipline, by imitating the Japanese . . . . The qualities of good teachers, the cultivation of the conditions in which they might flourish in the workplace, the appropriate modes of their preparation: these things earned hardly a mention.

Then there came what several of the authors in this volume characterize as "the second wave" of reform. This, it appears, is marked by a recognition that if schools are failing this must be because good teachers are not sufficiently numerous, do not stay in teaching long enough, and, perhaps most important, are inhibited from performing well by some of the most powerful structural characteristics of schooling in America. So there emerges a new reform agenda, very different from its more punitive and prescriptive predecessor, at the very heart of which lies the imperative of this volume: building a professional culture in schools.

What makes this new agenda at once impressive and uniquely vulnerable is its integrity and coherence. The various parts of the agenda are, it appears, interdependent. What are these principal components, running through the previous chapters as interlocking themes?

First comes the underlying assumption that teachers capable of building a professional culture will themselves need to be well educated. Such an assertion, frequently made in the United States, is neither obvious nor silly. The openness of higher education is often reflected in the absence of anything that other societies would regard as a curriculum; in this sense colleges and universities reflect and are reflected in the shopping-mall high schools. When reformers assert or imply that teachers should be well educated, they are, in effect, offering a critique of higher education as it is at present delivered in the United States. They claim that a miscellaneous collection of unarticulated courses does not represent a systematic and rigorous education and therefore cannot be a suitable formation for a future teacher. (It is, for a foreigner, not yet clear why, in that case, it should be a suitable formation for anybody else either; but, at the moment, such an extended attack on some of the key principles of an undergraduate education is not being mounted). If the problem-solving teachers of the future need a good liberal arts and science education for this general reason, they need it for a more immediately professional reason as well. It is needed to provide expertise in the subject matter of subsequent teaching: teachers, it seems plausible to assert, can only teach well what they know and understand profoundly. This emphasis upon specific subject-based knowledge is becoming highly fashionable; few questions are yet being asked about the continuities and discontinuities between the subject (e.g., mathematics, history) as mediated by universities and the subject (with the same name) as taught in K–12. This may prove to be a question, a problem even, for the third or fourth wave of reform. For the moment, there is enough to chew in what has already been bitten off: professional teachers need to be well educated and to master the subject matter of their teaching.

It follows conveniently, although this happens not to emerge as one of the key themes of this particular volume, that the undergraduate major in education now falls into disrepute—both to clear the field for a desired expansion of the imperial territory of the arts and sciences and to nudge the preparation of professional teachers into the graduate arena. The way is then open for the evolution, untidy and incomplete as it must certainly be, of the graduate school of education as the professional peer of its cousins in law, business, or medicine. The politics of professionalization is as important as its culture.

These agenda items—an emphasis on a quality education in the arts and sciences, the decline of the undergraduate major in education, the emergence of the model graduate professional school—are the necessary but not sufficient conditions of the building of a professional culture in elementary and secondary schools. It is at this point that, in one or another of its forms, the professional development school emerges as an integrating concept. There are, I believe, two reasons for this emergence, and they are related in reality although not in logic.

The first relates to the nature of professionalization and to a skepticism about the effectiveness of conventional theory-into-practice models of professional education. If, more specifically, the relationship between subject-matter studies, methods courses, student teaching, and foundations (all four being dubious if serviceable labels) is to be creatively redefined, then new sites for the delivery of a professional teacher education will need to be designed. This is a belief that is coming to be widely shared outside the United States. But the professional development school is more than a new training site, more than teacher education's cloudy version of the teaching hospital. It is also, and most significantly, a model of change for the public schools themselves and of a profound mutation in their culture. Unless, so the second argument runs, those schools do begin rapidly to change, then the lively and innovative teachers of the new dispensation will (like many of their idealistic predecessors) fade into disenchantment, and fold their tents. They, too, will have joined a procession and not a profession.

Crucial in this perception of the reshaped school (as a site for teacher preparation, as a model of innovation) is the restructuring of relationships among teachers. This can, and doubtless will, take many forms. For some advocates it may require no more than a full development of the significant role of mentorship and a recognition that experienced and successful teachers have much to offer to neophytes. The implications of such a change—for the enclosed privacy of the classroom, for the nature of collegiality in schools, for the celebration of success and leadership, for the autonomy and dignity of the teacher—have been vividly explored within the covers of this book.

Some advocates of change—more ferocious, more organizational in their thinking, more suspicious of change that might terminate in sentiment—will press further. For them, the hierarchization of the profession may be a necessary condition of structural change. They will argue that the coffee pot may be hot, and the cookie jar filled, and the soup brought from the deli, and the fire chief's hat bestowed, but that such symbolic changes will, by themselves, be episodic and ephemeral. Some teachers, not all, should earn professional status, and others will perform more effectively under professional supervision. Levels, strata, new certifications, new degrees and roles, new definitions of teaching and functions—not only will these emerge, but they will need to be codified. For those who argue, convincingly, in these terms, the self-regulation of the profession (or a part of it) and the creation of statewide *and* national standards boards for professional teachers are an indispensable part of building new professional cultures. The deregulation of teaching, which is what so many of these pages are about, requires the greater regulation of teachers. And that may prove to be problematical.

Will, then, professional cultures be built successfully in American schools? If commitment and enthusiasm are sufficient they may be—in some places. Certainly there will be significant changes. There remain, however, deep conflicts within the so-called reform movement, and some of these may need to be more openly addressed. Their ineluctable character is revealed, as was suggested at the beginning of this afterword, when the structural characteristics of schooling in America are compared to those in Europe. It is not clear that professional cultures can be built without a redefinition, and possibly a restriction, of the aspiring workforce. Are all teachers or only some teachers to be admitted to the charmed circle? The notion of teachers as executives rather than as workers is powerful and persuasive, but (like leadership itself) may not be applicable to all. Collegiality, as a negotiated form of collective autonomy, might be sold to the public—but a price. That price may well include describing levels of responsibility and accountability for lead teachers, or career professional teachers, or master teachers, or whatever they may be called. If such is indeed the case, then much well-conceptualized development work needs to be undertaken before the historically agglomerated tasks of teaching can be expressed in more refined form. That effort will arouse suspicion and opposition. The teachers' unions in particular face some unpalatable choices. Is it to be claimed (as some of these pages come close to implying) that all teachers are already good enough to be entrusted with the rights to exercise their discretion that effective schooling requires? And if not, then by what new process and under what governance will complex and discriminatory decisions be taken?

Nor are such choices limited in scope to questions of trade-union power, or rivalries, or enrollments. On the contrary. Lying beneath them is a long tradition of openness with regard to the teaching "profession." Lay and professional prejudices have combined to strengthen the doctrine that all teachers are equal—elementary and secondary, effective and excellent, experienced and raw—and should be required to operate within similar guidelines. What is more, the definition of these guidelines and the protection of the expectations of pupils are perceived as properly being expressions of lay rather than of professional authority.

The democratic/bureaucratic tradition is a powerful one, and one in which Americans take a great deal of legitimate pride. The schools belong to the communities that found and fund them, not to teachers who work in them. School boards in the United States are unlikely to take kindly to the notion that—even when and if teachers become "better" than they are currently perceived to be—their own responsibilities should be handed over to groups of teachers operating autonomously within schools. This is one of the reasons why other levels of collegiality—and notably the school district—deserve the attention they receive in at least two of the chapters of this book. The school may prove to be not the only, and perhaps not the best, setting within which (in some insular sense) to encourage the growth of a professional culture. Legitimate leadership exercised by expert teachers may be more acceptable in the wider arena of the school district, or even the state, than within the confines of each school. The important principle is that the best teachers should be providing the leadership for other teachers in curriculum development, research, inservice consultancy, and curriculum coordination. It may be more important to stimulate the growth of a professional culture in teaching than in schools themselves, viewed as discrete institutions.

The potential conflict between the interests of teachers (and therefore of schools) and those of the lay community (and therefore also of schools) is not the only example of an area in which new accommodations will be needed. There are several suggestions in this book of other cherished (and, at least in their origins, benevolent) habits of mind and action that are likely to inhibit teachers and to discourage bright people from becoming or continuing as teachers. Two in particular relate to the ideology of accountability and efficiency.

The origins of these habits have been well documented. The best yardstick by which to judge the performance of teachers is held to be the performance in tests of that teacher's students. That latter performance is commonly held to justify any claim for extra resources for schools, and in particular for any increase in the financial or other rewards (smaller classes, for example) to be conceded to teachers. But, in the longer perspective, the weight and bureaucracy of testing constrain those very qualities in teaching that articulate reformers most wish to encourage.

Similar considerations may apply to the place in American schooling of principals, superintendents, and administrators generally. I doubt whether the special nature of that place finds any real analogy in other educational systems. The administrator, I would argue, is perceived as the agent of a providing and supportive authority ensuring that standards are maintained by teachers (as validated by tests) and that value for money is delivered. Democratic control and bureaucratic surveillance are in this enterprise natural allies. Only in the United States would it be common to hear a principal observing, without any sense of incongruity or apology, "I was a teacher before I became an administrator." What such a statement exposes, of course, is the dissonance within schools between the emerging emphasis on responsible teacher leadership and a traditional insistence that leadership is something that needs to be imposed on teachers, from outside the school culture and within the school and the system, by the professional agent of that nonprofessional authority.

These comments across 3,000 miles of ocean are not intended to question either the wisdom or the practicability of the pursuit of a cultural regeneration in schools. Quite the contrary: if I had a vote and a voice, I would use both in support of the radical changes about which you have just been reading. But it might, I hope, be helpful (and limit the risks of premature disillusionment) for a foreigner to draw attention to other countervailing forces (also with virtuous origins) with which accommodation will have to be found. Here, as so often, the forces of light have to contend not with those of darkness, but with their own natural allies. Building professional cultures in schools will need somehow to be harmonized with the pursuit of egalitarianism and openness, with traditions of popular control, with principles of accountability and honest management.

It will also need to take account of some of the conflict implied in what I would wish to call "professionism," as distinguished from "professionalism." By professionism, I mean those frequently self-serving efforts of privileged groups to preserve a mystique, to delineate a monopoly, to restrict access to their ranks, to resist external controls. The trouble with professionalism in teaching, and the root of a general suspicion about professionism within it, is that the activity is so hard to specify in quasi-legal terms. The universities and colleges are full of people who teach, many of them with devotion and good effect, but who are neither licensed nor certified. The same is, and should be, true of authors, journalists, media-dwellers, museum keepers, politicians, preachers, sales directors, and (perhaps above all) families.

Not all efforts to restrict the right to teach deserve an unambiguous welcome. The public has much sympathy with those who argue against an excessive effort to insist upon credentialing. If capable liberal arts graduates can be attracted into teaching for a few years, is that not good? Or a middle-aged industrial scientist who discovers an interest in communicating knowledge to be stronger than the interest on a bank account? Or an able person who, without having received any professional training as a teacher, can nevertheless pass a rigorous national examination and demonstrate considerable practical competence? To deny such valuable people employment as teachers is, it can be argued, to mistake professionism for professionalism.

Well, perhaps it is. But those who argue in these terms (and, even in this book, there are a few slighting references to degreed consultants and university theorists generally) should pause and take a more distant view of the matter. While it is true that schools are unlikely to reject able helpers, wherever they come from, the abiding problems of schooling will not be solved until there is an adequate flow into them of well-educated people dedicated to becoming lifelong professionals in a high calling and receiving adequate extrinsic and intrinsic rewards.

The maintenance of such a flow depends in the long run on the capacity of universities, and specifically of schools of education, to attract good people and then to prepare them better than ever before. Fulfilling that mission requires a whole set of changes in the culture of the schools of education. Such changes might fill another book (or at least another afterword), but they would include a new respect for the practitioner and for pedagogy, a reorientation of the research agenda, and a fresh definition of the relationship between the skills and capacities of teachers and administrators in K–12 schools.

To conclude on such a note is not to distract attention from the strategic importance of building professional cultures in schools. That is indeed the key task, and one of profound and problematic difficulty. It is more likely of achievement if accompanied by closely related efforts to harmonize change in the other related cultures—that of "downtown" and that of the ivory tower. The agenda of the second wave of reform proves indeed to be integrated, and for that reason both potent and vulnerable. It also turns out to be even wider than might have been anticipated by those of us accustomed to study and to seek to change the culture of schools standing as lonely islands.

Current Issues
in Restructuring the Teaching Profession:
An Annotated Bibliography

PATRICIA A. WASLEY

Bacharach, S. "The Learning Workplace: The Conditions and Resources of Teaching." Research report, The National Education Association, Washington, DC, April 1986.

Through this national study of teaching, Bacharach attempts to identify the problems teachers have with the working conditions in schools. Using four principles of organizational effectiveness to survey teachers, Bacharach finds that school organizations do not provide the conditions and resources necessary for teachers to do their jobs well. Resources are too limited, decision making takes place at a level far removed from the classroom, and communication within organizations seldom takes place in a way that would assure common goals and objectives. Survey questions and an analysis of the responses are included in the report.

Cohn, M., et al. "Teachers' Perspectives on the Problems in Their Profession: Implications for Policymakers and Practitioners." (Contract No. H-ERI-D-86-3090). Washington, DC: U.S. Department of Education, Office of Educational Research and Improvement, 1987.

Through interviews and surveys conducted with the same Dade County teachers used in Dan Lortie's 1975 study, the focus of this work is to ascertain whether (1) the problems identified in the current reform reports reflect the problems as teachers see them; (2) it is possible to prioritize these problems; (3) the problems that cause people to leave the profession are the same as those that discourage people from entering the profession; and (4) we can distinguish the coping patterns of those teachers who are satisfied from those who are not. After a summary of the issues contained in the reform reports, the study isolates problems that affect all teachers: (1) parents are uncooperative partners; (2) students are unwilling partners; (3) the role of teacher has become less professional, more bounded by paperwork and central-office decision making. Those factors that discouraged people from entering the profession were money and status, while those that caused people to leave the profession were mentioned above. Dissatisfied teachers differed in coping mechanisms in that they believed that they could make no difference, while satisfied teachers believed that they could.

In conclusion, the study suggests that sociocultural differences cannot be dealt with by legislative mandate. Nor can improvement of instruction be guaranteed by greater regulation. Recommendations are made in the areas of recruitment, selection, and retention of teachers.

Corey, S. *Helping Other People Change.* Columbus: Ohio State University Press, 1963.

In this study change is defined and explored in the context of public schools. The fact that few changes actually take place in most school settings is a major point of the investigation. Corey delineates a process that avoids superficial treatment of complex issues and also delineates the role of the outside consultant. The author's central point is that change must take place with the involvement of those who will be affected by the change.

Darling-Hammond, L. "Beyond the Commission Reports: The Coming Crisis in Teaching." Santa Monica, California: Rand Corporation, July 1984.

The author outlines the contributing factors that are leading to the most serious teacher shortage the country has experienced. In addition, current reform efforts, aimed at improving the quality of teachers in public schools, will be thwarted unless teaching is made more attractive as a profession. After discussing those conditions that have made teaching less desirable as a profession, recommendations are made for the professionalization of teaching.

Devaney, K. "The Lead Teacher." Paper prepared for the Task Force on Teaching as a Profession, Carnegie Forum on Education and the Economy, New York, 1987.

This paper outlines the conditions and responsibilities that must be attended to if we are to restructure the teaching profession in order to reform schools. In order to explain how new roles created for "lead teachers" would generate greater professionalism in public schools, the author summarizes the literature that describes what teachers say they want for enhanced professionalism. Susan Rosenholtz's work indicated that teachers in learning-enriched schools were characterized by task autonomy, certainty about helping students, and personal opportunities to grow. Teachers in these schools engaged in greater collaboration both with other teachers and with their principals. Judith Warren Little and Tom Bird found that organizations that provided teachers with frequent time to talk about teaching, the ability to observe each other, opportunities to work together on curriculum and instruction, and opportunities to teach each other and learn together encouraged collegiality and experimentation. In such places, teachers were more satisfied. Linda Darling-Hammond states that in order to build professionalism, teachers must be involved in (1) the selection of new teachers; (2) providing assistance to new teachers; (3) the generation of performance evaluation that is tied to professional improvement plane; (4) frequent school site reviews; (5) building-based decision making.

The role of the lead teacher would be to establish working conditions that promote greater professionalization for the entire teaching staff in new and different ways. While current differentiated positions exist widely in schools, the author indicates that they are generally unsatisfactory in that they do not meet the demands of increased professionalism. Descriptions of new lead positions must be crafted by a respected group of teachers, who should also conduct the selection. Lead-teachers roles would include mentoring, coaching, developing better performance measures, designing and organizing in-service, and facilitating staff as well as school reviews of curricula.

Lead teachers should be selected based on their teaching competence, interactiveness, ability to understand schools, willingness to experiment, and ability to develop the trust of others.

In order to begin these kinds of positions, boards, superintendents, principals, and teachers' associations must forge new kinds of agreements and provide the necessary funding to support the kinds of activities that would foster greater professionalism for all teachers.

Goodlad, J. *A Place Called School*. New York: McGraw-Hill, 1984.

In this large-scale study of public schools in the United States, the author outlines the complexity of clearly ascertaining the purpose of public schools and the difficulty in identifying the constituents. In order to gather concrete data on the conditions that exist in public schools, researchers observed in numerous classrooms across the country. Passive places where students have little responsibility for learning, today's classrooms seem not to have changed at all despite the numerous reports of and challenges for reform. The author discusses problems with both instructional repertoire and curriculum. In addition, he points out that those closest to classrooms, teachers and school administrators, are seldom involved in efforts to reform schools. Finally, the author suggests possible solutions for positive change.

Green, J., ed. *What Next? More Leverage for Teachers*. Denver, CO: Education Commission of the States, 1986.

This report is the result of collaboration and dialogue among national experts concerned with teachers and the teaching profession. Centralized policy making has virtually ignored the people it most affects, the teachers. Piecemeal policy has hampered the abilities of classroom teachers. In order to be more effective in the future, policy makers should look toward restructuring training, altering working conditions, and improving the professionalism of teaching. These kinds of directions will require that policy makers (1) shift their viewpoint from regulatory to supportive; (2) create a climate conducive to experimentation; and (3) try novel approaches.

Hatfield, R., C. Blackman, C. Claypool, and F. Master. "Extended Professional Roles of Teacher Leaders in the Public Schools." Unpublished paper, Michigan State University, East Lansing, 1987.

Leadership in schools has changed relatively infrequently. As schools became more complex, superintendents assumed responsibility for school management from school boards, and then principals assumed building responsibility on the behalf of superintendents. Since that time, teachers have begun to fill a number of leadership functions about which we have very little information. The authors collected information from a wide selection of teachers who hold differentiated positions in order to determine the commonalities and differences in these roles. Their findings indicate that between 10 and 20 percent of the teaching workforce hold differentiated positions. Primary responsibilities involve staff development, curriculum development, and instructional improvement. While these positions often carry multiple responsibilities, the more focused the role, the more successful the teachers were likely to be.

Joyce, B. *Improving America's Schools.* New York: Longman, 1986.

Joyce proposes that schools be joyful places that utilize the best practices in the field, have the capacity to be self-renewing, and closely link policy and practice. In pursuit of how we get there, Joyce describes society's growing expectations from teachers as well as the constraints teachers face within the system. Very little time is built in for planning or studying either academic content or the instructional process. No time is allocated for collaborative work, curriculum articulation, or mutual problem solving. Because of his strong belief that change will not occur in schools unless it involves teachers in a significant way, the author describes possible roles for teachers that provide greater opportunities for decision making and for collegial responsibility for the standards in the classroom. The author concludes with the 3 R's of school improvement: refine, renovate, and redesign.

Kerr, D. "Authority and Responsibility in Public Schooling." In *The Ecology of School Renewal: NSSE Yearbook,* edited by John I. Goodlad, 20–40. Chicago: University of Chicago Press, 1987.

Kerr states that reform requires that we clearly understand who has responsibility and authority for our schools. Responsibility belongs both to the public and to the profession. Public agents have responsibility for equitably distributing appropriate resources and for supporting human resources. The profession has responsibility for ensuring high standards and expertise within the profession. The public at large has responsibility for supporting public education. Authority in schools belongs to the teachers who work directly with students. Teachers have three areas of responsibility when exercising their authority: epistemic, moral, and political—all of which take into account the complexity of the act of teaching. Reform that is mandated by distant, nonexpert sources and that attempts to automate the teaching profession does little to support the kind of education desirable for our nation's children.

Lieberman, A. "Enhancing School Improvement Through Collaboration."
     Paper presented at the Allerton Symposium on Illinois Educational Im-
     provement, Champaign, June 1985.
   The call for reform has made collaboration an important issue. Lieberman
dispels traditional myths surrounding collaboration and lists the following
criteria as necessary in order to begin: (1) a commitment to collaboration; (2)
a small group of activists; (3) some beginning activities; (4) enormous flexibility; and (5) a willingness to learn from mistakes. In addition, Lieberman
discusses the characteristics of good collaboration as well as the need for incentives to participate.

Lieberman, A., and L. Miller. *Teachers, Their World and Their Work: Im-
     plications for School Improvement.* Alexandria, VA: ASCD, 1984.
   The authors describe the complexity of teaching by first describing the social realities of the classroom: teaching and learning links are unclear; rewards generally come from the students; the knowledge base is weak; goals
are vague and conflicting; professional support is lacking; and teaching is a
craft rather than a formula. A description of the dailiness of teaching outlines
the constraints under which teachers work: five or six hours with students;
little or no opportunity to work with other adults; the need to be practical in
the face of constant decisions; and uncertainty about effectiveness. In separate chapters, the authors describe the working conditions that are specific to
elementary schools and secondary schools and the implications for staff development at both levels. Because the conditions are quite different at each
level, different concerns surface when a district begins to approach a school-
improvement project.
   Six critical components for change that blend with teacher descriptions
of change processes are outlined, in addition to a review of the research conducted on change in schools. Finally, Lieberman and Miller discuss teachers
as adult learners, review the successful strategies and organizing frameworks
for school-improvement projects, and review numerous projects that trans-
late research into practical, school-based strategies.

Lieberman, A., and S. Rosenholtz. "The Road to School Improvement: Bar-
     riers and Bridges." In *The Ecology of School Renewal: NSSE Yearbook,*
     edited by John I. Goodland, 79–98. Chicago: University of Chicago Press,
     1987.
   The authors indicate that the major organizational dilemma and the greatest barrier to school improvement deals with how change is controlled while
ensuring participant autonomy and job satisfaction. In light of what we know
about schools—that change is very difficult because of longstanding norms
and the lack of collegial interaction—the definition of effective schools must
be broader. The most effective schools are those which are constantly in a
state of "becoming" more effective and which do that by building bridges
toward a more professional culture. The authors describe several examples

of enhanced professional culture in schools that break down the barriers to improvement.

Little, J. "Seductive Images and Organizational Realities in Professional Development." In *Rethinking School Improvement,* edited by Ann Lieberman, 26–44. New York: Teachers College Press, 1986.

As it becomes apparent that staff-development programs are sometimes less effective than anticipated, this comparison of two programs helps shed light on what constitutes successful programs. Little identifies the following criteria as indicative of successful staff-development programs: (1) they ensure adequate collegial working conditions to guarantee shared understanding and commitment; (2) they require staff participation in both training and implementation; (3) they focus on critical problems of curriculum and instruction; (4) they guarantee long-term commitment and continuous involvement to ensure progressive gains in knowledge; (5) they create an environment congruent with the norms of collegiality and experimentation. Problems that hamper staff-development programs are funding and the demands placed on principals to function in new ways.

Lortie, D. *Schoolteacher.* Chicago: University of Chicago Press, 1975.

In this major sociological study of the teaching profession, Lortie outlines the history of the teaching profession in the United States, recruitment, current working conditions (including those for beginning teachers), the influence of the administration, the effect of isolation, and the rewards of teaching. While describing the endemic uncertainties of teaching, the author discusses why it is so difficult to reach the goals we have for public schools. In addition, monitoring teaching is difficult and subjective, while curricular goals are unclear and left to the individual. Lortie illustrates how teachers feel about their work and points out that when asked about change, teachers indicate minor rather than major changes. Parent/teacher relations are characterized as strained, while teachers view their colleagues as helpful (though they have little opportunity to work together). Teachers indicate that principals should be fair and supportive and should allow for teacher autonomy. Lortie speculates that while teaching has not changed in the past, changes in our society coupled with public pressure will force a restructuring.

McLaughlin, M., R. Wallin, S. Pfeifer, D. Swanson-Owens, and S. Yee. "Why Teachers Won't Teach." *Phi Delta Kappan,* 67 (6), 420–426, 1986.

The authors investigate the structural problems in the United States' educational system that make it impossible for teachers to meet their own goals. Teachers daily face problems of class size, varying ability levels, lack of resources, problems with the administration, isolation, poor initiation into the profession, and lack of recognition. These conditions provide few opportunities for success and spawn apathy or an exodus from the profession.

Popkewitz, T., B. Tabachnick, and G. Wehlage. *The Myth of Educational Reform: A Study of School Response to a Program of Change.* Madison: University of Wisconsin Press, 1982.

In a four-year study of schools that were implementing the Individually Guided Instruction (IGE) program developed by the federal government in the 1960s, the authors attempted to assess the success of a comprehensive school reform effort. The authors found three types of schools: (1) technical schools, which adopted the curricular program in its totality and focused on following implementation plans to the tee; (2) constructive schools, which adopted the parts of IGE that complemented their existing program; and (3) illusory schools, which adopted the curriculum in a ceremonial fashion only. While the appropriate language was in place, teachers did not change their traditional habits at all. As a result, the researchers concluded that any reform effort involves teachers' and administrators' underlying assumptions about knowledge, their concepts of teachers' working responsibilities, and their personal ideologies. While schools engage in reform efforts because they are legitimating, unless these underlying assumptions are dealt with, no real reform takes place at all.

Porter, A. "Teacher Collaboration: New Partnerships to Attack Old Problems." *Phi Delta Kappan,* 69 (2), 147–152, October 1987.

For the past ten years Michigan State University has brought classroom teachers to the university on half-time release assignments to collaborate with researchers. Teachers typically stay three years before returning to the classroom. The purpose of the collaboration has been to bridge the gap between educational research and practice. In this paper, Porter analyzes the costs and benefits of such collaboration. Conclusions indicate that while the collaboration is expensive ($20,000 per half-time teacher), the benefits appear equally distributed between university faculty and released teachers. Both groups agree that the collaboration strengthens the quality of educational research. In addition, Porter outlines the sources of frustration such collaborations entail—additional time on the part of teachers and researchers, lack of response from school systems to teacher's work, and so on.

Rosenholtz, S. "Political Myths About Reforming the Teaching Profession." Working Paper #4, prepared for the Education Commission of the States, Denver, CO, 1984.

The author notes that in a period of intense criticism of the teaching profession reform efforts generally oversimplify solutions to the problems. Then common myths are identified, such as "pay teachers more and they'll teach better" and "career ladders will encourage people to improve." Each of the myths is explored through current research on teaching. The author recommends that reform proposals be evaluated in light of these myths and calls for greater involvement of the educational community in the development of solutions to the problems in public education.

Rosenholtz, S. *Teachers' Workplace: A Social Organizational Analysis*. New
York: Longman, forthcoming.

This very significant book summarizes the findings of a major study of the
teachers' workplace and how their reality is shaped within. The "reality" of
school life and the definitions that teachers hold of their teaching is socially
constructed.

Critical questions are asked in this study: (1) To what extent do teachers'
potentials for growth and development depend on prevailing structures,
norms and patterns of interaction? (2) What formal and informal mechanisms
shape teachers' beliefs about the definition of what good teaching is?

Four social-organizational variables influenced teachers' perceived opportunities to learn: goal-setting activities, teacher evaluation, shared goals, and
teacher collaboration. In collaborative settings, teachers define their work as
inherently difficult. In isolated settings, teachers believe that learning to teach
would require an average of only two years. "Learning-enriched" schools as
opposed to "learning-impoverished" schools have major effects on teachers'
views of teaching and their work.

Sarason, S. *The Culture of the School and the Problem of Change*. Boston:
Allyn and Bacon, 1982.

Sarason describes the complexity of instituting change in public schools.
The constituency is broad and not clearly defined; change is often mandated
by people who come from outside the schools; change is often conceived of
in an oversimplistic manner without considering the realities of schools. The
author further describes two types of regularities that are affected by change
but seldom given adequate consideration: (1) programmatic regularities—the
fact that the curriculum is divided into isolated subjects, with a major emphasis on content as opposed to processes; and (2) behavioral regularities—
the fact that teachers lecture to students a majority of the time and test for
knowledge retention. Behavioral and programmatic regularities seldom match
the intended outcomes, and yet change efforts seldom encourage the kind of
planning and support that would make it possible to bring these essential
factors closer together.

To add further complexity to the problem of change, outside influences such
as the court system have engaged in decision making that will have far-
reaching implications for schools and the people in them. In addition, the
author outlines the growing responsibilities of principals, the inappropriate-
ness of their training, and their lack of control over what happens in their
buildings. Teachers, too, hold little power to change or to engage in meaningful decision making and are unused to participating in any kind of reflective or evaluative discussion. Finally, the author outlines the critical
components of a successful change process that requires constant involvement of those who work in schools.

Schlechty, P. "Schools for the 21st Century: The Conditions for Invention."
Unpublished manuscript, Gheens Professional Development Academy,
Louisville, KY, 1986.

The reform movement indicates that for public education to continue, a comprehensive restructuring of schools must take place. Schlechty points out that all the reform literature to date has ignored the role of superintendents and boards of education in that change. He indicates that reform is impossible unless superintendents and boards of education are willing to reconceptualize their roles. The author outlines the changes in role functions for students, teachers, principals, superintendents, and boards in light of a business metaphor. Decisions appropriate for centralized and decentralized control are discussed, as are the conditions that must exist if schools are to solve problems and to grow.

Schon, D. *The Reflective Practitioner: How Professionals Think in Action.* New York: Basic Books, 1983.

The author studied a number of professions in order to explore the function of reflection in action. He begins by noting that there has long been a discrepancy between university epistemology and the knowledge of practitioners. Furthermore, there appears to be a universal crisis in confidence in the professions in that solutions promoted often create problems bigger than the initial dilemma. The changing character of the situations of practice is steeped in complexity, uncertainty, instability, and uniqueness, making simplistic solutions unrealistic. Schon traces the development of the technical-rational approach to problem solving and notes that people raised in this way of thinking are uncomfortable with the combination of intuition and past experience that figures heavily in actual practice. Schon describes the kind of intellectual rigor that exists in reflective practice and calls for closer collaboration between the world of epistemology and the world of practice. He further outlines the characteristics of reflective institutions and the changing responsibilities of a reflective practitioner that would help resolve the crisis in confidence.

Shulman, L. "Autonomy and Obligation: The Remote Control of Teaching." In *Handbook of Teaching and Policy*, edited by Lee S. Shulman and Gary Sykes, 484–504. New York: Longman, 1983.

Shulman suggests that three parties are involved in the process of educational reform: policy makers, teachers, and educational scholars and researchers. Each faces the question of autonomy in the educational workplace in light of the obligation each has to reform public schools. Each feels frustration at the lack of perceived responsiveness of the other parties. Through an example of effective schools research, Schulman outlines the problems with school reform. Reform is itself a complex process that is compounded by the fact that research in education is not as forthright as research in other fields. The author suggests that a loosely coupled system where policy forms the shell in which practice can be comfortably planted and cultivated would constitute a more productive working relationship.

Sirotnik, K. "Evaluation in the Ecology of Schooling: The Process of School Renewal." In *The Ecology of School Renewal: NSSE Yearbook*, edited

by John I. Goodlad, 41–62. Chicago: University of Chicago Press, 1987.
The basic premise of this article is that school improvement must be conducted by the people in schools. In order to gain an appropriate perspective for school renewal, the author distinguishes among information, knowledge, and evaluation and suggests a method of continuous renewal through a process of critical inquiry. Sirotnik stresses that the process of inquiry recognizes that change occurs slowly and that it should be a continuous activity by and for the people who work in schools. As a result, inquiry stresses collegiality and reflection in the midst of practice, thus fostering the kinds of dynamics that lead people to constant renewal and improvement.

Sykes, G. "Public Policy and the Problem of Teacher Quality: The Need for Screens and Magnets." In *Handbook of Teaching and Policy,* edited by Lee S. Shulman and Gary Sykes, 97–125. New York: Longman, 1983.
In a summary essay, Sykes describes the current problems facing the teacher workforce. Good teachers are leaving the profession, and young people are not entering. Public policy, in response to the demands for better-quality education, has imposed a number of measures to screen out poor teachers at both the preservice and inservice levels. Such solutions are simplistic in that they ignore the need to create magnets to draw people to the profession. Sykes discusses and suggests more comprehensive solutions and roles for current policy makers.

Sykes, G. "Teaching Incentives: Constraint and Variety." Paper presented at the AERA Conference, Washington, DC, April 1987.
Incentives in teaching are treated from one of two perspectives: (1) the constraint perspective, which indicates that conditions in the teaching profession are so resistant to change that it is difficult to generate more meaningful incentives; or (2) the variety perspective, which holds that if we focus on the unusual, rather than the commonplace, we may be able to find new kinds of incentives to help in the restructuring of schools. Incentives, tools used to encourage particular kinds of behaviors, affect teaching in the following areas: (1) recruitment and retainment of teachers in the profession; (2) equitable distribution of the workforce; (3) disposition of the workforce to perform effectively; and (4) student learning and other outcomes of schools.
From the constraint perspective, teachers face the same dilemmas as other public servants—the chronic shortage of supplies and resources, their pursuit of ambiguous and hard-to-evaluate goals, and their attempt to deliver personal services in a large, impersonal bureaucracy. The teaching profession has additional constraints. Teachers have traditionally focused on psychic rewards, with little emphasis on extrinsic rewards. Teachers face daily uncertainty, low salaries, and few career opportunities. They work in isolation from other adults with conscripted clients. The author speculates that perhaps low incentives serve a variety of purposes. Weak incentives allow teachers to concentrate greater effort in other areas and promote greater turnover, which in turn keeps the cost of education down. The complexity of dealing with incentives from this vantage point seems overwhelming.

When looking at incentives from the variety perspective, Sykes looks to what teachers claim motivates them—greater opportunities for decision making, collaboration with fellow teachers in order to improve their own abilities to help students. The works of both Rosenholtz and Little and Bird indicate that when schools are organized to provide these opportunities, teachers feel more efficacious and more successful and, therefore, experience greater incentives to stay in the profession and maintain a high level of commitment.

Because little work done in education deals with incentives, Sykes concludes with an agenda for further research.

Wigginton, E. *Sometimes a Shining Moment: The Foxfire Experience.* New York: Anchor Books, 1986.

Documenting 20 years of experience in a high school classroom, the author divides the book into three distinct sections. In Book I, he shares with the reader his own account of becoming a teacher through recollections, journal entries, letters to friends, and student accomplishments. The reader watches his philosophy of teaching and learning unfold as his remarkable experience with the Foxfire project gains momentum. In Book II, he outlines the enormous responsibility of being a teacher and describes the characteristics of good teachers through a series of overarching truths such as: fine teachers see their subject matter whole; they are not afraid to be seen as fallible and human; they are constantly engaged in the process of professional growth; and they know how to avoid teacher burnout. Each of these overarching truths is the subject of a chapter illustrated by clear identification of the problems teachers face and their ultimate responsibility in solving them. Book III outlines how one goes about developing an integrative, participatory curriculum that allows teachers and students to work together in more meaningful ways.

About the Contributors

Roland S. Barth is Senior Lecturer on Education and Co-Director of the Principals' Center, Harvard University. He is the author of *Open Education and the American School, Run School Run,* and numerous articles.

Myrna Cooper is Director of the New York City Teacher Center Consortium, which is the oldest collaboration between a teacher organization and a school system. She has taught from kindergarten through eighth grade. Her current interests and contributions are in the areas of collaboration and translating research into practice.

Linda Darling-Hammond is Senior Social Scientist at the Rand Corporation in Washington, DC, and Director of Rand's Education Program. She has conducted many studies of teachers and teaching policy and is the author of numerous articles exploring how public policies can support effective teaching.

Kathleen Devaney, an education writer and consultant who lives in Berkeley, California, has recently become the editor of publications of the Holmes Group. In 1985 she was a research associate with the California Commission on the Teaching Profession, and from 1974 to 1982 she directed the Teachers' Center Exchange at the Far West Laboratory in San Francisco.

Holly M. Houston is Executive Director of the Coalition of Essential Schools at Brown University.

Harry Judge is Director of the University of Oxford Department of Educational Studies and the author of *A Generation of Schooling: English Secondary Schools since 1944* (1984) and *American Graduate Schools of Education: A View from Abroad* (1982). He is at present engaged in planning a cross-national study of teachers and teacher education.

Judith Warren Little is Assistant Professor of Education at the University of California, Berkeley. She formerly directed the Professional Development Studies Group at the Far West Laboratory for Educational Research and Development. Dr. Little's own research has focused on the professional "workplace" environment of schools, support for beginning teachers, and instructional leadership by administrators and teachers.

Ann Lieberman is Professor of Education at the University of Washington and Executive Director of the Puget Sound Educational Consortium, a partnership between the university and 13 school districts. Although she has written numerous articles, she is best known as the co-author (with Lynne Miller) of *Teachers, their world and their work* (1984) and as editor of *Rethinking School Improvement: Research, Craft, and Concept* (1986).

Milbrey Wallin McLaughlin is Associate Professor of Education at Stanford University. Her research interests focus on planned change in education, intergovernmental relations, the organizational context of teaching, and evaluation. Prior to joining the Stanford faculty, she was a policy analyst with the Rand Corporation, where her research centered on federal and state efforts to promote educational change and improvement.

Matthew B. Miles, a social psychologist, has been Senior Research Associate at the Center for Policy Research, New York, since 1970, and was Professor of Psychology and Education at Teachers College from 1953 to 1970. During the past three decades, he has been active in research, development, and consulting in the field of planned change in education; he has led major studies of leadership and intensive group training, school organizational renewal, educational innovation, program implementation, "school architecture" (the creation of new schools), effective schools programs, and school improvement, in addition to training educational consultants in North America and Western Europe. His current project focuses on the process of reform in urban high schools.

Lynne Miller has earned degrees from the University of Pennsylvania (B.A.), Harvard University (M.A.T.), and the University of Massachusetts (Ed.D.) and has served as an NIE Postdoctoral Research Fellow at Northwestern University. She has held a variety of teaching and administrative positions; most recently she was Assistant Superintendent of Curriculum in South Bend, Indiana. She is currently Associate Professor of Education at the University of Southern Maine. She is co-author (with Ann Lieberman) of *Teachers, their world and their work* (1984) and has written about life in schools, school improvement, and staff development.

Ellen R. Saxl is currently Senior Research Associate at the Center for Policy Research and is also Adjunct Assistant Professor of Education, Curriculum, and Teaching at Teachers College. Her work and interests concern program evaluation of large-scale urban improvement programs as they relate to staff development and change.

Phillip Schlechty is Executive Director of the Jefferson County (Kentucky) Public School System's Gheens Professional Development Academy. He received the American Federation of Teachers (AFT) Quest citation for the year 1985–1986. He is best known for the development of the Charlotte-Mecklenburg Career Development Program.

Gary Sykes is Assistant Professor in the Department of Teacher Education at Michigan State University. He is best known for his articles on policy on teaching.

Patricia A. Wasley has held a variety of positions in public schools, including administrative assistant for curriculum and instruction in a regional educational agency. She is currently a research assistant at the University of Washington, where she is completing her doctoral work on teacher leadership.

Sylvia Mei-ling Yee is a Ph.D. candidate in the Administration and Policy Analysis Program at Stanford University. She has taught at the elementary, secondary, and university levels (including three years in the People's Republic of China); she has also been an administrator in special programs for disadvantaged students. Her current areas of interest include career issues for teachers and dropout prevention.

Index

23.45